"If you think you know Luther, read this book. illuminating piece of work. Displaying the intere historian, Carl Trueman provides us with an analys that is as 'human' as the German Reformer himself. ... it s far more than Luther on the Christian life. It's one of the very best summaries of Luther in context."

> **Michael Horton,** J. Gresham Machen Professor of Systematic Theology and Apologetics, Westminster Seminary California; author, *Calvin on the Christian Life*

"Carl Trueman has pulled off a tremendous feat: he's not only given us a volume that is scholarly and historically nuanced while still accessible and refreshingly contemporary; he's also managed to capture the brilliance and boldness of Martin Luther in a relatively short space. Trueman is to be commended for presenting a Luther who is unlike us in so many ways, and yet a Luther from whom we can learn so much."

> **Kevin DeYoung,** Senior Pastor, University Reformed Church, East Lansing, Michigan

"This book illustrates again why Martin Luther remains a nearly inexhaustible resource. Trueman explains why Luther can be such a perceptive, encouraging, human, and even humorous guide to the Christian life. Especially important is Trueman's clear communication of why the cross of Christ grounded Luther's approach to almost everything and why a 'theology of the cross' might powerfully motivate believers today as well."

> **Mark A. Noll,** Francis A. McAnaney Professor of History, University of Notre Dame

"Trueman gives us not only Luther's theology, but Luther as a theologian, which in turn connects with us as theologians. We learn from Trueman's insight into Luther that theology isn't just what we know about God, or even how we know it, but is intimately connected to who we are. Trueman gives us Luther—constipation, wit, contradictions, and all. We also finally get a theological apologetic for a robust sense of humor."

> **Aimee Byrd,** author, *Housewife Theologian* and *Theological Fitness*

"It is no easy task to write a small volume summing up the theology and significance for the Christian life of Martin Luther. Yet Trueman has done it superbly with aplomb and verve. Highly recommended as an excellent introduction to a remarkable Christian and human being."

> **Michael A. G. Haykin,** Professor of Church History and Biblical Spirituality, The Southern Baptist Theological Seminary

"This book takes us on an engaging, enjoyable tour of the thought of one of Christianity's most influential theologians. Writing with wisdom and accessible style, Trueman gets to the heart of Luther's theology, showing how his teachings in areas like law and gospel, justification by grace through faith, and the means of grace connect with the everyday Christian life of believers. Trueman's insightful scholarship and clear writing give us a wonderful introduction to Luther's thought. I highly recommend it."

Justin S. Holcomb, Episcopal Priest; Professor of Christian Thought, Gordon-Conwell Theological Seminary; author, *On the Grace of God*

"In this compelling book, we encounter an arresting portrait of Luther the pastor, a full-blooded man who knew the spiritual and physical joys and pains of life and the formidable daily challenges of being a Christian in a fallen world. In elegant, bracing prose full of pastoral and theological insight and leavened with his characteristic humor, Trueman both keeps Luther in his time and engages us in conversation about how the German doctor speaks to ours. Trueman's profound exploration of one of the great writers on the Christian life challenges all of us to cancel our tickets for journeys of self-exploration and self-expression to pursue something more authentic. From a distance of five hundred years, Luther tells us that the story is not about us; it's about what God has done for us."

Bruce Gordon, Titus Street Professor of Ecclesiastical History, Yale Divinity School; author, *Calvin*

"This book deftly combines deep historical learning with sage pastoral wisdom to present us with an unaccommodated Luther—one who is sure to surprise as well as offend those only familiar with sanitized portraits of the Wittenberg Reformer. But this is the Luther that we need, for it is the real Luther—not the fictions of hagiographers—who has the most to teach us about the Christian life. Both new and longtime readers of Luther will derive much benefit from Trueman's book."

Scott R. Swain, Associate Professor of Systematic Theology and Academic Dean, Reformed Theological Seminary, Orlando, Florida

"Eminently readable, humorous, and always with an eye to the church today, Trueman brings us into Luther's world, devils and all, and shows us the centrality of the cross and the objective power of God's Word for Luther's understanding of the Christian life. Most importantly, we meet Luther on Luther's terms. His high view of the liturgy and sacraments stands alongside his more familiar views on the authority of Scripture and justification by faith alone. All those interested in Luther or the Reformation need to read this excellent book."

Carl Beckwith, Associate Professor of History and Doctrine, Beeson Divinity School; author, *Hilary of Poitiers on the Trinity*

LUTHER

on the Christian Life

THEOLOGIANS ON THE CHRISTIAN LIFE

EDITED BY STEPHEN J. NICHOLS AND JUSTIN TAYLOR

Augustine on the Christian Life:
Transformed by the Power of God,
Gerald Bray

Bavinck on the Christian Life:
Following Jesus in Faithful Service,
John Bolt

Bonhoeffer on the Christian Life:
From the Cross, for the World,
Stephen J. Nichols

Calvin on the Christian Life:
Glorifying and Enjoying God Forever,
Michael Horton

Edwards on the Christian Life:
Alive to the Beauty of God,
Dane C. Ortlund

Luther on the Christian Life:
Cross and Freedom,
Carl R. Trueman

Newton on the Christian Life:
To Live Is Christ,
Tony Reinke

Owen on the Christian Life:
Living for the Glory of God in Christ,
Matthew Barrett and Michael A. G. Haykin

Packer on the Christian Life:
Knowing God in Christ, Walking by the Spirit,
Sam Storms

Schaeffer on the Christian Life:
Countercultural Spirituality,
William Edgar

Warfield on the Christian Life:
Living in Light of the Gospel,
Fred G. Zaspel

Wesley on the Christian Life:
The Heart Renewed in Love,
Fred Sanders

LUTHER

on the Christian Life

CROSS AND FREEDOM

CARL R. TRUEMAN

FOREWORD BY ROBERT KOLB

AFTERWORD BY MARTIN E. MARTY

CROSSWAY®

WHEATON, ILLINOIS

Luther on the Christian Life: Cross and Freedom

Copyright © 2015 by Carl R. Trueman

Published by Crossway
           1300 Crescent Street
           Wheaton, Illinois 60187

Cover design: Josh Dennis
Cover image: Richard Solomon Artists, Mark Summers

First printing 2015

Printed in the United States of America

The author's Scripture quotations are from the ESV® Bible (The Holy Bible, English Standard Version®), copyright © 2001 by Crossway, a publishing ministry of Good News Publishers. Used by permission. All rights reserved.

Trade paperback ISBN: 978-1-4335-2502-5
PDF ISBN: 978-1-4335-2504-9
Mobipocket ISBN: 978-1-4335-2506-3
ePub ISBN: 978-1-4335-2510-0

Library of Congress Cataloging-in-Publication Data

Trueman, Carl R.
   Luther on the Christian life : cross and freedom / Carl R.
Trueman ; foreword by Robert Kolb.
      pages cm. — (Theologians on the Christian life)
   Includes bibliographical references and index.
   ISBN 978-1-4335-2502-5 (tp)
   1. Luther, Martin, 1483–1546. 2. Christian life. 3. Theology of the cross. I. Title.
BR333.3.T78   2015
248.4—dc23   2014020705

Crossway is a publishing ministry of Good News Publishers.

VP		25	24	23	22	21	20	19	18	17	16
15	14	13	12	11	10	9	8	7	6	5	4	3	2

For Catriona.

Which is Gaelic for Katherine.
Which rhymes with the Latin word catena.

Enough said.

CONTENTS

SERIES PREFACE

Some might call us spoiled. We live in an era of significant and substantial resources for Christians on living the Christian life. We have ready access to books, DVD series, online material, seminars—all in the interest of encouraging us in our daily walk with Christ. The laity, the people in the pew, have access to more information than scholars dreamed of having in previous centuries.

Yet for all our abundance of resources, we also lack something. We tend to lack the perspectives from the past, perspectives from a different time and place than our own. To put the matter differently, we have so many riches in our current horizon that we tend not to look to the horizons of the past.

That is unfortunate, especially when it comes to learning about and practicing discipleship. It's like owning a mansion and choosing to live in only one room. This series invites you to explore the other rooms.

As we go exploring, we will visit places and times different from our own. We will see different models, approaches, and emphases. This series does not intend for these models to be copied uncritically, and it certainly does not intend to put these figures from the past high upon a pedestal like some race of super-Christians. This series intends, however, to help us in the present listen to the past. We believe there is wisdom in the past twenty centuries of the church, wisdom for living the Christian life.

Stephen J. Nichols and Justin Taylor

FOREWORD

The little Augustinian friar who could hardly bring his sighs and cries over his lips to God finally found a voice that echoed across all of western Europe in his own day. His words are still addressing the Christian church in all corners of the world today.

Some Lutherans like to make a proprietary claim on Martin Luther as their own possession. Carl Trueman demonstrates that the Reformer from Wittenberg belongs to the whole church of Jesus Christ. When printers teamed Luther with Johannes Gutenberg, they broadcast his conversations with God and with fellow believers through print not only across their time but into ours. Trueman takes advantage of this and passes the conversation on to us, his readers. From his standpoint as a historian committed to the Reformed confession of the faith, he sensitively approaches this figure separated from twenty-first-century Christians by centuries and contrasting cultures. Nonetheless, he interprets this thinker with whom he does not always agree as a worthy, engaging, and lively conversation partner. Trueman here illuminates for both Lutherans and Christians of other traditions how Luther engaged Holy Scripture and lived out its message of God's creative and re-creative power and profound mercy.

From a perspective outside the tradition that claims Luther's name (and has sometimes even taken his message seriously), Trueman leads the reader into the twists and turns of Luther's career. He explains how the context of German Occamist thought and monastic piety interacted with the biblical texts that Luther pledged to interpret for the benefit of the people of God when he took his oath as a doctor of Bible, a teacher of the Word of God. This study perceptively traces the interaction of Luther's turbulent and tender conscience with the writers of the Scriptures and with a wide variety of religious sensibilities of his peasant relatives and his princely rulers alike. Trueman's judiciously chosen quotations from Luther's own pen enliven his account.

Luther found in Scripture that God is not pleased with external sacrifices, with mere ritual performance of religious duty. God is a God of conversation and community, a God whose words create and constitute reality. Luther finally was plunged into conversation with this God, who had come into human existence to die on a cross and reclaim life for his people. We often think of Luther as a theologian so fixated on Jesus Christ and his cross that he could not pay much attention to the fruits of faith and the life of new obedience to the Creator's plans for human living. In fact, Trueman elucidates the fact that as the professor preached to the Wittenberg congregation and wrote for the instruction of readers across the German lands, Luther emphasized living as the reborn children of God. His strong doctrine of Creation led him to enjoy the Creator's gifts of both material blessings and the relationships woven into the very essence of human life in community. Therefore, he spoke to human need and human desires within the warp and woof of daily life, with all its temptations and all its divine callings to serve as God's masks in his creation. In all Luther's struggles with his own conscience, with stubborn peasants and arrogant princes, with powers of Satan ranged against him and ready to burn him at the stake, Trueman finds "one of us" (p. 55), from whom we can learn much, whether we agree with him at all points or not.

Thus, this volume presents us with a conversation of another "one of us" who has over the years watched Luther closely, listened carefully, and now shares more than only nuggets of insight. This book lays out a plan for living the godly life on the basis of God's address to his human creatures as a Word made flesh, a Word that delivers a promise in oral, written, and sacramental forms. It concretizes wisdom from another era that fits our own because it is mined from the Word of God. In this study Trueman facilitates a rewarding conversation across the ages and leads the reader into eavesdropping on Luther as he listened to and talked with his Lord and the Lord's faithful people.

Robert Kolb
Concordia Seminary, Saint Louis
Herzog August Bibliothek, Wolfenbüttel

PREFACE

I have loved Luther almost since the moment I first grasped the gospel. Along with Augustine, Aquinas, Owen, Warfield, Lloyd-Jones, and Packer, he has been one of my private theological companions. And he has made me laugh far more frequently than any of those other auspicious names. Thus, to be asked to write on him for this Crossway series was both an honor and a delight. I am, nonetheless, tempted to suggest you cast this book aside and read Luther for yourself, for who would want to look at a photograph of the Grand Canyon or Mount Everest when they have the chance to see it for themselves? But for those who want an introduction to the great, flawed genius of the Wittenberg Reformation, I trust this book will serve its purpose and indeed whet their appetite for the real thing.

I would like to thank Steve Nichols and Justin Taylor for inviting me to write this book and then being exceptionally patient as I missed deadline after deadline. They took a risk in asking someone outside the Lutheran tradition to do it, but I hope the final product passes muster even among the true Lutherans out there. And as always, I would like to thank the other staff at Crossway who helped to pilot the book from manuscript to publication.

I would also like to express my deep gratitude to Robert Kolb for taking the time to read the manuscript and write a delightful and kind foreword. Bob is a great Lutheran churchman and scholar. He has taught me through his writings how to love and understand Luther, and it is a privilege to have his imprimatur on this Reformed churchman's labors. In a similar vein, I am also grateful, delighted, and honored that Martin Marty provided such a kind afterword.

Some of the ideas in this book were tested out at the Southern Baptist

Theological Seminary in Louisville, Kentucky, where I was honored to give the Gheens Lectures in the fall of 2012 on the topic of Luther as theological pastor. Thus, I am grateful to President Mohler and (then) Dean Russell Moore for the kind invitation to spend time with their students.

I am also grateful to the trustees and faculty of Westminster Theological Seminary for granting me study leave in the spring of 2014 to finish this book; and also to Ben, Charles, Cris, Dick, Sandy, and Tom. As members of the session of Cornerstone Presbyterian Church (OPC), Ambler, Pennsylvania, along with the congregation, they have provided a happy spiritual home where my family and I have been regularly fed with the Word and sacrament for over a decade now, even if in a way that Dr. Martin would not wholly approve.

Thanks are also due to friends who have taught me much about the Christian life, especially the place of laughter, so central to Dr. Martin himself: Todd, Aimee, Matt, Max, Paul, and Alicia. Keep the jokes coming! Finally, I dedicate this work to my own "Lord Katie." As I wrote in the last book I dedicated to her some sixteen years ago: *sine qua non*. That is even truer today than it was back then.

ABBREVIATIONS

Sources abbreviated *LW*, followed by volume numbers, are from *Luther's Works*, American edition, vols. 1–55, ed. Jaroslav Pelikan and Helmut T. Lehmann (Philadelphia: Muhlenberg and Fortress; St. Louis: Concordia, 1955–). Titles of volumes cited are included in this list:

BC	*The Book of Concord: The Confessions of the Evangelical Lutheran Church*, ed. Theodore G. Tappert (Philadelphia: Mühlenberg, 1959).
LW, 1	*Lectures on Genesis, Chapters 1–5*, ed. Jaroslav Pelikan, 1958.
LW, 11	*First Lectures on the Psalms II, 76–126*, ed. Hilton C. Oswald, 1976.
LW, 14	*Selected Psalms III*, ed. Jaroslav Pelikan, 1958.
LW, 18	*Lectures on the Minor Prophets I: Hosea–Malachi*, ed. Hilton C. Oswald, 1975.
LW, 21	*The Sermon on the Mount (Sermons) and the Magnificat*, ed. Jaroslav Pelikan, 1956.
LW, 26	*Lectures on Galatians, 1535, Chapters 1–4*, ed. Walter A. Hansen, 1963.
LW, 27	*Lectures on Galatians, 1535, Chapters 5–6; Lectures on Galatians, 1519, Chapters 1–6*, ed. Walter A. Hansen, 1964.
LW, 31	*Career of the Reformer I*, ed. Harold J. Grimm, 1957.
LW, 32	*Career of the Reformer II*, ed. George W. Forell, 1958.
LW, 33	*Career of the Reformer III*, ed. Philip S. Watson, 1972.
LW, 34	*Career of the Reformer IV*, ed. Lewis W. Spitz, 1960.
LW, 35	*Word and Sacrament I*, ed. E. Theodore Bachman, 1960.

LW, 36   *Word and Sacrament II*, ed. Abdel Ross Wentz, 1959.

LW, 38   *Word and Sacrament IV*, ed. Martin E. Lehmann, 1971.

LW, 40   *Church and Ministry II*, ed. Conrad Bergendoff, 1958.

LW, 41   *Church and Ministry III*, ed. Eric W. Gritsch, 1966.

LW, 42   *Devotional Writings I*, ed. Martin O. Dietrich, 1969.

LW, 43   *Devotional Writings II*, ed. Gustav K. Wiencke, 1968.

LW, 44   *The Christian in Society I*, ed. James Atkinson, 1966.

LW, 45   *The Christian in Society II*, ed. Walther I. Brandt, 1962.

LW, 46   *The Christian in Society III*, ed. Robert C. Schultz, 1967.

LW, 47   *The Christian in Society IV*, ed. Franklin Sherman, 1971.

LW, 49   *Letters II*, ed. and trans. Gottfried G. Krodel, 1972.

LW, 50   *Letters III*, ed. and trans. Gottfried G. Krodel, 1975.

LW, 51   *Sermons I*, ed. and trans. John W. Doberstein, 1959.

LW, 53   *Liturgy and Hymns*, ed. Ulrich S. Leupold, 1965.

LW, 54   *Table Talk*, ed. and trans. Theodore G. Tappert, 1967.

Cited cities in the life of Luther
on a map of modern Germany

Magdeburg

Wittenberg

Mansfeld

Frankenhausen
Eisleben

Leipzig

Eisenach Erfurt

Dresden

Marburg
Wartburg

Weimar

Zwickau

Coburg

Worms
Heidelberg

Nuremberg

Augsburg

kilometers   100   200   300
miles   50   100   150   200

INTRODUCTION

WHAT HAS GENEVA TO DO
WITH WITTENBERG?

It was long ago and it was far away,
and it was so much better than it is today.

MEATLOAF, "PARADISE BY THE DASHBOARD LIGHT"[1]

It is traditional to start a book such as this by asking, why write a book on Luther on the Christian life? But in the case of the Reformer of Wittenberg, that would seem pointless. After Augustine, no single churchman-theologian has influenced the Western church more than Luther over the centuries. Not only did his pastoral protest in the sixteenth century precipitate the shattering of the medieval church, but many of his own particular concerns—the clarity of Scripture, the centrality of the preached Word, justification by grace through faith, and the Lord's Supper—helped to define Protestantism in relation to Roman Catholicism and to determine how different Protestant communions came to understand themselves in relation to each other. In short, an understanding of Luther's approach to the Christian life is fundamental to understanding the varieties of practical Western Christianity over the last five hundred years.

Yet, readers of Luther should be aware of a number of problems from the start. The first is that his theology lends itself to dramatic sound bites. Many who have never read Luther in any great depth will be familiar with various phrases that he used or that are popularly ascribed to him: "theologian of glory," "theologian of the cross," "justification by grace through

---

[1] Lyrics by James "Jim" Steinman.

faith alone," "the hidden God and the revealed God," "the bondage of the will," "the epistle of straw." No Christian with an interest in theology can fail to be intrigued by such vocabulary; but being intrigued by or familiar with these phrases is not the same as understanding exactly what they mean, still less how they fit into a comprehensive view of the Christian life.

This problem is particularly acute when we take into account the evangelical propensity to reinvent heroes of the past as modern-day evangelicals. Numerous characters have been subjected to this over the years, Dietrich Bonhoeffer and C. S. Lewis, to name but two of the most obvious. Why this should be the case is not immediately obvious, but perhaps it has something to do with the current reluctance in American culture to relate positively to anyone with whom one has serious ideological differences. Sadly, this often means that one cannot learn from others: if we always re-create others in our own image, we can never be truly challenged by the ways in which they differ from us.

Luther was not a modern American evangelical. Indeed, neither his thought world nor his physical world were those of American evangelicalism. For many modern evangelicals, for example, private Bible study is central to their understanding of the Christian life, while sacraments are peripheral. The tradition, in some Baptist circles, of allowing repeated baptisms for those who keep repenting and being unsure of whether their earlier baptism truly followed a real profession of faith shows just how low a view of baptism evangelicals can have. And few, if any, evangelicals regard the Lord's Supper as anything other than a mere symbolic display.

For Luther, however, the idea that private Bible study might be a universal staple of the Christian life would have been bizarre: after all, few of his parishioners would have been able to read, even if they could afford a book. As to sacraments, Luther's understanding of justification is driven in large part by his changing view of baptism; "I have been baptized" was his chosen defense against the temptations that the Devil whispered in his ear; and he was adamant that Huldrych Zwingli was of a "different spirit," thus calling into question his Christianity, precisely because the Swiss theologian argued that the Lord's Supper was symbolic. In short, Luther would not have recognized typical evangelical piety or attitudes about baptism; and if consistent with his rhetoric against Zwingli, he would actually have dismissed all evangelicals, Prayer Book Anglicans, and Presbyterians as "of another spirit" because of their failure to agree with him on the Supper. Of course, Luther was often bombastic, and we should not always take him at his word. But even if he would not have denied the Christianity of all those who differed with him on the Supper, he would nonetheless have regarded them as seriously deficient in their understanding of the Christian faith.

In fact, Luther and his world are deeply alien to the sensibilities of modern evangelicalism. Luther's piety was rooted in the gathering of the church, in the Word preached more than the Word read, and in the sacraments of baptism and the Lord's Supper. Further, his world was one where the Devil walked abroad, where the supernatural permeated the natural, where the battle in the human breast between the old man and the new was also paralleled by the larger cosmic struggle between God and the Devil over the fate of the soul of every individual. Luther the familiar hero of evangelical mythology needs to be set aside if we are to learn about Luther the theologian of the Christian life.

This problem of familiarity and quotability is compounded by a second problem in approaching Luther: the common belief that he was not a systematic thinker. There is a sense in which this claim is true: Luther did not write a comprehensive *summa* or systematic theology of the kind produced by Aquinas. In the early Lutheran tradition, that task fell to his brilliant younger colleague Philipp Melanchthon (1497–1560), whose *Loci Communes* fulfilled that role from 1521 onward. Yet one should not make the mistake of assuming that because he wrote no system of theology, his thought was not remarkably consistent in both its content and, indeed, its development. Over many decades, Luther wrote a vast amount of theology in a wide variety of genres, from sermons to polemical treatises, to pastoral letters, to hymns, to catechisms. Does he contradict himself at points? Probably. Who would not after writing millions of words on a vast spectrum of topics over nearly forty years? But is the overall content of his thought both consistent and sophisticated? Absolutely, as witnessed to by the large number of syntheses of his thought that have been produced over the years.[2] The fact that his thought is elaborate and consistent, then, demands that readers of his work—and even more so those who quote his

---

[2] See the "Further Reading" section at the end of this introduction. The meaning of Luther's theology was even a source of controversy almost from the moment of his death, when his followers rapidly divided into two broad groups: the Philippists (who read Luther in terms of the concerns of Melanchthon) and the Gnesio-Lutherans (or "real Lutherans"). The former tended to be more open to the Reformed on the issue of the Lord's Supper, more Erasmian on the issue of the human will, and more concessive to the Roman Catholics on issues of liturgical aesthetics; the latter maintained a strict opposition to Reformed views of the Lord's Supper and firmly upheld Luther's teaching on the will as expressed in his 1525 treatise *The Bondage of the Will*.

well-known terms and phrases—make sure they set it into the overall context of his theology lest they put it to a purpose Luther himself would have
repudiated.

This in turn leads to a third problem, which is generated by the su-
perficial familiarity many of Luther's fans have with his thought: Luther's
own personal biography is crucial to understanding the nature and development of his thought. To make the point specifically with regard to the
topic of this volume: we cannot understand Luther's view of the Christian
life in general without understanding his own Christian life in particular.

One of the interesting things about the reception of Luther in contemporary evangelical Protestant circles is that it is the *early* Reformation Luther—
the Luther of the Heidelberg Disputation, of *The Freedom of the Christian
Man*, and of *The Bondage of the Will*—who generally provides the quotations,
the sound bites, and the clichés. Thus, it is the Luther of 1525 and earlier
who receives all the attention. The problem with this approach is that Luther
lived for another twenty-one years after his clash with Desiderius Erasmus,
years marked not only by the doctrinally defining conflict with Zwingli but
also by the institutional and practical consolidation of the Lutheran Reformation at ground level. The Reformation was, after all, a work in progress
in Luther's lifetime: his theology shattered old pastoral patterns and transformed the practical and experiential expectations of Christians. Even as
it resolved some of the difficult issues generated by late medieval Catholicism, it asked new questions and created new problems, which then had to
be addressed. It is not enough to quote Luther's *Heidelberg Disputation* or
The Freedom of the Christian Man without seeing how the theology of these
documents affected the world of their own day and how Luther and his colleagues had to refine their thought and practices in light of this.

To give the reader a little foretaste of what I wish to argue in later chapters, it seems to me that the post-1525 Luther is vital for understanding
his view of the Christian life. By that time, he was growing old and feeling
the effects of the aging process. He had also suffered chronic bouts of constipation ever since his sedentary sojourn at the Wartburg Castle in 1521.
Furthermore, it was becoming increasingly clear to Luther that he was not
living on the threshold of Christ's return, that the mere preaching of the
Word would not guarantee the progress of the kingdom and the good order
of the church. In 1522, Luther could lightheartedly explain the success of
the Reformation by commenting that he just sat around in the pub drink-

ing beer with Amsdorf and Melanchthon while God's Word was out doing all the work;[3] the years after 1525 taught Luther that it was a whole lot more difficult than that. The Peasants' War of 1525 and the dispute with Zwingli throughout the latter half of the 1520s demonstrated how illusory was the Protestant consensus and how socially dangerous were the times. The rising antinomianism in the parishes showed how the preaching of the Word needed to be set within a more disciplined pastoral and ecclesiastical framework. The failure of the emperor to subscribe to the Augsburg Confession, of the pope to acknowledge the correctness of Luther's stand, and of the Jews to convert to Christianity all indicated that the Reformation was going to be a long haul.

If the young Luther had, like the British soldiers of 1914, assumed that the conflict would all be over by Christmas, the later Luther knew that the struggle was actually going to last until the end of time—and that that was much further into the future than he had ever imagined in even his worst nightmares. In the interim, moral imperatives, coherent pedagogy, and church structures had to reenter the picture in order to guarantee the preservation of the gospel for future generations.

Given all of the caveats necessary when the modern reader approaches Luther, what is unique about this man that makes him particularly useful as a dialogue partner on the Christian life today? Obviously, as noted above, he defined many of the terms of Protestant debates about Christianity in general. Yet there is much more to him than this. As a theologian who was also a pastor, he was continually wrestling with how his theological insights connected to the lives and experiences of the people under his care. This gave much of his writing a distinctly pastoral dimension. Further, he was (for a theologian) unusually forthcoming about his own life and experiences. There was a personal passion to Luther that finds no obvious counterpart in the writings of other significant Reformers. Calvin's letters contain insights into his private life, but his lectures, commentaries, and treatises offer little or no light on the inner life of the man himself. John Owen outlived all eleven of his children, yet he never once mentioned the personal devastation that this must have brought to his world. Luther was different: he lived his inner life as a public drama. Unlike many today on chat shows and Twitter and personal blogs, he did not do so in a way that boosted his own prestige; he did it with irony, humor, and occasional

---

[3] *LW*, 51:77.

pathos. But he did it nonetheless, and this makes him a fascinating case study in self-reflection on the Christian life.

In the eight chapters that follow, I offer an account of Luther's understanding of the Christian life that takes as its cue the fact that he himself lived a dramatic Christian life. Too often theologians are treated as if they were simply abstract collections of ideas. Luther was a man of real flesh and blood; he was a son, a priest, a pastor, a preacher, a politician, a controversialist, a professor, a husband, a father, a drinking companion, a humorist, a depressive, a man who was to stand more than once at the grave of one of his beloved children. He baptized babies, performed marriages, heard confessions, presided at funerals. All of these things shaped his theology. Indeed, he wrote theology from the position of being immersed in the mucky reality of everyday life.

It is perhaps helpful to mention, at this point, what I do not do in this work. First, I do not interact extensively with the vast and ever-growing scholarship on Luther. My purpose is to expound Luther in a way that introduces his thinking on the Christian life to a thoughtful Christian audience. Thus, debates over contested points of interpretation of his work do not generally fall within my purview. The one exception is perhaps his view of holiness in the Christian life, but that is driven more by contemporary debates in the church than by the dynamics of Luther scholarship.

Second, I do not offer significant critique of Luther. I could have spent time offering an analysis of those points where Lutherans and Presbyterians disagree and used the opportunity to promote my own confessional position. I have tried hard to avoid that temptation. What I have done is offered an exposition of Luther's theology on its own terms. Yes, I have significant disagreements with Luther on matters such as baptism and the Lord's Supper, but they do not feature in the following chapters.

At the end of each chapter, I have included a brief section in which I offer some reflections on how the subject matter of the chapter might apply to the church and to Christians today. There is always the possibility of anachronism here. As in the quotation from Meatloaf at the head of this introduction, there can be a tendency to idealize the past and simply use studies like this one as an excuse for nostalgia and lamenting the loss of a bygone golden age. That is pointless and historically fallacious: the past was not that good, after all. Nevertheless, as Christians we have the responsibility, indeed the privilege and the imperative, of dialoguing constructively with the saints of the past in a way that can help us to think clearly in the present. Given Luther's seminal importance for Protestantism, engaging with his thought is vital. I trust that these sections of reflection will provide both challenge and encouragement.

As far as the overall content of the chapters is concerned, in chapter 1 I describe Luther's life in terms of its many dramatic episodes. This chapter is very lightly footnoted, as the reader should really turn to the works by Bainton, Marty, and, above all, Brecht listed at the end of this introduction for the full details on Luther's life. Nevertheless, some knowledge of his biography is necessary for understanding his theology. Luther's own wrestling with God shaped his understanding of God's Word in profound ways. Further, an understanding of both his strengths and his terrible flaws will help the reader have a realistic understanding of the man, warts and all.

In chapter 2, I examine some of the foundational theological concepts in Luther's thinking. Taking the Heidelberg Disputation as my starting point, I explore the key distinction between the theologian of glory and the theologian of the cross. Those basic categories shape all of Luther's understanding of life as it is lived before God. Then, I outline his understanding of justification, as well as his understanding of human beings as simultaneously both righteous and sinners, before looking at his notion of the priesthood and kingship of all believers. Weakness is strength—this is the overall message of God in Christ, a powerful antidote to the Nietzschean excesses of our current world.

In chapter 3, I focus on the Word preached. Luther had a profoundly theological understanding of God's Word. It shaped his views of creation, of God's action in general, and of his specific action in salvation. There is real value in reflecting upon Luther's insights here, for they remind the preacher that his task rests not in his own strength or eloquence but in the power of the God who speaks through him.

In chapter 4, we see how, for Luther, the Christian life had a strongly liturgical aspect to it. The basics of the Christian life were routine and ordinary: learning the Decalogue, the Apostles' Creed, and the Lord's Prayer. Luther designed liturgies and catechisms to do this. We may live in an age when everything has to be "radical" and "revolutionary." For Luther the most radical thing one could do was to learn the basics of the faith with the simple trust of a little child.

In chapter 5, I examine how the Word works in the lives of individuals. Central to this is Luther's idea that hearing God's Word involves speech, meditation, and "trials" (or, to use the German, *Anfechtungen*). The Word addresses us at the core of our being; learning it is never a purely cerebral or rote exercise. It grips our souls, drives us to despair and lifts us up to the very portals of heaven.

In chapter 6, we come to the area where modern evangelicals will have least sympathy with Luther: the sacraments. Yet here we can learn from him even as we differ. The great objectivity of God's gift to us in Christ undergirds Luther's thinking, as does his absolute conviction that the incarnation means that God deals with broken sinners in tangible, weak forms that are despised by the theologians of glory.

In chapter 7, I address the tricky set of issues surrounding Luther's thinking on actual, intrinsic righteousness. Here I make the case to which I alluded above, that the popular Luther canon of a select few pre-1525 works is not a sufficient evidential base for drawing wider conclusions about his mature theology.

Finally, in chapter 8, I look at Luther and real life: life in the public sphere, earthly callings, marriage, and family. Luther, perhaps more than anyone else in the sixteenth century, revolutionized thinking on all these matters and thus deserves attention.

As I draw this introduction to a close, it is perhaps time to mention why I myself find Luther such a worthy subject of personal study. I am not exactly promising Luther territory: a Reformed Presbyterian who holds a view of the Lord's Supper, and correlative christology, that Luther would have decried as positively unchristian. Indeed, as I noted above, when I survey the series of which this volume is a part, it seems that I am the only author who might say that he stands clearly outside the broad tradition that his chosen subject represents. Further, I have rarely if ever used any of Luther's commentaries or lectures in order to help clarify an exegetical point. Frankly, he lacks the precision and sensitivity to the biblical text that one finds in Calvin. So why is it that, despite many attempts over the years to move on from studying Luther, I find myself drawn back to him again and again? And why have I been teaching his thought every year now for over two decades to classes of undergraduate and graduate students on both sides of the Atlantic?

First, I was profoundly influenced as a student by a comment made to me by my own doctoral supervisor, the Zwingli scholar Peter Stephens. Peter is a highly sacramental Arminian Methodist with little personal sympathy for Zwingli. Yet he told me that he considered it an appropriate challenge for a Christian to see if he could write with fairness and enthusiasm about someone with whom he radically disagreed. That way, he said, he could be sure his analysis and conclusions were not driven by special pleading.

I have always valued that comment as sage advice and now have an opportunity to see if I am worthy of standing in the tradition of my own academic mentor's approach. I would not say that I am in *radical* disagreement with much of Luther, other than his view of the sacraments (though that would be enough to render me a Radical in Luther's eyes). But he is not my tradition, even as I find him useful. Thus, I agreed to write the book out of a certain methodological contrarianism.

Second, I find Luther to be one of the most human theologians there is, certainly among Protestants. His humor alone endears him to me. His last written words—"We are beggars: this is true"—set all human pretensions to greatness and divinity in tragicomic perspective. A theologian who ultimately helps us to remember that we are of no lasting earthly importance whatsoever has crucial importance in an era obsessed with numbers of Twitter followers and Facebook friends.

Third, I find Luther to address some of the most basic questions of human existence: despair, illness, sex, love, bereavement, children, enemies, danger, death. Luther touches on them all, and always with an unusual anecdote, an insightful comment, a human touch. There is no false, desiccated, tedious piety about the man. He lived his Christian life to the full, red in tooth and claw.

Fourth, I find Luther to be fun. Who else would describe how a woman scared the Devil away by breaking wind in his face, but then caution his listeners not to do the same as it could prove lethal? Any theologian with advice like that has to be worth reading.

Finally, I love Luther because it was his highest ambition to let God be God. And in doing so he realized that the love of God does not find but creates that which is lovely to it.

And with that thought, to which we shall return, let us turn to Luther's life.

Further Reading

Two useful selections of Luther's major writings are

> Dillenberger, John, ed. *Martin Luther: Selections from His Writings*. Garden City, NY: Doubleday, 1961.
>
> Lull, Timothy F., ed. *Martin Luther's Basic Theological Writings*. Minneapolis: Fortress, 1989.

Throughout this book, I cite the standard multivolume English translation, *Luther's Works*, which was initially produced under the general editorship of Jaroslav Pelikan and is now published by Concordia (for specific volume titles, see the table of abbreviations, above).

The best introductory biographies in English are

> Bainton, Roland H. *Here I Stand: A Life of Martin Luther*. London: Forgotten Books, 2012.
>
> Marty, Martin E. *Martin Luther: A Life*. New York: Penguin, 2004.

For the really serious Luther aficionado, however, the best biography in English is

> Brecht, Martin. *Martin Luther*. 3 vols. Minneapolis: Fortress, 1985–1993.

Summaries of Luther's theology abound. Among the best are

> Kolb, Robert. *Martin Luther: Confessor of the Faith*. New York: Oxford University Press, 2009.
>
> Lohse, Bernhard. *Martin Luther's Theology: Its Historical and Systematic Development*. Translated and edited by Roy A. Harrisville. Edinburgh: T&T Clark, 1999.

Finally, for anyone interested in how Luther's theology can be used to inform church life today, see

> Kolb, Robert, and Charles P. Arand. *The Genius of Luther's Theology: A Wittenberg Way of Thinking for the Contemporary Church*. Grand Rapids: Baker, 2008.

CHAPTER 1

MARTIN LUTHER'S CHRISTIAN LIFE

The past is a foreign country; they do things differently there.

L. P. HARTLEY, *THE GO-BETWEEN*

Martin Luther, the man who should perhaps shoulder the greatest responsibility for rupturing the Western church in the Reformation, came from a relatively humble background that gave no hint of the controversial stature he would later achieve. He was born on November 10, 1483, to Hans and Margaret Luther in the town of Eisleben. Ironically, while this town played little role in Luther's life as a whole, he was to die there in 1546, shortly after preaching his last sermon in the local church.

Hans Luther was a son of the soil, but in accordance with medieval inheritance laws, he did not inherit the family farm. Instead, as the oldest son, he was expected to make his own way in the world. This he did, first as a miner and then as a mine manager. The need for work meant that the Luther family had to leave Eisleben for Mansfeld just a few weeks after Martin's birth, but Hans ultimately did well and rose to the level of his managerial position.

Like many parents who have worked hard and enjoyed social mobility, Hans Luther had greater hopes for his son. Thus, he decided that the young Martin would not have to work at the physically hard labor that had marked his own early life but would go to university to study for a career in law. And so it was in 1501 that Martin left home and matriculated at the University of Erfurt.

Studies at the university were typical of late medieval institutions. Law was one of the three higher faculties, along with medicine and theology, and in order to qualify to study it, the student first had to pass through the general arts curriculum, which Luther did. Thus, he was typical of his age in pursuing an unexceptional education. This ordinary start, however, was to be dramatically disrupted.

It was in 1505, while returning to the university after a visit to his parents, that Luther found himself in a situation which changed his life forever. Caught in a thunderstorm, he was almost killed when a bolt of lightning came crashing down at his side. Today, we regard such things as natural phenomena, the result of massive ionic imbalances in the atmosphere created by the collision of ice crystals at high altitude; in Luther's day, such things were supernatural acts of God, intimations of divine judgment. Consequently, as the lightning bolt earthed beside him, Luther threw himself to the ground and screamed, "St. Anne, save me and I will become a monk!" St. Anne being the patron saint of miners, it was quite probably instinctive for Luther to call upon the saint who was presumably central to the piety of the household in which he had grown up.

All the evidence suggests that Luther was rather earnest and an intense young man. Such a vow to God, even when made in panic at what he must have thought could be his moment of death, was to him a very serious matter, and within a few days he presented himself at the door of the Augustinian cloister in Erfurt.

The choice of the Augustinian Order might at first appear to be significant. As it bears the name of the great Bishop Augustine of Hippo, the great opponent of Pelagius, might not Luther have chosen this order because of its view of God's grace? This is unlikely. The name was certainly taken from Augustine, but the order itself was not particularly committed to an especially pristine Augustinianism. In fact, as all medieval theology was to some extent a dialogue with Augustine, one might say that all medieval theology could be categorized as broadly Augustinian.

Luther's decision to abandon a potentially lucrative career in law and pursue a monastic vocation proved extremely upsetting to Hans, and the relationship between father and son was badly disrupted for some years.

In modern Luther studies this has led the psychoanalyst and writer Erik Erikson to argue that Luther's theological struggles were really a projection of his dispute with his father onto God.[1] Thus, Luther ostensibly sought to be right with God when, in reality, he was seeking to be right with his earthly father.

Evangelical Christians have tended to dismiss Erikson's thesis as speculative and reductionist. In fact, while it is undoubtedly reductionist to make Luther's theology merely a cipher for his personal anxieties about his family, it is surely also true that the relationship between a father and a son is both complex and important. Thus, it stands to reason that Hans's disapproval of his son's move to the cloister impacted Luther's life in significant ways.

Perhaps the most dramatic moment in the father-son drama came as a result of another decision Luther made: to become a priest. Monks were members of religious orders but were not necessarily ordained to the priesthood and thus would not have the sacramental duties and pastoral responsibilities of the parish priest. Luther, however, was ordained as priest in 1507 and officiated at his first Mass. The moment was one of high drama for him: not only was his father present, but Luther was also aware that as a priest he was in effect making, touching, and holding the real body and blood of Christ in the bread and the cup. The question that burned Luther's soul for many years became acute at this point: how could he, knowing how sinful he was, possibly stand in such proximity to a holy and righteous God?

Later Protestants have often forgotten that Luther's existential struggles with God's righteousness cannot be separated from his sacramental theology. The Mass left a lasting impression on his soul, not only on the grounds that he was making God but also because he later came to see the medieval view of it as the centerpiece of a works righteousness that served only to fool individuals into thinking they were doing good works. It was never transubstantiation that he found so obnoxious in the medieval sacrament; it was the implication of sacrifice, of offering something to God, that was so disturbing to him.

In 1508, Luther was transferred from Erfurt to the relatively new University of Wittenberg. Founded in 1502 by Frederick the Wise, the Elector of Saxony, this was to be Luther's home, with brief exceptions, for the rest of his days. Later in Luther's story, this university had two particular points

---

[1] See Erik H. Erikson, *Young Man Luther: A Study in Psychoanalysis and History* (New York: Norton, 1958).

of significance. First, it was a new foundation and, as such, its founder was eager for it to make its name. When Luther became infamous in 1517 and beyond, it is thus not so surprising that Frederick would exert his influence to protect his controversial professor. Then, as now, there was a sense that all publicity could at least be made into good publicity, if the time was right.

The other significant factor was the location of the institution in Electoral Saxony. While the Holy Roman Empire had been founded by Charlemagne in 800, it had undergone considerable political development in the Middle Ages. Under the Golden Bull of 1356, it was established that the emperor should be appointed by a vote of a college of seven electors, among whom was numbered the prince of Saxony. Thus, when Luther moved to Wittenberg in 1508, he came under the authority—and, crucially, the protection—of an imperial elector. This position effectively gave Frederick the Wise political power and influence beyond what the economic and military strength of his territory might have suggested. As history played out, it also meant that Luther was far safer there than he might have been elsewhere.

For the rest of his life, Luther would have the dual role of professor of theology and pastor. As professor, he followed the standard career path of a late medieval theologian, lecturing on Peter Lombard's *Four Books of Sentences* and then on large sections of Scripture. It is the ignorance and snobbery of modern Protestantism which derides the Middle Ages for a failure to engage with the text of Scripture. While it is true that the text of choice—indeed, for most, the only accessible text—was the Latin Vulgate, the average medieval professor was expected to have exegeted his way through more Scripture before he was deemed remotely competent as a theologian than any seminary professor in North America today.

The years 1510–1511 saw Luther traveling to Rome on business for the Augustinian Order. As for many before and since, his visit to the Eternal City was a profoundly moving and conflicted experience. In addition to its obvious historical and theological significance, he was impressed by the opportunities for piety that the city represented, with its multitude of relics and religious artifacts. Nevertheless, he also witnessed firsthand the corruption that coexisted amid the piety. The images of excess that the papal court presented to him would shape his later opinions of the papacy and, indeed, fuel the kind of rhetoric he was happy to deploy against it.

Back in the classroom, Luther continued to exegete his way through books of Scripture, particularly the Psalms and Romans. This routine work was to have a major impact upon his theology, as it led to two significant changes in his thinking between 1512 and 1517. First, he changed his mind on the nature of sin and baptism. He had been taught that sin was a *fomes*, akin to a piece of tinder. The implication was that sin was a weakness that needed to be dealt with via the sacraments. One might say that such an understanding of sin meant baptism was understood as a kind of damping down of the problem or a temporary fix. Once sin reared its ugly head within the life of the subject after baptism, then there was need for further moral triage in the form of the other sacraments. Luther, however, became convinced that sin meant that human beings were morally dead. We will explore this in more detail in the later chapters, but the key point to note here is that this change in thinking came about through his wrestling with the teaching of the Psalms and with Paul. These labors in exegesis intensified his understanding of the seriousness of sin: no longer were sinners highly defective; they were dead. Sin is a root problem. It defines human beings before God in a profound and radical manner. And that has all manner of implications for how fallen humanity and salvation are to be understood.

One immediate implication is that one's understanding of baptism needs to be changed: baptism can no longer be simply a damping down of sinful weakness and tendencies. If the sinner is dead, then he needs more than cleaning or even healing; he needs to be resurrected. Luther thus moved from seeing baptism as primarily indicating a washing or a cleansing to signifying death and resurrection.

This points to the second change that this alteration on baptism and sin required: a critical reevaluation of the way of salvation Luther had learned at the hands of his medieval teachers. Luther was schooled in what later scholars have come to term the *via moderna*, or "modern way." This tradition of theology is closely associated with later medieval theologians such as William of Occam (1288–1347) and Gabriel Biel (c. 1420–1495). The latter was particularly important to Luther as he would have had to study and lecture upon Biel's seminal text *The Canon of the Mass* (1488). Basically, Biel understood God as being utterly transcendent and sovereign, able to do anything he chose with the exception of logically contradicting himself. So, for example, he could make a world where human beings have four legs, but he could not make a world where triangles have four sides. This is what medieval theologians typically referred to as God's *absolute power.*

Yet the world is stable, contains a finite number of objects, and thus witnesses to the fact that God's absolute power is not fully realized. Thus, medieval theologians posited that God also has an *ordained power,* a finite set of possibilities that God has actually chosen to realize. Biel applied this to the realm of salvation: God can demand perfection from human beings prior to giving them grace but, in fact, has condescended via means of a *pactum* (or covenant) to give grace to "the one who does what is in oneself," a literal translation of the first part of the Latin phrase, *facienti quod in se est, Deus gratiam non denegat.*

This concept seems at first to be very useful. In answer to Luther's question, How can I be right before a righteous God? one might respond, "Do what is in you," that is, do your best. We should also note that the underlying understanding of what makes a human being right before God is shifted in this system from being an intrinsic quality in the Christian (actual, intrinsic righteousness) to the external declaration of God: I am right with God not because my works are, in and of themselves, worthy of his favor but because he has decided to consider them so. That concept was to have a profound influence on Luther and to provide the foundation for his later Protestant understanding of justification.[2]

The pastoral problem generated by this *pactum* idea, of course, is that knowing how and when one has done one's best then becomes a highly subjective matter and, in the experience of Luther in the cloister, an increasingly terrifying one: the more Luther exerted himself in good works, the more he became certain that he had fallen catastrophically short of meeting the minimum condition of the *pactum.* This situation became much worse, of course, when Luther came to identify sin as death. How can a dead person do his or her best? This led to perhaps the most significant move in Luther's thinking, which is detectable in his lectures on Romans during 1515–1516: Luther came to identify the condition of the *pactum* as being humility, utter despair in oneself as a condition for throwing oneself entirely and without reserve upon God's mercy. This crucial insight paved the way for his later understanding of the necessary condition as faith, trust in God, a concept very closely related to this earlier understanding of humility.

---

[2] This is discussed in more detail in chapter 2.

The Indulgence Controversy

While Luther was undergoing this theological transformation, events in the wider European scene were conspiring to bring him to a much wider audience than might fit into the lecture hall at the University of Wittenberg or the parish church. Pope Leo X (1475–1521) was presiding over a Roman church that had exhausted its finances in wars and later in the massive building project of St. Peter's and the Vatican. Then, in the German lands to the north, an ambitious cleric, Albrecht of Brandenburg (1490–1545), was looking to add a third bishopric to his tally. Bishoprics brought revenue and were thus desirable; but the canon law of the church prevented anyone from holding three simultaneously without a license from the pope. Thus, there was a happy confluence of interest at this point between the financial needs of the papacy and the ecclesiastical aspirations of Albrecht. In short, the pope granted Albrecht permission to take the third bishopric, and Albrecht paid the pope a handsome sum for the privilege. To finance the deal, Albrecht borrowed a significant sum of money from the Fuggers bank, and the pope allowed Albrecht to raise an indulgence, half of the proceeds of which could be used to pay down the loan, and half of which would go straight into the papal coffers.

Indulgences were certificates sold by the church, and they guaranteed the purchaser, or the designated beneficiary, relief from a stipulated period of time in purgatory. In medieval Catholic eschatology, when people died, they went to hell, to heaven, or more likely, to purgatory, a place where the godly might be purged of their remaining impurities before being translated into paradise. The concept of purgatory found its origin in the Apocrypha and was present in the work of numerous early church fathers, including Augustine. In the early church, however, the doctrine had functioned merely as part of individual eschatology; by the late Middle Ages it had been connected to the penitential system of the church. Two papal bulls in particular are of relevance to this: *Unigenitus* (1343) and *Salvator Noster* (1476). The former established the dogma of the treasury of merits, consisting of the merits of Christ, the Virgin Mary, and all the great saints of the church, which could be distributed by the pope. The latter connected the treasury of merits to financial gifts to the church, such that those giving such money might enjoy eschatological benefit in the form of reduced time in purgatory. Thus, the dogmatic foundation of indulgences was established.

The sale of Albrecht's indulgence was entrusted to a Dominican friar,

Johann Tetzel (1465–1519). He was a profane man but a brilliant salesman, using jingles (according to Luther's *Ninety-Five Theses*) such as the gem "As soon as a coin in the coffer rings, a soul from purgatory springs," and asserting that even if one had raped the Virgin Mary, one of his indulgences would be sufficient to cover the sin.

While Tetzel was not allowed to sell his indulgences in Electoral Saxony (the elector having his own collection of sacred relics, which he did not want eclipsed by some rival object of piety), the issue was one of some pastoral urgency for Luther. Having concluded that God's grace was so costly that only the death and resurrection of the Son of God himself could deal with the human dilemma of death in sin, and only total despair of oneself and consequent humility before God were sufficient to meet the conditions of the *pactum*, Luther inevitably saw the cash transactions of a Tetzel as cheapening grace. More than that, Tetzel was selling false security to people; and as Luther's parishioners crossed the river into the neighboring territory of Ducal Saxony where the Dominican salesman was plying his trade, Luther would inevitably have to take a stand.

Luther preached on indulgences at Easter of 1517 and then was strangely silent on the matter. In September 1517, he delivered his *Disputation against Scholastic Theology*, which, of all the writings of the year, was the most radical in its full-orbed attack on late medieval theological method; but it was not directly aimed at the indulgence issue, and it stirred up no significant controversy. Then, on October 31, 1517, in accordance with standard academic protocol for announcing a debate, he nailed to the door of the Castle Church in Wittenberg ninety-five theses against the practice of the sale of indulgences.

In the history of the Reformation, this document has taken on almost mythical status as the writing that triggered the whole crisis. In fact, while some of the theses sparkle with the rhetoric that would become the hallmark of the later Luther, some are more obscure. Indeed, unless the modern reader of the missive has a good working knowledge of late medieval theology and piety, a number of its theses will be incomprehensible. Further, Luther's own approach at this point was arguably fairly cautious: he was attacking what he perceived to be the abuse of indulgences in fleecing the flock of money and selling God's grace for cash; whether indulgences could have a legitimate use was a question about which he was undecided and unclear.

In a sense, the details are no longer important: the precise issues and practices to which Luther was reacting have long since vanished. What is important is the theology on which the theses were built: the theology of humility and the costliness of grace. Though Luther probably did not realize it at the time, these struck at the heart of the medieval sacramental system and thus at the authority of the church. In criticizing indulgences, Luther also did what is always guaranteed to precipitate a reaction: he hit the church where it hurts most, in her revenue department.

From Heidelberg to the Death of Maximilian

While the *Ninety-Five Theses* rapidly became a popular tract and a rallying point for protest, the church was slow to act. Indeed, in April 1518, Luther traveled to the city of Heidelberg for a regular chapter meeting of the Augustinian Order. It was here that he presided over what is now the famous Heidelberg Disputation, where Augustinian friar Leonhard Beier presented a set of theses Luther had prepared on philosophy and theology. We will examine these in detail in chapter 2. Here it is simply worth noting that these theses represented a return to, and a radicalization of, the theology of his *Disputation against Scholastic Theology* of 1517. While the *Ninety-Five Theses* were making Luther a significant public figure, his real theological agenda was much more radical than anything that tract might have suggested.

In the summer of 1518, the controversy was now spilling beyond the borders of Electoral Saxony, and it was clear that the church would have to act. At around this time, there was a strange incident at a monastery in Dresden. Invited to a party there, Luther drank too much and waxed eloquent about Thomas Aquinas and the use of Aristotle in theology. Behind a curtain in the room sat a Dominican friar, taking down notes on what the increasingly voluble Augustinian was saying. These notes were later made public and further enhanced Luther's reputation for dangerous heterodoxy.

At the same time the Dominicans were playing nasty tricks on Luther, the church was starting a more formal process. In August, Luther was summoned to appear in Rome. This was almost certainly an automatic procedure, triggered by the complaint from Albrecht against Luther of the previous December. The pope also commissioned Sylvester Mazzolini, better known as Prierias, to form a theological opinion on Luther. This was published under the title *Dialogue against the Presumptuous Conclusions of Martin Luther*. In it, Prierias boasted that Luther was so incompetent a theologian that he, Prierias, had written the refutation in just three days.

Luther's response was brilliant and demonstrated an instinctive grasp of the nature of the print medium. Rather than have the book burned—the typical approach of the church of the time—he had it reprinted with his own response, which, he declared, he had written in just two days. Game, set, and match to the wit from Wittenberg.

The summons, however, shook Luther, who wrote immediately to George Spalatin, Frederick the Wise's secretary, to the effect that the honor of Wittenberg was at stake and that whatever proceedings were to take place should happen on German soil.[3] Given Frederick's status as an elector, along with the emperor's need for support against the Turks, who were placing the eastern flank of the empire under pressure, the Wittenbergers were able to persuade church and empire that the place to deal with Luther would be at the Imperial Diet of Augsburg in October 1518.[4]

Thus, Luther traveled to Augsburg in October and was there interrogated by Cardinal Cajetan, one of the great intellects of the Renaissance and perhaps the most influential interpreter of Thomas Aquinas in the history of the church. He was charged with taking Luther into custody, but after failing to elicit a recantation from the troublesome Augustinian, he then found that Frederick the Wise would not surrender Luther into his custody because the Saxons did not consider him a heretic. This was a significant moment: it showed where Frederick's loyalties were likely to lie in the future; and it crystallized the notion of Luther as a Saxon hero.

Thus, Luther returned safely to Wittenberg. And it was then that fate dealt a vital card to the Wittenbergers: in January 1519, Emperor Maximilian died. This had a twofold effect: it effectively stalled all imperial action on the Luther case until a new emperor could be appointed; and it made Frederick the Wise, as one of the seven electors of the empire, a peculiarly significant and powerful person, at least for a time.

Reforms at Wittenberg

Even as the Luther drama played out on the main stage of the politics of church and empire, back at Wittenberg the Reformation started to take in-

---

[3] Though Wittenberg was a tiny town, Luther never actually met Frederick the Wise. All communication between the two was mediated, typically through Spalatin. This allowed Frederick to have sufficient distance from Luther, what we might today call "plausible deniability," when it came to the Reformation, in that he could always claim that it really had nothing to do with him.

[4] The word *diet* means a formal deliberative assembly and was typically used for official meetings of the leading officials of the Holy Roman Empire.

stitutional shape. In 1518, the university, on Luther's advice, stopped the lectures on physics and logic that followed the teaching of Aquinas. Then, campaigns were launched to fill chairs in Hebrew and Greek. This was not simply a pedagogical move: as Luther and his colleagues became convinced that Scripture in the original languages was the revelation of God, it became necessary to capitalize on the rising popularity of linguistic studies and fold them into the theological curriculum. The Hebrew chair was to be filled by Matthaeus Goldhahn, a competent if uninspiring Hebraist. The Greek chair, however, was filled by Philipp Melanchthon, a twenty-one-year-old prodigy who was to become Luther's second-in-command and whose theology was eventually to split Lutheranism after the death of its founder in 1546.

The Leipzig Debate

After the Heidelberg Disputation, the next most significant public airing of Luther's theology took place in 1519 in the so-called Leipzig Debate. John Eck, a leading Dominican theologian, had been a friendly acquaintance of Luther's prior to the indulgence controversy. Since that time, however, he had been looking for ways to strike at the Wittenbergers. In 1518, he published a work against the Wittenberg theology, *Obelisks*, to which Luther had replied with a privately circulated book, *Asterisks*. Eck's work, however, had really annoyed one of Luther's colleagues, Andreas Bodenstein von Karlstadt, who had responded by publishing 380 theses against Eck. Even by the standards of the time, that was pretty excessive.

In response, Eck challenged the Wittenbergers to an intellectual dual, a debate to take place at the University of Leipzig. This occurred in June amid much drama as Luther and Karlstadt arrived in town surrounded by an armed cortege of Wittenberg students. Whether there was any real threat to their safety is beside the point: this was theological debate as public entertainment and propaganda.

While the debate itself was something of a stalemate, it represented a crucial development in Luther's thinking. Up until this point, the controversy surrounding him had focused on occasional issues of practice. Underlying these, though, was an implicit critique of the nature of the church and of church authority as then understood. It was only at Leipzig that this point became explicit, in part through the incisive attack of Eck, which forced Luther's assumptions to the surface. Hints of this were provided at the predebate sermon that Luther preached on Matthew 16:13–19. Originally scheduled for the Castle Church, it had to be moved to the university lecture hall because of the number who wished to attend. There, to a packed house, Luther laid out the notion that God would be gracious to all who humbled themselves before him, and that the keys of which Christ spoke were given to all Christians and not simply to the priestly hierarchy.

Eck heard the sermon and left the hall with the ominous declaration that what he had just heard was "completely Bohemian." In doing so, Eck was drawing attention to the connection between Luther's understanding of the church and that put forward by John Hus, the Bohemian church leader a century before. Hus's understanding of the church accented the importance of predestination and thus undermined the authority of the visible structures. Crucially, Hus's views had been condemned as heresy, and he had been burned at the stake at the Council of Constance in 1415. If Luther was teaching Hus's doctrine, then he was clearly a heretic and subject to the precedent already established.

This was the approach Eck adopted in the debate, pressing Luther on where he saw authority lying in the church. When he declared Luther to be teaching matters that had been condemned at Constance, Luther fell into the trap and responded that Constance had condemned many articles that simply were sound Catholic teaching. He also added that papal supremacy was a relatively recent innovation.

Arguably, this is the moment when the Reformation truly began in earnest, for it was then that the implications of Luther's otherwise piecemeal attacks on indulgences and theological method became clear. If Luther was right, if humility was the key to salvation, then the whole medieval system needed to be rejected, and the papacy was wrong. Leipzig made this clear, along with the fact that there was no middle ground.

While the result of the actual debate at Leipzig was somewhat equivocal, Luther returned to Wittenberg as the clear champion of the new Reformation movement.

1520: The Year of Dreaming Dreams

In many ways, Luther was never to have a more glorious theological year than 1520. It is true that the year began in an ominous way. Charles V had been elected emperor in the late summer of 1519, and thus formal proceedings against Luther within church and empire could begin again. This took place in January 1520, when an assembly of cardinals and diplomats in Rome demanded that the pope proceed against the Reformer. Later that spring, Eck arrived to report firsthand on the Leipzig Debate and to join a committee tasked with drawing up charges against him.

All of this served to indicate that the chances of a peaceful resolution to the Luther crisis were all but gone. In this context, Luther embarked upon laying out his manifesto for what a Reformation church should look like in the three great treatises of 1520: *The Babylonian Captivity of the Church*; *The Freedom of the Christian Man*; and *An Appeal to the German Nobility*. All three of these treatises will be discussed in some detail in subsequent chapters, but it is useful to know from a biographical perspective what topics they covered.

The Babylonian Captivity was Luther's sacramental manifesto, in which he not only reduced the number of sacraments from seven (baptism, confirmation, holy orders, marriage, penance, the Mass, and final unction) to three, or possibly two (baptism, the Mass, and perhaps penance), but also restructured his sacramental thinking around promise and faith. The implications of his new soteriology, so ably exposed by Eck at Leipzig, were now allowed to reshape the very heart of medieval devotion: the sacraments.

The Freedom of the Christian Man was Luther's application of his insights on justification to the realm of ethics. Unlike the medieval system, where the motive for good works was not knowledge of being in a state of grace but rather a means to move into or to maintain a state of grace, Luther's approach turned everything on its head. He argued that it was because one has been justified without works that one is then free to do good works for one's neighbor, in a manner analogous to that of Adam before the fall.

Finally, realizing that the church was not going to reform itself, Luther turned his mind to the civil magistrate as a means of achieving this in *An Appeal to the German Nobility*. Given that he saw a lot of the confusion of the time as originating in the church's incursion into areas belonging properly to the civil magistrate, Luther argued that the magistrates needed to take back what properly belonged to them, thus clearing the way for the church to be once again a truly spiritual entity.

These three works, taken together, represent perhaps Luther's most sustained and positive vision for what reformation should be. It is arguable that he never again presented such a comprehensive view of Christianity in such a positive way. While Luther was engaged in this positive construction, however, the church issued its long-awaited condemnation of his thought. The papal bull *Exsurge Domine* was proclaimed in July 1520 and then began its long journey toward Wittenberg, carried there by, among others, John Eck.

It finally arrived in Wittenberg on October 10, when it was presented to the rector of the university, Peter Burckhard. Interestingly enough, it was not Eck who presented it. He had wisely stayed outside of Electoral Saxony, presumably knowing that it would not have been a safe place for him to travel. In fact, it was the Leipzig militia who delivered the bull, another sign of the hostility between the two cities since the debate of 1519.

Luther must have heard of the bull's arrival almost immediately. Wittenberg was—and still is—a very tiny town where nothing of any great consequence could happen in secret. Further, we know that he wrote to Spalatin on October 11, informing him of the bull's advent at the university. In the coming months, Luther wrote an explanation of the articles condemned by the bull and reiterated his call for a German council on German soil to resolve what he claimed was a German problem. He was very keen to play the ethnic card as a means of keeping himself out of the hands of the papacy.

Then, on December 10, 1520, Luther led a procession to the town square in Wittenberg and publicly burned both the bull and the books of canon law. Now there was no turning back.

The Diet of Worms

The church had now exhausted its options for handling Luther. Excommunication was the final sanction, and yet he was still free to write and preach with impunity in Wittenberg. As a result, a new strategy had to be devised. Charles V was convening an imperial diet in the city of Worms in April 1521, and it was decided to summon Luther to appear there. This was a controversial decision. First, Luther's excommunication meant that he was a nonperson, and the technical question of how one issues a summons to a nonperson was a problem. Second, the growing popularity of Luther as the people's champion against a corrupt and moribund church meant that such a move was potentially dangerous. Ultimately, however, the pragmatic need to deal with Luther overrode these concerns, and he was summoned. Thus, in April 1521, Luther arrived in the city to face his greatest challenge so far.

The hearing itself was an impressive affair. At the front sat the youthful Emperor Charles V, coming face-to-face with the troublemaking monk whose religious innovations would ruin his rule and ultimately drive him to abdication. Around the hall stood the most powerful politicians of the day. On a table before the emperor were laid all of Luther's books. And there stood Luther himself, apparently surrounded by his enemies and dangerously exposed.

The man leading the questioning of Luther was John Eck, though not the John Eck of Leipzig fame. This John Eck was an employee in the household of the archbishop of Trier. At the start of the proceedings on April 17, Eck asked two simple questions: whether the books on display were Luther's, and whether he would recant their content. These were obvious questions that Luther must have expected. His answer, however, was anything but what one might have anticipated: he declared that, because the matters concerned salvation, he needed time to think about his response.

No one knows why he gave this response. Perhaps it was part of a strategy that the team from Electoral Saxony had designed to surprise their opponents. A more prosaic explanation might be that Luther was simply scared at what must have been a moment of intense personal pressure. We shall never know. In any event, the assembly recessed and reconvened on the following day. Then, faced with the same questions, Luther offered a trenchant response: some of the works dealt with piety and morals that even his opponents had liked, and thus he should not be the only one to retract their contents; some criticized the papacy, but the papacy was notoriously corrupt and destroyed many souls, so he could not retract those; and some attacked individuals who defended Roman tyranny but, while occasionally excessive in language used, were fundamentally sound and could not be retracted.

Eck refused to accept these arguments. Then, at the end of a vigorous exchange, Luther made his famous speech (which probably did not end with the claim "Here I stand! I can do no other"):

> Unless I am convinced by the testimony of the Scriptures or by clear reason (for I do not trust either in the pope or in councils alone, since it is well known that they have often erred and contradicted themselves), I am bound by the Scriptures I have quoted and my conscience is captive to the

Word of God. I cannot and I will not retract anything, since it is neither safe nor right to go against conscience.[5]

After this dramatic stand, Luther was ushered from the hall, amid cries from the Spanish delegation that he should be burned at the stake. It was not to be, however. As he left Worms to return to Wittenberg, he was surrounded by a group of armed men and kidnapped. After nearly four years as the center of attention for both church and empire, Luther would vanish from the public eye for the better part of a year.

Sir George, Resident Knight of the Wartburg

Luther spent the rest of 1521 incognito in the Wartburg, the medieval castle atop the mountain over the town of Eisenach. Growing a beard and dressing as a knight, he enjoyed a brief but relatively peaceful time, although it was here that he first developed chronic constipation, which was to become something of an obsession.

While in the Wartburg, Luther engaged in numerous theological writings that indicated the way his mind was moving. There he addressed the issue of religious vows and responded to the significant criticisms of the Catholic theologian Latomus. The former of these was triggered by the fact that in May 1521, priests started to marry, which demanded that the Reformation leadership clarify its position on the matter. Luther also wrote a defense of oral confession at this time. The need to balance established practice with new Reformation content was acute.

Perhaps most significant, however, was his translation of the New Testament into German. As his Reformation theology developed and placed an increasing emphasis upon the objective Word of God, in sermon and in sacrament, as the means of salvation, so the need for Scripture in the vernacular became urgent. As with the King James Version in English and Calvin's *Institutes* in French, the Luther Bible was to prove foundational in the development of the modern German language.

Meanwhile, back in Wittenberg, the leadership of the Reformation passed to Karlstadt, Melanchthon, and Konrad Zwilling. Under these men, things took a more radical turn. Karlstadt started to develop novel ideas about the Eucharist, emphasizing the symbolic nature of the words of institution. By the end of the year he was also parading around Wittenberg

---

[5] *LW*, 32:112.

dressed as a peasant and officiating at Mass in a plain robe. In addition, the leadership at Wittenberg turned against images, and iconoclastic rioting resulted. Then came the final straw: three men from Zwickau, the so-called Zwickau Prophets, arrived in Wittenberg. Led by one Nicholas Storch, these men combined apocalyptic visions and claims to be led directly by the Spirit with political and social radicalism. Karlstadt and Zwilling were enamored of the three; gentle Melanchthon, out of his depth, had no option but to ask Frederick the Wise to recall Luther from the Wartburg to reassert control over the Wittenberg Reformation and bring things back to a more moderate path. Frederick took little persuading, for he did not want the emperor taking an undue interest in the internal affairs of his territory, something that would certainly have resulted if anarchy had triumphed.

Luther had visited Wittenberg in disguise in December 1521 to observe the nascent radicalism firsthand. Now, in January 1522, he returned to take back the leadership. This is probably the point at which he was most vulnerable, as success came down to whether he could preach the people away from social revolution and back to proper reformation. This he did over the next few months, in a stunning display of what personal presence can do. The Zwickau Prophets were put to flight, and Karlstadt and Zwilling, toppled from their positions of leadership, both left town shortly thereafter.

Along with the Leipzig Debate and the Heidelberg Disputation, the conflict of 1522 is perhaps the most important moment of Luther's early Reformation career. It fixed in his mind the connection between symbolic views of the Lord's Supper and social revolution, a connection that helps to explain the passion of his conflict with Zwingli. It also left him with a lasting hatred of anyone who talked about the Spirit rather than the Word. For Luther, the Spirit only works in and through the Word. To allow otherwise is to open a Pandora's box of subjectivity that leads to the kind of riots and chaos he witnessed in Wittenberg in early 1522.

1525: The Year of Brilliance, Joy, and Hatred

After 1522, Luther's position in Wittenberg was relatively secure. Further, after the exuberance of his early theological breakthroughs, he settled into a routine of teaching, preaching, and pastoring which, with a couple of exceptions, meant that his life was never to have quite the same level of drama again. Nevertheless, the year 1525 was, in its own way, as significant for his theology and his reputation as the years 1520–1521. Indeed, it was marked by three major events: his clash with Erasmus; his marriage to Katie; and his ill-fated intervention in the Peasants' War.

In retrospect, the clash with Erasmus was inevitable—if not in 1525, then at some point. Erasmus was the man who had produced a Greek New Testament and had thus laid the textual foundation for the Reformation. He was also the man whose dazzling scholarship and wit had made him an implacable critic of the Renaissance church. Yet his personality was that of the supercilious satirist who would criticize and mock the church but ultimately remain within its bounds. Erasmus had no intention of risking life or even career for the cause of the Reformation.

At one point in the early Lutheran Reformation, Frederick the Wise had asked Erasmus his opinion of the troublesome monk. His response was that Luther had committed two sins: he had criticized the pope's power and the monks' bellies. These comments, given confidentially to Frederick, had been leaked to the public, and from that time on Erasmus had been under pressure to declare his position with respect to the Wittenberg Reformation. Finally, in 1524 he did so in his *Diatribe on Free Will*, where he argued for the basic opacity of Scripture on the issue of the role of the human will in salvation. Whether one characterizes his position as agnostic, semi-Pelagian, or semi-Augustinian depends on how charitable one wishes to be. What is certain is that Erasmus had placed his finger on the conceptual underpinnings of Luther's whole theology: the basic clarity of Scripture and the need for salvation to be all of God.

When the book arrived in Wittenberg, Melanchthon greeted it with enthusiasm. When Luther read it, however, his heart fell: not only did he see the devastating implications of denying scriptural clarity and the bondage of the will; he also knew that Erasmus was too big a critic to ignore. The result was *The Bondage of the Will*, a veritable sledge-hammer of a book, which contains Luther's most brilliant defense of his doctrines of Scripture, of the human will, and of the divine initiative in salvation. Along with his catechisms, it was one of his few books that he himself considered worthy of outliving him.

The second great event of 1525 was his marriage to Katharine von Bora, also known as "my Lord Katie" and "the Chain." She was one of a group of Cistercian nuns who had escaped from the cloister in Nimbschen in 1523 and arrived in Wittenberg in April of that year. Luther arranged for the nuns to be married off, but Katie proved a problem. Initially she had been placed in the household of the artist Lucas Cranach. After various abortive attempts to marry her off, Katie expressed her desire to marry either Luther or one of his colleagues, Nicholas von Amsdorf. Having had the idea of marriage placed in his mind by the redoubtable female reformer Argula von Grumbach, Luther finally acceded to the idea in 1525 and, on June 13 of that year, married Katie. We will look at the marriage in more detail in chapter 8. Suffice it here to say that it appears to have been happy and fruitful.

It was at the time, however, a public-relations disaster. This was not because Luther as a monk was marrying. That issue had long been resolved in Wittenberg. It was because the nuptials occurred during the Peasants' War, a major outbreak of rebellion across the German territories of the Holy Roman Empire. The rebels were united by a set of economic grievances, many of which focused on the corruption of the church. Thus, it was natural that they used Lutheran-style rhetoric of freedom and that many of them (though not all) expected Luther to speak for them. After initial sympathy for their cause, Luther, ever fearful of chaos and anarchy and upset that the peasants had, against his counsel, resorted to violence, swung hard against them and published one of his most notorious treatises, *An Admonition to Peace, against the Robbing and Murdering Hordes of Peasants*, which was a call to the nobles to suppress the rebellion in as ferocious a way as was necessary. This work tarnished Luther's reputation in a way matched only by his later attacks on the Jews. The peasants were ultimately crushed at the Battle of Frankenhausen, and their leaders, such as Thomas Müntzer, put to death. That Luther was celebrating his marriage as the Peasants' War moved to its bloody conclusion was deemed profoundly insensitive.

The Conflict with Zwingli

Even as Luther consolidated the Reformation in Saxony after 1522, other reformations were beginning to take shape elsewhere in Europe. Most significant from the Lutheran perspective was the rise of Huldrych Zwingli in Zurich. Zwingli was from a very different background than Luther, since his education was shaped by the humanism of Erasmus, whom he greatly admired. The Reformation in Zurich was also of a different cast than the one in Wittenberg. Zurich was a rising modern city ruled by a town council and with an economy increasingly based upon skilled labor, not a medieval feudal context like Electoral Saxony. Where the Wittenberg Reformation

had started with a call for a medieval university debate, its Zurich counterpart began with the breaking of the Lenten fast by workers in that most
early modern of industries, printing. Zwingli then worked closely with the
town council in the implementation of a reform more radical than its Wittenberg counterpart (they outlawed images and even banned music and
singing from worship services).

What caused Luther and Zwingli to collide, however, was the latter's
belief that the word "is" in "This is my body," the words of eucharistic institution, meant "symbolizes," an insight Zwingli apparently gleaned from
a letter written by the humanist scholar Cornelius Hön in 1524. For the
Zurichers, the Lord's Supper was symbolic; it was mainly a horizontal statement of loyalty between Christians, akin to a military oath (which was the
meaning of the Latin word *sacramentum*). If Christ was present, then he
could only be thought of as present spiritually.

For Luther, this teaching was toxic. It was reminiscent of the spiritual
approach of Karlstadt and thus indicative to him of a revolutionary attitude. Further, in taking the real presence of Christ out of the bread and
the wine, Zwingli removed the gospel. The bread and the wine no longer
became the means of God's feeding his people with Christ but something
they do for God or for each other. To use Lutheran terminology, Zwingli
took the gospel and turned it into law.

From 1527 onward, Luther and Zwingli engaged in a bitter pamphlet
war against each other. Yet division in the Protestant ranks was not desirable, and the possibility of an alliance between the Lutheran princes in the
north and the Reformed Swiss cities in the south was very attractive. As
a result, in 1529 Landgrave Philip of Hesse persuaded the two factions to
meet at the castle in the city of Marburg to debate theology with a view to
producing a common statement of faith that could then provide the basis
for a political/military alliance.

The cast of characters at the Marburg Colloquy was impressive, including Zwingli; Oecolampadius, the brilliant Patristic scholar; Bucer, the
Reformation's passionate ecumenist; Melanchthon; and, of course, Luther
himself. While agreement was reached on fourteen and a half of fifteen
points, the outstanding half point—that of the nature of Christ's presence
in the Supper—was the crucial one. No meaningful alliance was possible,
and Luther dramatically declared that Zwingli was of a different spirit, that
is, not a true believer. The breach at Marburg was the point at which Prot-

estantism divided into Lutheran and Reformed, a breach that continues to this day.

When Zwingli died on the battlefield at Kappel in 1531 and the news reached Luther, his comment was simple and to the point: "Those who live by the sword shall die by the sword." Till his dying day, Luther regarded Zwingli as the epitome of evil fanaticism.

One other reason for failure to find agreement at Marburg was the fact that the German Lutheran princes were slowly starting to move toward a military alliance of their own, and this inevitably weakened the pressure for an alliance with the Swiss. After the imperial Diet of Augsburg in 1530 this German alliance took form as the Schmalkaldic League.

Charles V had asked the Lutheran princes to provide him with a statement of their beliefs. This was drawn up by Melanchthon and became known as the Augsburg Confession, or *Augustana*. The confession was presented to Charles V at the diet, though Luther was absent, sequestered in the nearby castle at Coburg. He was, after all, officially an outlaw in the empire, and his presence at Augsburg would have been both an affront to the emperor and more than likely a death sentence for himself. At the diet, the emperor refused to subscribe to the confession but it was adopted by the Lutheran princes and cities. This formed part of the basis for the military alliance that Philip of Hesse established in 1531, the Schmalkaldic League, which guaranteed the safety of Lutheranism (and thus of Luther) within the Lutheran territories up until Luther's death in 1546.

Later Years

The last fifteen years of Luther's life were in many ways far less exciting than the period 1517–1531. With Lutheranism at least temporarily secure, thanks to the league, Luther was free to continue his Reformation with a great level of protection. Financial worries continued to dog the Luther household. He and Katie took in student lodgers and also worked at times as gardeners in the town. It is perhaps good to remember that being a Reformer was not necessarily a lucrative career move, and that Luther was not immune to the routine economic hardships that afflict most ministers at various points.

What is perhaps saddest about this period are the notes of bitterness that crept into Luther's works. He, of course, had held high hopes for the Reformation at its inception. Standing in the late medieval tradition of eschatological expectation, he had assumed that the Reformation was part of the great revival that was to come at the end of time and to herald the second coming of Christ. By the 1530s, however, these hopes were dying. Rome had not fallen, and indeed Roman Catholicism was beginning to show early signs of the resurgence that was to mark the century from the 1540s onward. The Protestants were divided among themselves, not simply Lutherans versus Reformed but also growing sectarian elements such as spiritualists and Anabaptists. The situation was no longer that of the dramatic and wonderful possibilities Luther saw before him in 1520; it was the cold, hard reality of life in a fallen world that was pressing in on him, at the same time as his own mortality.

Two events of Luther's later years tarnished his reputation. The first has an almost comical dimension to it. Landgrave Philip of Hesse was a constant actor in the Luther story. He was the man with the vision behind the Marburg Colloquy and the driving force in the formation of the Schmalkaldic League. He was also a man with what Americans would today euphemistically call "issues." There were perhaps hints of this in his first encounter with Luther at the Diet of Worms. When Luther arrived in Worms, one of the first of the great and the good to seek him out was Philip, who had not at that point turned to the Reformation. He was intrigued by a comment Luther had made in *The Babylonian Captivity* to the effect that a woman married to an impotent husband could remarry.

That this question perhaps adumbrated later "issues" is suggested by the events of 1539. Philip had been married to Christina of Saxony since 1523. The marriage produced seven children but was by all accounts unhappy, and Philip was a serial adulterer. This philandering had given him syphilis but had also affected his conscience, and he rarely went to communion. Then, in 1539 he fell in love with Margaret von der Sale, the seventeen-year-old daughter of a Saxon nobleman. He then appealed to Bucer, Melanchthon, and Luther for advice and help. Eventually, Melanchthon formulated an opinion to which the other two agreed, that Philip should simply marry the girl in secret under the seal of the confessional. In short, in what the Reformers regarded as extraordinary circumstances, they sanctioned bigamy. The marriage took place in March 1540, with Melanchthon and Bucer among the witnesses.

Of course, it is a truth universally agreed upon that three men can keep a secret if two of them are dead. This was too good a story to keep quiet, and word slipped out in the public realm via Philip's sister, the duchess of Rochlitz. The result was a furious and uncontrollable scandal in which it looked very much as if the typical Roman propaganda about the Reformation—that it was motivated by a desire to unleash sexual license upon society—was true. Though Melanchthon was the one Wittenberger most deeply involved in the disaster, it was Luther's reputation that took the hardest knocks.

The second issue, which still (rightly) impacts Luther's reputation, was his growing animosity toward the Jews. In 1523, he had written what was, for the time, a very progressive treatise, *That Jesus Christ Was Born a Jew*. In this work, Luther broke with the dominant attitudes of the age and encouraged Christians to be good, loving neighbors to the Jews, so as to build bridges for the gospel.

By the early 1540s, however, the Jews were becoming for Luther a constant and bitter obsession. Notoriously, he wrote another major treatise on them, *On the Jews and Their Lies*, which represented a repudiation of his earlier work and a return to the standards of the day, only in an even more violent and hateful way than was typical. This latter work advocated murder and went on to enjoy a notorious career, not least as a staple of Nazi propaganda in the 1930s and '40s, and as a common feature on anti-Semitic websites today. That it represented Luther's mature opinion can be in no doubt: his final sermon in Eisleben in 1546 included an anti-Jewish appendix.

There is not space here to address the matter of Luther on the Jews. My own views on the subject can be found in *Histories and Fallacies*.[6] Suffice it to say two things here. First, Luther's later attitude toward the Jews shows that even the greatest of men can have catastrophic moral blindness on certain issues. Second, when assessing a historical figure's life, we must not ignore or exclude the problems in the interest of presenting an inspiring picture. Luther believed that, outside of Christ, he was dead in trespasses and sins and desperately wicked. His attitude toward the Jews confirms his own opinion of himself.

Luther's Death

In January 1546, Luther traveled to his birthplace to mediate in a dispute between local counts, much to the consternation of Katie, who was concerned about his health—rightly so, as it turned out. While at Eisleben, he

---

[6] Carl R. Trueman, *Histories and Fallacies: Problems Faced in the Writing of History* (Wheaton, IL: Crossway, 2011).

preached four times, the last on either February 14 (when he also ordained two priests) or 15. The assistant accompanying him, John Aurifaber, copied a slip of paper on February 16, which contained Luther's last written statement, ending in the famous phrase "We are beggars: this is true." The first clause was in German, the second in Latin. On February 17, he was feeling unwell and unable to transact any business that day. He was to die the following day, in the presence of a number of friends. Having reaffirmed his confidence in the gospel, he uttered his very last words, a threefold repetition of Psalm 31:5:

> Into your hand I commit my spirit;
>> you have redeemed me, O LORD, faithful God.

It was a quintessential Protestant end: faith in the Word—no final unction, last rites, or final communion. Luther had received the Lord's Supper the previous Sunday, and that was quite enough. Indeed, his own way of dying exemplified how he had himself transformed pastoral care and, indeed, the piety of dying.

As a last, sad postscript, though, the greatest personal trophy of his Protestantism, the beloved woman he had broken his monastic vows to marry, could not be there. Katie was brokenhearted when the news reached her, distraught that she could not comfort him in his final moments. Yet he died, as she was to die, safe in the knowledge that they were united in Christ and would be reunited in the hereafter, when they would attend a greater wedding feast than their own had been so many years earlier.

Concluding Reflections

With a figure like Martin Luther, the tendency will always be to make him a hero or a villain. The stakes are so high in the Reformation debate, and Protestant and Roman Catholic identities so wrapped up in responses to him, that the temptation of a black-and-white, morally and theologically straightforward approach is significant. Yet even this brief overview of his life reveals not only the connections between his biography and his theology but also the human contradictions and failings that were part of who he was and what he did. His stand at Worms is magnificent; his later writings against the Jews are nauseating. What are we to do with him?

The answer, I believe, is actually very simple: we are to see him as one of us. One might note that, as with the rest of the human race, his strengths were his weaknesses. The hardheaded stubbornness and conviction that he was right—which meant he could face down the combined might of church and empire at Worms in 1521 and put the Wittenberg radicals to flight in 1522—was the same character trait that shaped his arrogant attacks on the Jews. We can all learn from seeing how strength in one area can be dramatic weakness in another.

But at a deeper, theological level, we should see Luther as one of us in the way he wrestled with the deepest perennial questions of human, Christian existence. How can I find a gracious God? What and where is grace? In what does true happiness consist? How am I to connect the mundane and often tedious realities of daily life to my faith? How can I face the death of loved ones and eventually the death of myself without going completely insane with grief? Luther's life was full of these questions. And his theology is one extended reflection upon them. It is to these matters that we now turn.

CHAPTER 2

THEOLOGIANS, PRIESTS, AND KINGS

All I want is to enter my house justified.

JOEL MCCREA, *RIDE THE HIGH COUNTRY*

The Heidelberg Disputation

In chapter 1, I briefly noted that shortly after he became a controversial figure through his call for a debate on indulgences, Luther had an opportunity to present a more positive exposition of his theology at a meeting of the Augustinian Order in the city of Heidelberg in April 1518. At this meeting, called to transact regular order business, Luther presided at a disputation in which a colleague, Leonhard Beier, defended a set of theses that Luther had prepared in advance.

The event has come to be known as the Heidelberg Disputation, and it can be regarded as one of the theologically foundational events for later Lutheranism. The debate consisted of forty theses, the first twenty-eight being theological, and the last twelve being philosophical and particularly concerned with the damaging influence of Aristotelianism on Christian theology. In many ways, the theses represent an extension and elaboration of the positions adumbrated in the *Disputation against Scholastic Theology* of September 1517.

At the heart of the theology elaborated that day is one of the most famous distinctions Luther makes, and one that is of fundamental importance to his theology in general: that between the theologian of glory and the theologian of the cross. He defines these in theses 19 and following, but before we can understand what Luther means by this somewhat enigmatic terminology, it is important to understand how it fits into the overall argument of the disputation.

Luther starts the disputation by examining the role of God's law. The foundation is laid in the first two theses, which propose that the law of God is indeed salutary and good but that it is not able to advance human beings toward salvation (thesis 1), and that good works are even less capable of achieving that end (thesis 2). These theses summarize Luther's new theological convictions, which had emerged as a result of his immersion in the writings of Paul in the immediately preceding years. God is righteous and his law is an expression of his holy character, but human beings are incapable of making themselves worthy in his sight. The next pair of theses draws epistemological conclusions from this foundation: human works appear attractive but are actually "likely to be mortal sins" (thesis 3). Luther means here that human works seem to us to be worthy of God's acceptance but are in fact as filthy rags before him. There is a disconnect between our perception of their merit and the reality, which points toward the moral nature of human knowledge. The same is true, in reverse, of God's works, which appear sinful to human beings but are actually meritorious before God (thesis 4).

Thesis 5 is, on the surface, a quite confusing statement: "The works of men are thus not mortal sins (we speak of works which are apparently good), as though they were crimes."[1] Luther's own published explanation of this thesis is that mortal sins, those which damn us before God, are not what we might think—outrageous acts such as adultery or murder—but rather any acts, even those which seem good, that flow from a sinful heart.[2] Luther is both deepening the understanding of what constitutes sin and at the same time pointing to the profound epistemological corruption to which human beings are subject. We might say that he is emphasizing that the theologies we create for ourselves are false in that they fail to understand the seriousness of the fallen human condition. This is reinforced in thesis 6, which declares that the works God does through human beings are not meritorious.

---

[1] *LW*, 31:39.
[2] *LW*, 31:45. In medieval theology, *mortal sins* were serious and deliberate breaches of God's law that caused the Christian to fall from a state of grace. Such things would have included idolatry, murder, and adultery. *Venial sins* were trivial sins that did not involve a fall from the state of grace. Such sins might have included an act of trivial gossip.

This latter point is, of course, crucial for Luther's mature Protestant theology. In the system of the *via moderna* the one who does what is in him or her receives grace on the basis of congruent, not condign, merit. Now for Luther the work that God does through human beings can never be strictly meritorious in a condign sense. As he comments in his explanation of this thesis, human beings are like damaged and defective tools, and however perfect the workman might be, any work he does with such implements is inevitably flawed.[3]

Theses 7 to 12 further elaborate the issue of mortal sin, specifically in relation to human attitudes toward and understanding of good works. Luther's key if somewhat paradoxical point here is that it is precisely those works which we do not regard as mortal sins that are in fact mortal and soul damning. Here we see the emergence of a constant theme in Luther's theology: the fear of self-righteousness. It is of a piece with his theology of humility: if it is only as we completely despair of our own works and cast ourselves onto God's mercy in all humility that we are made right with him, then our attitude toward our own works will be a key indicator of how real that humility is. The true Christian lives in a place of great tension: fear of God as righteous and holy is central to understanding the unrighteousness of our own works. With logic reminiscent of the old saying that the wise man is the one who knows that he knows nothing, thesis 12 captures Luther's understanding of works well: in the sight of God, sins are then truly venial when they are feared by men to be mortal.[4]

In theses 13–15, Luther now draws out the conceptual framework for what he has said thus far by attacking the notion of free will. Luther does believe in post-fall free will, but only insofar as it is able to do evil. There is no active disposition of the human will toward the good, only a passive one. As a corpse can stand only in a passive relationship toward the possibility of life, so we stand only in a passive relationship toward God. This is the inference of his changed understanding of baptism: if baptism is about cleansing, then there is some active principle in the subject of baptism toward the good; but if, as Luther has become convinced that Paul taught, baptism is about death and resurrection, then the subjects of baptism are, like Lazarus, utterly and passively dependent upon the unilateral and sovereign action of God.

---

[3] *LW*, 31:45.
[4] *LW*, 31:40.

In 1525, this would form part of the debate with Erasmus, when Luther responded to his *Diatribe on Free Will* with his own masterpiece of theological polemic, *The Bondage of the Will*. As mentioned earlier, this, along with his two catechisms, was one of the few works Luther considered worthy of outliving him. He also famously thanked Erasmus in the work for being the only one who had actually engaged him on the point on which all the rest of his Reformation theology turned.[5] Thus, it is important that we understand the structural importance of the bondage of the will to Luther's overall theological project.

The bondage of the post-fall will is foundational for Christian certainty, for how can we ever be certain of our salvation if even a fraction of it depends upon ourselves, weak, sinful, and vacillating as we are? Here, in the Heidelberg Disputation, it undergirds all that Luther has thus far said about good works and, indeed, intensifies the point: good works are an impossibility not just because our wills are corrupted; they are an impossibility because our wills are utterly bound to sinful ends.

This leads Luther to the most directly polemical thesis so far, number 16: "The person who believes that he can obtain grace by doing what is in him adds sin to sin so that he becomes doubly guilty."[6]

This thesis is a fearsome attack on the theology Luther learned from his medieval masters. The language used is clearly associated with the *pactum* theology of Gabriel Biel and the *via moderna*, and the conclusion Luther draws could scarcely be more offensive: such theology involves a compounding of humanity's sinful state. There is no ground for compromise or for agreeing to differ at this point: Luther has made his position very clear and allowed himself no escape route from confrontation. He then proceeds to reject a potential false inference from this by stating that such a manner of speaking does not lead to despair (thesis 17) but actually paves the way for the abject humility that is the precondition for receiving the grace of Christ (thesis 18).

This brings Luther to the point where he makes the famous distinction between theologians of glory and theologians of the cross. In short, this distinction rests upon a view of salvation that assumes various truths.

---

[5] "I praise and commend you highly for this also, that unlike all the rest you alone have attacked the real issue, the essence of the matter in dispute, and have not wearied me with irrelevancies about the papacy, purgatory, indulgences, and such like trifles (for trifles they are rather than basic issues), with which almost everyone hitherto has gone hunting for me without success. You and you alone have seen the question on which everything hinges, and have aimed at the vital spot." *LW*, 33:294.
[6] *LW*, 31:40.

First, he radicalizes sin such that it is equivalent to being morally dead before God, as revealed to us by the holy law of God. Second, the will is entirely impotent for salvation. Third, the rejection of these basic truths is a moral issue that itself involves the compounding of sin and guilt before God.

The Two Theologians

Against this background Luther now introduces one of his most famous theological distinctions:

> 19. That person does not deserve to be called a theologian who looks upon the invisible things of God as though they were clearly perceptible in those things which have actually happened [Rom. 1:20].

> 20. He deserves to be called a theologian, however, who comprehends the visible and manifest things of God seen through suffering and the cross.

> 21. A theologian of glory calls evil good and good evil. A theologian of the cross calls the thing what it actually is.[7]

The theology of these theses is an extraordinarily rich starting point for reflection upon Luther's theology in general, and it has very particular implications for his understanding of the Christian life. It is important at the outset to note that he does not speak here of an abstract theology of the cross, even though the term "theology of the cross"—or, more pompously, *theologia crucis*—occurs with some frequency in discussions of Luther. Instead, Luther speaks of *theologians* of the cross and *theologians* of glory. That is a reminder that he is not speaking here about something that can be reduced to the level of an intellectual technique or method. Theology is thought by real, embodied people, and it is thus a part of what makes them who they are. Theology (as the act of theologizing) and anthropology are thus indissolubly connected.

Before returning to this last point, we should note the theological points underlying Luther's statement. First, he is making a plea for theology based on God's revelation of himself. In terms of the objective sources of theology, the distinction turns upon the theologian's identification of

---
[7] *LW*, 31:40.

the sources for knowledge of God. The mistake the theologian of glory makes is to think that the way the world appears to be is actually an accurate account of who God is.

As we will note below, this clearly connects to Luther's understanding of justification. It is sufficient here to note that the world around us operates on the basis of reciprocity: those who do good are the ones who consequently receive a reward; those who do evil receive punishment. Thus, by identifying the world around us as providing the basic criteria for understanding the actions of God, the theologian of glory assumes that the same dynamic exists between human beings and the Creator in matters of salvation. In short, if I want God to look with kindness upon me, then I need to do something good to earn his favor.

The theologian of the cross, by contrast, draws his understanding of God from looking at how God has revealed himself in the place where God has chosen to do so. On this point, Luther exhibits considerable continuity with the theology of the *via moderna*. Late medieval voluntarism accented, from a human perspective, the priority of God's will in determining God's actions. This was an important epistemological development, as it preserved the otherness of God's actions. From the perspective of human knowledge, it made God's actions unpredictable in advance of how he had actually revealed himself to act. Thus, in stressing the need for what we might call special revelation in order to understand salvation, Luther builds here on his medieval training: if one wishes to know how God acts, one must look at how God has revealed to us that he will act.

Yet even as he develops this late medieval emphasis on revelation, Luther goes further than his medieval masters, intensifying this point in two ways. First, he has made it clear from the argument of the earlier theses that he regards the distinction between theologians as having not simply an epistemological dimension but also a moral one. Indeed, we might say that Luther has made epistemology a moral issue. Anything less than Luther's view of the moral death that sin involves and the moral bondage that thus flows from it compounds sin. Those who do not despair but who think that doing what is in them will lead God to give them grace are actually engaged in a sinful act of rebellious self-deception. Luther's theology here connects to that of Paul in Romans 1. For his medieval masters, knowledge of God was essentially an epistemological issue: because God is omnipotent, he appears from a human perspective to be unpredictable; thus, his revelation binds him to being a certain kind of God toward us. The moral crisis of sin does not have a great impact on this picture. For Luther, it is not simply God's apparent unpredictability that makes it necessary to pay attention to how he has revealed himself; it is the fact that human beings are dead in sin and ever inclined to invent a god who conforms to their expectations.

This is clear in the second way in which he goes beyond the teaching of his medieval masters: he focuses the revelation of God on the crucifixion of Christ on the cross. Of course, Luther does not reduce God's revelation to the cross in such a manner that God is not revealed elsewhere, but he does make it the fundamental criterion for the theology of the gospel, in light of which God's revelation as a whole must be understood. The fact that God humbled himself, took flesh, and died a painful death via a method typically reserved for the scum of the earth is itself a powerful revelation of who God actually is and how he acts. Christ's hanging on the cross is constitutive of the very identity of God toward fallen human beings. Further, by setting the cross at the center, Luther reinforces the fact that the knowledge of God is a moral issue. For him, epistemology is not something that can be abstracted from the moral stance of the knowing subject. In short, in line with Paul's teaching, Luther sees theology as a function of a person's basic moral orientation.

We might note that what Luther says at Heidelberg stands in particularly positive relation to Paul's teaching in 1 Corinthians. There the cross is presented as the moral and epistemological test for the human race, with responses to the cross placing human beings in one of two camps. That Jews sees the cross as an offense and Greeks see it as foolishness (1 Cor. 1:23) actually reveals the state of their hearts and their attitudes toward Jesus Christ and his gospel: they are perishing because they fail to see the cross for what it is, the power of God for salvation (Rom. 1:16). Their respective interpretations of the cross are no doubt grounded in their own cultural contexts, but these contexts explain only the specifics of their views and do not excuse, relativize, or legitimize them. They are still perishing. In short, the Jews and the Greeks refuse to accept God on his own terms, as he has revealed himself; they instead demand that he must be measured by their own cultural criteria. It is only those who start with the cross and accept that it is what God has declared it to be—the power of God for salvation—rather than what it appears outwardly to be—the execution of a filthy sinner—who are being saved.

This distinction has both theological and existential implications for Luther. Theologically, it demands a basic rethinking of vocabulary in light of the cross. This is the teaching of thesis 21, where Luther plays with the language of good and evil. The theologian of glory appears to call things what they are because his sinful nature causes him to operate within the canons of meaning operative in the world around him; but the cross stands as a contradiction of these canons and thus requires a counterintuitive use of standard vocabulary when applied to God and his actions. Luther presses this point home in thesis 22, where he defines such theological errors as having their origin in humanity's basic sinfulness and rebellion.[8]

Theologians—whether of glory or the cross—use words to express their beliefs. For Luther, the conceptual content of these words needs to be defined by the act of God's revelation that takes place in Jesus Christ upon the cross. Thus, the theologian of glory will no doubt understand the word *power*, when applied to God, as referring to something analogous to a king's power: imposing and coercive. Yet the theologian of the cross gives the word different content: power is there revealed in and through weakness. Then there is the idea of *wisdom*. The theologian of glory will understand wisdom in terms set by the world around, perhaps seeing it as intelligence or the knowledge of how to play the system. The theologian of the cross understands wisdom in terms of the incarnate God hanging weak and broken on a cross: a contradiction of all that the wise of the world around us would expect from the sovereign Creator. The theologian of glory will understand *righteousness* as an outward, visible quality constituted by good works. The theologian of the cross sees it in the one who is sinless yet made sin for others. The theologian of glory sees *life* and *death* as antitheses, and the latter as something to be avoided. The theologian of the cross understands that death is actually the gateway to true life.

Later in his career, while commenting on Paul's letter to the Galatians, Luther makes this comment:

> But true Christian theology, as I often warn you, does not present God to us in His majesty, as Moses and other teachings do, but Christ born of the Virgin as our Mediator and High Priest. Therefore when we are embattled against the Law, sin, and death in the presence of God, nothing is more dangerous than to stray into heaven with our idle speculations, there to

---

[8] "22. That wisdom which sees the invisible things of God in works as perceived by man is completely puffed up, blinded, and hardened." *LW*, 31:40–41.

investigate God in His incomprehensible power, wisdom, and majesty, to ask how He created the world and how He governs it. If you attempt to comprehend God this way and want to make atonement to Him apart from Christ the Mediator, making your works, fasts, cowl, and tonsure the mediation between Him and yourself, you will inevitably fall, as Lucifer did (Is. 14:12), and in horrible despair lose God and everything. For as in His own nature God is immense, incomprehensible, and infinite, so to man's nature He is intolerable. Therefore if you want to be safe and out of danger to your conscience and your salvation, put a check on this speculative spirit. Take hold of God as Scripture instructs you (1 Cor. 1:21, [23–]24): "Since, in wisdom, the world did not know God through wisdom, it pleased God through the folly of what we preach to save those who believe. We preach Christ crucified, a stumbling block to Jews and folly to Gentiles, but to those who are called, both Jews and Greeks, Christ the power of God and the wisdom of God." Therefore begin where Christ began—in the Virgin's womb, in the manger, and at His mother's breasts. For this purpose He came down, was born, lived among men, suffered, was crucified, and died, so that in every possible way He might present Himself to our sight. He wanted us to fix the gaze of our hearts upon Himself and thus to prevent us from clambering into heaven and speculating about the Divine Majesty.[9]

This is really an extension and elaboration of the understanding of the theologian of the cross. God in his majesty, apart from the flesh of Christ, is a terrifying, unknowable, powerful God before whom no fallen human can stand. The terror of coming before this God is the terror induced by trying to build a relationship with him on the basis of law and thus to make God's perfect righteousness and naked power the context for approaching him. The idea of the incarnation is utter foolishness, for it contradicts all expectation of what a powerful, terrifying God would do. Yet it is there—in the weakness of human flesh, and especially in the supreme moment of that flesh's weakness, the agonizing death on the cross—that God has come to his people as a God of grace and tender mercy.

This is where Luther sees the law as playing a key role: the law—that expression of God's holiness, a standard utterly unattainable by any sinful human being—is good and necessary because it is the great reminder of human limitations and of the inability of men and women to aspire to God

---

[9] *LW*, 26:28–29.

in their own power. Luther makes this clear at Heidelberg. Neither in their thoughts nor in their actions are people commensurable with the divine, and the law operates to keep that continually before our gaze; and only in the context of the cross can this be properly understood (theses 23 and 24).

Before noting the greatest piece of theological redefinition demanded by Luther's use of the cross as the criterion for theological vocabulary, we should also note that this also has significance for the believer's life in terms of both expectations and experience. We shall return to this point in later chapters, but it is important to understand that the theology of the Heidelberg Disputation has implications not simply for the morality of Christian epistemology but also for the nature of the Christian life as a whole.

Redefining God's Love

Luther's radical redefinition of theological vocabulary demanded by the cross involves nothing short of a virtual inversion of meaning. This is most evident in the last of the theological theses. In fact, while the distinction between the two kinds of theologians has tended to grip the imagination of subsequent generations, the greatest thesis, the capstone of the whole Heidelberg theology, is arguably thesis 28: "The love of God does not find, but creates, that which is pleasing to it. The love of man comes into being through that which is pleasing to it."[10] Immediately prior to this, theses 25 and 26 adumbrate Luther's mature understanding of justification by faith: the doing of the law is seen as woefully inadequate as a means of being right with God and is contrasted with simply resting on God's Word by faith.[11] This is followed by thesis 27, which states that Christ's work is an active work, and our work in salvation should therefore be regarded as a passive, accomplished work. This then provides the platform for the thesis on God's love.

Here the glory-cross antithesis undergirds the distinction between human and divine love. Human love, Luther claims, is reactive: it responds to something intrinsically attractive in an object, which consequently draws it out. In other words, human love is attracted to what it first finds lovely. When a husband recalls the moment he fell in love with his wife,

---

[10] *LW*, 31:41.
[11] "25. He is not righteous who does much, but he who, without work, believes much in Christ." "26. The law says, 'do this,' and it is never done. Grace says, 'believe in this,' and everything is already done." *LW*, 31:41.

he remembers that he saw something intrinsically attractive within her—perhaps her physical beauty or her charming personality—and his heart was moved to love her. There was something in the object of his love that existed prior to his love and drew him toward her. This is the basic dynamic of human love; but we must remember that the revelation of God on the cross inverts such human logic.

Thus, divine love, by contrast, is not reactive but creative: God does not find that which is lovely and then move out in love toward it; something is made lovely by the fact that God first sets his love upon it. He does not look at sinful human beings and see among the mass of people some who are intrinsically more righteous or holy than others and thus find himself attracted to them. Rather, the lesson of the cross is that God chooses that which is unlovely and repulsive, unrighteous and with no redeeming quality, and lavishes his saving love in Christ upon it.

It is arguable that Luther never wrote a more profound or beautiful sentence than the first part of thesis 28. A moment of reflection indicates that it contains in embryonic form much of his mature Reformation theology. For example, given his position (already stated in earlier theses) on the impotence of the human will, it is theologically necessary that God take the sovereign, unilateral initiative in salvation. This thesis defines the content of the love of God in precisely such anti-Pelagian terms. Theologians often express God's sovereignty and predestination in somewhat abstract terms. Here, Luther articulates a doctrine of God's love that provides a framework for both with accents on the personal.

Justification

No doctrine is more commonly associated with the name of Martin Luther than justification by grace through faith. We noted in chapter 1 how a combination of his own existential issues, his exegetical studies of Scripture (especially the letters of Paul), and the wider politics of the European church all conspired to throw this obscure German monk and professor from an obscure university into the center of the great ecclesiastical drama of his time. And right at the doctrinal center of that drama was his notion of justification.

In the medieval understanding, justification was a process of growing righteous via the impartation of Christ's righteousness connected to the infusion of grace via the sacramental ministry of the church. Thus, justification was simply one part of a much larger structure. Strictly speaking, Luther could not be heretical on justification prior to the decrees on the doctrine approved by the Council of Trent at its sixth session in 1547, the year after Luther died. Before that—during the whole of Luther's lifetime!—the church really had no official position on the doctrine. Yet Luther's teaching on the topic had been highly controversial for many years. This was because his understanding of justification, rooted as it was in a divine declaration, undercut the significance of the sacraments and thus of the priesthood and, by implication, the papacy. It also had ethical implications that his Catholic opponents feared: if sinners are simply declared righteous, will they not be free to behave in any manner they choose?

Luther's mature understanding of justification by grace through faith emerges clearly in his 1520 treatise, *The Freedom of the Christian Man*. In a manner reminiscent of the cross, where outward appearance contradicts inward reality, Luther builds his argument in this treatise on the notion that human beings can be considered both as outer and as inner. This allows apparently contradictory things to be asserted about one and the same person.[12] Thus, a man may appear outwardly righteous (before the world) but in reality be inwardly unrighteous. Likewise, he may appear outwardly unrighteous and indeed despicable but inwardly be perfectly righteous before God. This distinction is absolutely basic to Luther's understanding of justification, for it is the basis upon which he asserts that no external thing (in terms of works righteousness) can actually affect standing before God.

For Luther, therefore, what makes the difference between the one who is justified and the one who remains in a state of sin is not infusion of grace or a slow transformation of moral being through the sacramental tutelage of the church. Rather it is grasping the Word of God by faith. We noted earlier how Luther in 1517, and even on into 1518, was committed to seeing humility as the key that made someone a passive recipient of God's grace. By 1520, humility had been absorbed into, and transformed by, his broader understanding of faith as trust in God's Word.

Such faith assumes humility, in that the Christian's life involves despair of one's own righteousness and repentance toward God; but it also involves the positive grasping of God's revelation of his gospel in the Lord Jesus Christ and trust in the promises that Christ embodies. One thing only is necessary for righteousness, Luther declares near the start of the treatise,

---

[12] *LW*, 31:344.

and that thing is the Word of God.[13] This means that Luther's understanding of the Christian life is very different at a practical level from that of late medieval Catholicism. As we will see in the next chapter, the centrality of the Word has implications for how the Christian life is understood and then lived.

Luther uses dramatic language to speak of the power of faith in the matter of justification. When faith grasps the Word, the power of the Word is imparted to the believer as heat is imparted to an iron placed in fire.[14] Then, faith gives the greatest honor possible to Christ by ascribing to him truth and trustworthiness.[15] Finally, and supremely, faith in God's Word unites the believer to Christ and thus provides the context for what Luther calls *the joyful exchange*, whereby the believer's sins are passed to Christ and Christ's righteousness is passed to the believer. Using his favored image of the bride and the groom, Luther gives a famous description of this in *The Freedom of the Christian Man*:

> The third incomparable benefit of faith is that it unites the soul with Christ as a bride is united with her bridegroom. By this mystery, as the Apostle teaches, Christ and the soul become one flesh [Eph. 5:31–32]. And if they are one flesh and there is between them a true marriage—indeed the most perfect of all marriages, since human marriages are but poor examples of this one true marriage—it follows that everything they have they hold in common, the good as well as the evil. Accordingly the believing soul can boast of and glory in whatever Christ has as though it were its own, and whatever the soul has Christ claims as his own. Let us compare these and we shall see inestimable benefits. Christ is full of grace, life, and salvation. The soul is full of sins, death, and damnation. Now let faith come between them and sins, death, and damnation will be Christ's, while grace, life, and salvation will be the soul's; for if Christ is a bridegroom, he must take upon himself the things which are his bride's and bestow upon her the things that are his. If he gives her his body and very self, how shall he not give her all that is his? And if he takes the body of the bride, how shall he not take all that is hers?[16]

---

[13] *LW*, 31:345–46.

[14] *LW*, 31:349.

[15] *LW*, 31:350.

[16] *LW*, 31:351. Luther uses the marital image in an adumbration of this later passage in the important 1519 sermon "Two Kinds of Righteousness," *LW*, 31:297. While Melanchthon, Luther's close colleague, preferred to use more strictly forensic analogies in his discussions of justification, there is no significant difference between the two men in terms of the underlying concept. This is clear from a postscript, written in Luther's own hand, that he appended to a letter from Melanchthon to the Lutheran theologian

This joyful exchange indicates that Luther's thinking on justification is in one sense driven very much by the late medieval notion of divine declaration. As the one who did what was in him was extrinsically declared by God to have merited grace even though intrinsically he did not merit it, so the one who has faith receives Christ's righteousness as an extrinsically declared reality parallel to Christ's reception of the believer's sin. As Christ died on the cross not because he was *intrinsically* sinful but rather because our sins were imputed to him, so the believer is declared righteous not because he is *intrinsically* righteous but rather because he receives Christ's righteousness by imputation. The whole matter is rooted in the external declaration of God, based upon the union of Christ and the believer. Luther calls this justifying righteousness, received by faith, *alien* righteousness.[17]

There are, however, significant differences between Luther's position and that of his medieval teachers. For them the instrument of justification was ultimately the sacraments. It is true that late medieval theology, with its emphasis upon the *pactum*, might be seen to have weakened that point: the necessity of the sacrament seemed thereby to have been subordinated to God's decree and to the individual's effort; but even in the circles of the *via moderna*, the importance of the sacrament was still maintained, however inconsistently. Further, medieval teachers regarded God's declaration that a person was in a state of grace as the foundation for actual consequent meritorious righteousness; thus justification remained a process by which the Christian became more and more actually, intrinsically, righteous over time.

For Luther, however, faith is the instrument, and there is no place for merit, either before or after the individual comes to trust in God's Word and be united to Christ. Justifying righteousness is alien righteousness, and justification is always the extrinsic declaration of God, not based upon any intrinsic quality. Further, while Luther does regard the sacraments as important, they are not strictly speaking necessary for salvation, since faith is the one thing needful in this regard.[18] As we shall see in chapter 6, Luther's theology of justification led him to a fundamental reconstruction, theologically and liturgically, of the sacraments.

Johannes Brenz, dated May 12, 1531. Here Luther comments that he and Melanchthon prefer to express the idea in different ways but are in conceptual agreement: see *Weimarer Ausgabe Briefwechsel* 6:98–101.
[17] *LW*, 31:297.
[18] Luther makes this clear in his 1521 treatise *Against Latomus*: "St. Paul says (Rom. 10[:10]) that, 'A man believes with his heart and so is justified.' He does not say that it is necessary that he receive the sacraments, for one can become righteous by faith without the bodily reception of the sacraments (so long as one does not despise them). But without faith, no sacrament is of any use, indeed, it is altogether deadly and pernicious." *LW*, 32:15.

Simul Justus et Peccator

One phrase that Luther used to characterize his understanding of justification is *simul justus et peccator*, Latin for "simultaneously righteous and a sinner." The phrase plays off of the classic Lutheran opposition between outward appearance and inward reality. The cross is again the supreme example of this: outwardly, Christ appears to be a sinner and cursed, though inwardly he is actually the only perfect man who ever lived and is blessed by the Father. By contrast, the religious rulers who gather at the cross that day are outwardly righteous (they are, after all, the religious elite) but inwardly sinful (they are responsible before God for the death of the Christ).

This notion is crucial to one's understanding of Luther. All human beings, the Christian and the non-Christian, are simultaneously righteous and sinners. The non-Christian, the theologian of glory, is righteous in his own eyes and, quite probably, in the eyes of the world around him. Any who are confident that, though not perfect, they will still be found acceptable by God on the day of judgment would be great examples of such. Christians, by way of contrast, know that they stand as sinful and condemned already, and that there is nothing in them that will lead to anything other than condemnation when they stand before God's throne. There is also a sense in which all Christians are people divided against themselves: clothed in the righteousness of Christ and yet always striving to justify themselves by their own righteousness. That inner conflict is part of the very essence of what it means to be a Christian in a fallen world this side of glory. As we will see in chapter 7, this is one reason why the law remains a permanent part of the arsenal of the Christian.

Numerous other aspects of justification need to be addressed. For example, how does the individual come to faith? And what place do good works have in the Christian life? These will be best addressed in subsequent chapters. There are, however, two further foundational points to make before we move on to more specific discussion of the theological practicalities of Christianity: the priesthood and kingship of all believers.

Priesthood and Kingship

At the heart of Luther's earliest Reformation battles in 1518 and 1519 lay a basic distrust and dislike of what the formal priesthood of the Roman Catholic Church represented. There was significant anticlericalism in the northern European air at this point anyway, and Luther's salvoes against priestly elitism played very well with the crowds.

By 1520, however, his critique of the priesthood was becoming much more theologically grounded. The debate with Eck at Leipzig in 1519 had brought matters of church authority to the fore in his mind, as the practical implications of his protest against indulgences and the theological implications of his emerging understanding of salvation became clearer. Thus, his three great writings of 1520, *The Babylonian Captivity of the Church*, *The Freedom of the Christian Man*, and *An Appeal to the German Nobility*, all in different ways offered critiques of church power and alternative approaches to the various issues addressed.

In *The Freedom of the Christian Man*, Luther draws out most clearly the implications of the cross as the criterion for theology as it relates to the self-understanding of the Christian. We noted above that the cross demands a counterintuitive inversion of meaning in standard terms when applied to the gospel. Power is seen in weakness, wisdom in foolishness, and so forth. As the believer is united to Christ and thus is to understand her identity in light of that union, thus her understanding is to be transformed too.

For Calvin and later Reformed theology, Christ's office of Mediator is typically divided into three: prophet, priest, and king.[19] Luther, however, divides the office of Mediator into two: priest and king.[20] Priests sacrifice and offer prayers; kings rule. Crucially, of course, Christ's priesthood and kingship need to be refracted through the revelation of the cross: Christ sacrifices himself and offers prayers for those who are his enemies; and his kingship is inaugurated not through the expected routing of his enemies but through his surprise submission to the will of his enemies and then to death itself.

Luther makes a provocative statement at the start of *The Freedom of the Christian Man*, which would appear at first glance incomprehensible:

> A Christian is a perfectly free lord of all, subject to none. A Christian is a perfectly dutiful servant of all, subject to all.[21]

In many ways this is vintage Luther: a dramatic, paradoxical statement that immediately grabs the reader's attention. To juxtapose lordship and

---

[19] For the distinction in Calvin, see his *Institutes*, 2:15; for a confessional statement of the same, see Westminster Confession of Faith, 8.1.
[20] *LW*, 31:353–54.
[21] *LW*, 31:344.

servitude in such a way seems to be playing with words. In fact, of course, it is entirely consistent with Luther's developing theology since it rests upon three basic theological assumptions: the cross is the criterion for theology; Christ is Lord, king, ruler; the Christian is united to Christ by faith.

Using 1 Peter 2:9 as textual support, Luther argues that all believers, united to Christ, are part of a royal priesthood and thus can be counted as kings and priests.[22] This must then be understood within the context of both the cross of Christ and Luther's related anthropology, which makes the clear distinction between the outward and the inward. Inwardly, by faith, the Christian rules over all things in the sense that nothing can happen to him that will harm him; moreover, all things, even the most evil, must actually serve to further his salvation (Rom. 8:28).[23] This point has powerful ethical significance.

First, it preempts any ambition Christians or the church may have to earthly, coercive power. This is not to say that Christians cannot hold high office in the state or become significant and powerful figures in their earthly callings, as we shall see in chapter 8. It is, however, to make clear that the Christian as a Christian has a power that is to be conceived of in cross-shaped terms, and the church, as the body of believers, is also to see its power and its role in a spiritual manner.

Second, it makes Christ the ethical paradigm for Christianity. Christ as example has been a commonplace throughout Christian history and in Luther's own day was central to the thinking of his greatest polemical opponent, Desiderius Erasmus. What Luther does, however, is make union with Christ the foundation for Christ as example and then make Christ's sufferings and death central to this exemplary role in a profoundly existential manner: because the believer is united to Christ, suffering is inevitable. Christian power in this context—indeed, Christian liberty—means that all this suffering, all these persecutions, all these painful wounds inflicted on body and mind by the forces of evil, can make no impact upon the state of the Christian's soul and in fact are harnessed to work to his ultimate salvation. For Luther, Christ is the great example of this: a life marked by suffering and rejection, culminating in death at the hands of deadly enemies, was in fact the means by which he inaugurated

---

[22] *LW*, 31:354.
[23] *LW*, 31:354.

his kingdom.[24] Christian kingship thus means an analogous life experience for those united to Christ. Indeed, in his treatise *On the Councils of the Church* (1539), Luther will make the cross—that is, suffering—one of the seven outward marks of the true church.[25]

If Christians as "lords of all" means that suffering and evil are subverted for the believer's good, Luther regards priesthood as an even greater privilege. The church of Luther's day made the priesthood an elite caste that actually held the power of salvation because it alone had the authority and the power to administer the sacraments. Yet, Luther argues, united to Christ, all believers are priests. This raises the immediate question, Is Luther simply universalizing the established pattern of medieval priesthood? Of course, this is not his meaning; again, "Christ on the cross" as the criterion of theology demands that the notion of priesthood be remade in accordance with this theological reality. Thus, priesthood for the believer means that we, through our union with Christ, can now appear in God's presence and intercede for others. In reformulating the notion of earthly priesthood, Luther has removed the sacrificial aspect of the role, as this is fulfilled in Christ, and instead focused on the ongoing intercession that now takes place.[26]

This latter concept, often known as "the priesthood of all believers" or "the general priesthood of all believers" was explosive in Luther's day because it struck at the very structure of medieval piety. By demolishing the notion of a special, sacramental priesthood, Luther effectively demolished the ecclesiology of his day. It was also a notion that would become increasingly controversial and problematic within Protestant ranks. One obvious question it raised was, Is there any need for a special, clerical calling? If all are priests, after all, why would one need to have some people ordained to conduct worship services and pastor the flock? Cannot all be preachers, all baptize, all administer the Lord's Supper and hear confession?

---

[24] The key passage on Christian power is worth quoting in full for its dramatic intensity: "As a matter of fact, the more Christian a man is, the more evils, sufferings, and deaths he must endure, as we see in Christ the first-born prince himself, and in all his brethren, the saints. The power of which we speak is spiritual. It rules in the midst of enemies and is powerful in the midst of oppression. This means nothing else than that 'power is made perfect in weakness' [II Cor. 12:9] and that in all things I can find profit toward salvation [Rom. 8:28], so that the cross and death itself are compelled to serve me and to work together with me for my salvation. This is a splendid privilege and hard to attain, a truly omnipotent power, a spiritual dominion in which there is nothing so good and nothing so evil but that it shall work together for good to me, if only I believe. Yes, since faith alone suffices for salvation, I need nothing except faith exercising the power and dominion of its own liberty. Lo, this is the inestimable power and liberty of Christians." *LW*, 31:354–55.

[25] *LW*, 41:164–65.

[26] *LW*, 31:355.

The problem became acutely significant for the Reformers, and especially Luther, in 1525, with the Peasants' War. At that time, radicals used Luther's language of freedom as part of the rhetoric of rebellion, for understandable reasons. Such language resonates powerfully with the oppressed and disenfranchised in every age. The problem, of course, was that Luther was using such words in a manner that assumed their refraction through the cross. The same applied to the language of universal priesthood: the obvious democratizing tendency of the language was popular with those seeking more social equality. Yet the anarchy of the war placed Luther in an impossible position: he was no democratizing radical; he needed to reassure his secular lords that reformation did not mean revolution; and he needed to make sure that his teaching was clearly understood. The result was that, from 1525 onward, language of universal priesthood was decidedly muted in Luther, as it was to be in other magisterial Reformers, such as John Calvin.

Luther would also proceed in later writings to develop a clearer understanding of the need for a properly constituted and ordained church leadership. In 1520, however, that line of argument was not strongly developed, with Luther simply commenting that not all can be public leaders in the church because not all are competent to teach.[27] Later, he would make ordination a mark of the true church.[28] He would also emphasize that ordination to an office is defined by functions, not by status or rank, as is clear from the ordination rite he composed in 1529.[29] Freedom for Luther must be understood through the incarnation and the cross: it is freedom to serve others and freedom to die for others. The whole of the Christian faith, and therefore the whole of Christian ministry, needs to be constructed in light of who God is for us as he is revealed in his incarnate Son hanging on the tree at Calvary.

Concluding Reflections

Luther's distinction between the theologian of glory and the theologian of the cross is foundational to his understanding of the Christian life because it makes clear the two—and only two—ways in which human beings

---

[27] *LW*, 31:356.
[28] *On the Councils of the Church*, in *LW*, 41:154. Here Luther emphasizes that Paul's teaching excludes from office women, children, and those who are simply incompetent, reserving ordination only for competent males.
[29] *LW*, 53:124–27.

can approach God. They do so either on their terms or on God's terms. For Luther, as for Paul, Christ on the cross is the watershed of the history of redemption and the discriminating factor regarding eternal destiny. And it is Christ in his flesh, crucified on the cross, that permeates Luther's entire theology.

Throughout the centuries, theologians have often been preoccupied with the cross for what it offers: penal substitutionary atonement, expiation of sin, triumph over the Devil, an example of devotion to God that others should strive to follow. Luther's understanding of the cross, however, brings out another important aspect: the cross as revelation of God toward us and also as an indicator of where we stand before God.

As the young Luther had been terrified of a righteous, holy, and wrathful God, so he was liberated by the discovery that God had made himself weak and vulnerable, subject to abuse and to death at the hands of the powers of evil. This transformed everything for Luther. Both theological language and human expectations of God are inverted by the great inversion of the cross. God's strength is revealed in God's weakness; and we are declared righteous extrinsically even as we are intrinsically sinful.

This offers Christians today a powerful foundation for theological reflection. What Luther provides is a theology that draws richly on Paul's teaching in 1 Corinthians. We have a perennial tendency to make human nature the measure of reality, but the cross stands as God's judgment against that and as his positive revelation of the right way to approach him and think of him. First Corinthians 1 is a reminder that the criteria for doing theology are not the expectations of human beings, whether we think of those expectations in terms of some transcendental human reason or the horizons of plausibility and particular norms of our own specific cultures.

The cross, however, is also an existential paradigm for the Christian. As noted above, it is significant that Luther talks in concrete, personal terms of theologians and not theologies when he makes the distinction between glory and the cross. Theology is thought and known by real, specific people. To be a theologian of glory is not simply to construct an image of God in one's own image; it is to *live* in line with that image, with all of the expectations and interpretations of experience that follow in its wake. The same is true for the theologian of the cross. So here is the rub: the theologian of glory will ultimately not be able to make any sense of this world, for this world ultimately ends for each of us in physical decline, weakness, and death. That is incomprehensible in terms of the theology believed by the theologian of glory. But the theologian of the cross knows that this world is fallen and evil; that life leads inexorably to the grave; that the longer one lives, the more loved ones one loses. Yet in the midst of this desolation, the theologian of the cross can see the logic of the cross at work.

This is not a logic that simplistically declares that all this misery is God's will and that one should stoically endure it. The logic of the cross says that weakness and death, painful as they are, have been utterly subverted by God in Christ, that pain and mortality have ironically become the means of strength and power, and that the grave itself has become the gateway to paradise. And that is the lesson of justification by grace through faith too: the outer man may well be fading away, but the inner man goes from strength to strength. Nothing can be done to the physical body that will ultimately jeopardize the soul. In fact, the greatest evil that can be inflicted on the body—death—is simply the pathway to resurrection.

This is powerful pastoral medicine. It can be preached to that single mother in the congregation who is poor, has a hard life, and sees little hope that these things will change. It can be applied to the old man whose body, full of years, is rapidly breaking down and racing only toward eternity. It can be applied to the widow and the orphan, to the despised and to the things that are not. It is, after all, simply the gospel of the Lord Jesus Christ whereby strength is made perfect through weakness. Suffering is not good in itself, but it has been subverted for good, as dying has been made the gateway to paradise through Christ's own death and resurrection.

Luther makes a significant statement of this in his 1539 work *On the Councils of the Church*, where suffering is made the seventh mark of the church:

> Seventh, the holy Christian people are externally recognized by the holy possession of the sacred cross. They must endure every misfortune and persecution, all kinds of trials and evil from the devil, the world, and the flesh (as the Lord's Prayer indicates) by inward sadness, timidity, fear, outward poverty, contempt, illness, and weakness, in order to become like their head, Christ. And the only reason they must suffer is that they steadfastly adhere to Christ and God's word, enduring this for the sake of Christ, Matthew 5[:11], "Blessed are you when men persecute you on my account." They must be pious, quiet, obedient, and prepared to serve

the government and everybody with life and goods, doing no one any harm. No people on earth have to endure such bitter hate; they must be accounted worse than Jews, heathen, and Turks. In summary, they must be called heretics, knaves, and devils, the most pernicious people on earth, to the point where those who hang, drown, murder, torture, banish, and plague them to death are rendering God a service. No one has compassion on them; they are given myrrh and gall to drink when they thirst. And all of this is done not because they are adulterers, murderers, thieves, or rogues, but because they want to have none but Christ, and no other God. Wherever you see or hear this, you may know that the holy Christian church is there, as Christ says in Matthew 5[:11–12], "Blessed are you when men revile you and utter all kinds of evil against you on my account. Rejoice and be glad, for your reward is great in heaven." This too is a holy possession whereby the Holy Spirit not only sanctifies his people, but also blesses them.[30]

As God himself suffered in Jesus Christ, hanging on a cross, reviled and despised by others, so the church, his body, can expect the same. Yet, as with the incarnate Christ, the church is blessed by God in harsh circumstances because her pain and her weakness are the points at which God is able to demonstrate most decisively his power and his strength. As vocabulary is inverted by the cross, so are the experiences and expectations of the church.

And it is now time to see what this life of the theologian of the cross, this life that leads through death to resurrection, looks like.

---

[30] LW, 41:164–65.

CHAPTER 3

THE THEOLOGY OF THE WORD PREACHED

Protestantism . . . is the work of a Prophet: the prophet-work of that sixteenth century.

THOMAS CARLYLE, *ON HEROES,*
HERO-WORSHIP AND THE HEROIC IN HISTORY

In the last chapter, we noted that a major factor driving Luther's foundational theology was the question of where we can find a gracious God. Luther's basic response was clear: in the incarnate and crucified Christ. This invites the follow-up question, And where do we find the incarnate and crucified Christ today, seeing that he has ascended to heaven? The answer to that question connects to Luther's theology of the Word: we find him in the Word preached and in the sacraments, and we find him there not by sight but by faith. It is here that Luther's theology of the creative Word and the crucified Christ come together; and this points toward the importance of the corporate, church context for the Christian life. For all of the post-Bultmannian criticisms of Luther for developing an individualistic theology, in practice his emphases are really rather corporate: Word and sacrament demand a corporate context.

This leads us inevitably to very practical questions: If the preached Word is the foundation of the Christian life, then what kind of sermons do preachers need to preach and congregations need to hear? In what kind of service context would the preaching take place? And how do other routines of daily Christian life connect to, and draw upon, this Word?

Before we can address these issues, though, we need to spend a little time reflecting on Luther's basic understanding of the Word of God in itself, and this requires that we know something about his theological background and context.

Luther's Christian life was in many ways exceptional for a man of his times. Obviously, few of his contemporaries enjoyed the kind of notoriety and influence that he commanded. Indeed, his life was rich with excitement. Yet it was exceptional for a more mundane reason too: he was able to read and write. Luther was a true intellectual in an era when literacy rates, while rising, were very low; and this meant that for most people the routines of their day-to-day Christian lives were very different from those of Christians today. Few would have read the Bible for themselves, and the church service would have been the main forum in which they were able to learn what the Bible actually said.

If the educational limitations of the times had such an influence on everyday Christian experience, it is also true that Luther's theology placed a great emphasis on the corporate aspects of the Christian life, especially in terms of Word and sacraments. Indeed, Word and sacrament were the two primary objective means of the Christian life. We shall look at the sacraments in later chapters; but for the next three chapters we must spend some time exploring the theological importance of the Word. For Luther, the Word not only describes reality but also determines reality, all reality; and if that is true in general, then how much more is it true for the reality of the Christian life?

Before engaging this subject, however, we should note that this will necessitate discussion of a few ideas that at first glance might seem rather arcane and of little relevance to the Christian life. The present age is one of a very pragmatic bent: we tend to judge the importance of any given idea on the basis of its immediate practical benefit, and this can make us impatient with what appear to be abstractions or ivory-tower speculation. Luther's understanding of the nature of the pastoral task, its objectives, and its tools was deeply theological. He gave priority to theology in that he understood the world and all that is in it first and foremost in theological terms. Because the world is God's creation, and because the church is God's special creation, both are to be understood in terms determined by God himself. Any response, whether to the world or the church, was thus, for Luther, determined by theology. Thus, it is vital for us to explore the theological foundations of Luther's thought before we can hope to understand his approach to the Christian life.

Two particular elements of Luther's theology are of special importance here: his understanding of the Word of God as powerful and creative; and the related distinction between theologians of glory and theologians of the cross. These two foundational components of his theology emerge early in his Reformation career and provide the basis for his later understanding of justification, the sacraments, the church, and thus the Christian life. To understand Luther's thinking in these areas, however, it is first of all necessary to understand something of his background in late medieval thought.

Luther and the Late Medieval God

Luther is famous as the man who started the Reformation. Even those who have never read a word he wrote know that his life and career marked a decisive moment in the church's history. At a popular level, this has often led to the assumption that Luther's thinking marks a clean break with all that went before it—that if his theology is to be connected to the past, it is by way of antithesis, not positive continuity. Popular Christian artwork has often reinforced this idea, with plentiful pictures showing Luther nailing the *Ninety-Five Theses* to the church door in Wittenberg and thus symbolically driving a nail into the coffin of a moribund church as a fresh, new era begins.

While such an opinion may still be in vogue in some quarters, the scholarly world has come to adopt a very different picture. Ever since the ground-breaking work of the Jesuit scholar Joseph Lortz in the 1940s, students of Luther have been aware of the positive connection between late medieval theology and Luther's Reformation thought.[1] Indeed, in many ways Luther remained a man of the Middle Ages: his politically conservative feudalism and his acute sense of the constant proximity and even physical presence of the Devil are just two examples of things that separate him from the other Reformers, with their Renaissance humanist

---

[1] Joseph Lortz, *The Reformation in Germany*, trans. Ronald Walls (London: Darton, Longman and Todd, 1968).

sympathies;[2] and, of course, while Melanchthon and Calvin found much in the work of Erasmus to admire, Luther despised that most modern of men with a vengeance and made him the constant butt of disparaging remarks in the *Table Talk*.[3]

Luther's theology connects to that of his late medieval teachers in a number of ways, both positive and negative. Most significant for his understanding of the power of the Word is the critical philosophy of language that developed in the fourteenth and fifteenth centuries and connected to the radical application of the dialectic of God's two powers. To summarize these late medieval approaches, theologians developed the dialectic of the two powers in an attempt to safeguard both God's infinite omnipotence and the stability of the finite created order.

As noted above, theologians posited two powers in God: an absolute power and an ordained power. According to God's *absolute power*, he could do anything, subject only to the law of noncontradiction. Thus, for example, he could have created a world where elephants did not exist, but he could not have created a world where Herod both existed and did not exist at the same time. According to his *ordained power*, however, God has realized a specific world with a finite set of possibilities. Thus, he has made human beings with two legs, rather than three, and apples that, when ripe, are green, yellow, or red, not black or silver. Of course, theologians did not think that God in himself really possessed two separate powers; the distinction was really an epistemological one framed from the human perspective that allowed us to protect God's omnipotence and omniscience while maintaining the fundamental stability of the universe as it is actually constituted. God did not have to make this world; but once he did, he was committed to it, and it was thus real and stable.

As confidence in human reason declined from the twelfth century onward, a decline driven both by internal logical pressure and by external catastrophes such as the Black Plague, the dialectic between the two powers was used in an increasingly sharp and critical way to articulate this increasing epistemological modesty with regard to God. To put it simply, the gap between the absolute and the ordained power became bigger. As a result, theologians came to regard reason as less and less competent, and they focused increasingly on revelation (that which discloses God's

---

[2] References to the presence of the Devil, and to conversations with him, occur throughout Luther's writings; e.g., *LW*, 54:78.
[3] E.g., "I hate Erasmus with all my heart." *LW*, 54:84.

ordained will, what he has *chosen* to do) as the source of knowledge of God rather than pure logical and metaphysical speculation (which might yield, at best, knowledge of God's absolute power, what he *could* do).

Of course, these late medieval theologians were not Protestants in even an embryonic sense, and they identified as a source of revelation the teaching of the church's Magisterium and not simply the words of Scripture. Yet the overall thrust of their theology was revelational, and that connection was to be developed and radicalized by Luther and his Reformation contemporaries.

One other point of interest in late medieval theology is of great relevance to our understanding Luther. Connected to the distinction between God's powers was a perennial linguistic debate about the nature and function of words. This debate might seem a little arcane at first glance, something of interest only to logicians and philosophers, but it would actually play a key role in the development of Luther's understanding of the power of God's Word.

The debate was about the referential nature of nouns. To put the matter simply, what gives a noun its meaning? Is it something in the object to which the word is applied? Or is it simply the application of the word itself? For example, does the word *dog* mean something because it refers to something real, a universal "dogginess" in which all dogs participate such that the word legitimately applies to them? Does each dog have something objectively in common with all other dogs that makes the application of the word *dog* to each of them appropriate? Or does the word simply refer to lots and lots of individual things we choose to bracket together— Fido, Rover, Tico, Butch—under the term *dog*, with no ideal "dogginess" out there in which they all participate? Taken to its extreme, this latter view became what philosophers call an antiessentialist ontology, which effectively made words, and not underlying essences or substances, the determiners of reality. We might put the matter this way: is dogginess something real and independent of any individual example of a dog, or is it merely a linguistic construct, created by the person or the community that uses the word?

Those who denied the existence of universal forms such as "dogginess" represented what is known as late medieval *nominalism*. This was the linguistic school in which Luther was trained and whose basic assumptions remained with him throughout his career. His theology may well have undergone remarkable changes over the years, but his commitment to nominalism, to the priority of words in determining reality, was unswerving.

Readers may well be familiar with some of the philosophical argument associated with the contemporary eclectic movement known as postmodernism. There are in fact potent similarities between late medieval nominalism and certain schools of postmodern linguistic theory. We might say that both envisage the world as a linguistic construct. Words, not essences, become determinative and constitutive of reality. I suspect that Luther would have little time for the excesses of postmodern antiessentialism and the kaleidoscopic anarchy it has created with regard to gender, sexuality, and even the notion of human nature. Nevertheless, we should note that Luther would not object to postmodernism by reasserting a kind of essentialist ontology. Rather, his rejection of postmodern anarchy would be based on his belief that God is the supreme reality and ultimately the one who speaks and whose speech is therefore the ground of existence and of difference. Reality is determined not by the linguistic proclivities of any human individual or community but by the Word of God. This point is absolutely crucial to understanding all of Luther's theology and thus his approach to the Christian life because it points to the vital and creative role of the Word of God.

The practical significance of this linguistic philosophy for Luther as pastor is that words become absolutely foundational to everything the pastor does; language is thus foundational to all aspects of the Christian life. If God's words determine reality, then of all the things a pastor does, speaking the words of God to the congregation is the most important. For the individual Christian, it is the words of God addressing him that determine his own reality. Thus, public and private reading of the Bible are vital. Preaching that Word and hearing that Word are vital. Applying the Word individually or having that Word applied to oneself by the pastor in the confessional is vital. Indeed, because each of these things involves God's Word, each also determines the reality of the church and of the individual Christian's life. In addition, it also points to the importance of the sacraments: those of us with less sacramental proclivity than Luther may find his views on these matters at first perplexing. But does it not make sense, within Luther's framework at least, that if God says the bread and wine are Christ's body and blood, given for you, then that is what they become at that moment, whatever our physical senses or the empirical data might suggest to the contrary?

The Theology of the Word

It would be wrong, however, to reduce Luther's Reformation theology to a particularly radical application of late medieval linguistic theory to theological language and the doctrine of God. If one wants to reduce Reformation theology to cultural factors, one might just as easily point to the growing prominence of words in a culture that, for its time, had access to relatively cheap print and was seeing literacy rates slowly start to climb. Luther's preoccupation with the Word and with divine speech, however, was not simply driven by his philosophical and cultural context; it was also theological. He saw the Word as powerful, creative, and definitive for reality because that is what the Bible itself teaches.

There is, of course, a happy coincidence or, perhaps better, an elective affinity between such critical linguistic philosophy of Luther's teachers and what Luther saw as the Bible's own teaching about the nature of God. For Luther, God in himself was utterly unknowable in any positive sense. He dwelt in deep darkness; he rode on the wings of the storm; like the God described by Job, he was invisible, unaccountable, infinitely powerful, and utterly incommensurable with anything or anyone else. Like a good late medieval theologian, Luther considered that God could be known as a certain kind of God only on the basis of how he had revealed himself to be according to his ordained power. In short, only as God spoke could he be known.

As we have seen, however, God's speech not only defined reality but also in a very real sense *made* reality. A thing is what it is because God says it is this thing and not another; but this thing exists only because God has first spoken it into existence. Luther saw the Bible as teaching that there could be a reality external to God only if God chose to speak such a reality. Thus, material reality exists external to God because God has chosen to speak it. We might perhaps say that the Creator-creature distinction in Luther is that between the One who speaks and that which is itself spoken.

The obvious place to go in Luther for statements on this role of speech in creation are his 1535 *Lectures on Genesis*. Speaking of the work of the fifth day, Luther says this:

> Who could conceive of the possibility of bringing forth from the water a being which clearly could not continue to exist in water? But God speaks a mere Word, and immediately the birds are brought forth from the water. If the Word is spoken, all things are possible, so that out of the water are made either fish or birds. Therefore any bird whatever and any fish whatever are nothing but nouns in the divine rule of language; through this rule of language those things that are impossible become very easy, while those that are clearly opposite become very much alike, and vice versa.[4]

The particular point he is making has general theological significance: when God speaks, that speech creatively determines reality; it is, to build on late medieval terminology, both the expression and the actualization of his ordained power. The substance of water, by every law of physics both in Luther's day and in our own, should lead to the conclusion that it is impossible to make from such a thing creatures like fish or birds. Yet when God speaks, these creatures are created and possess existence out of the water. The objective nature of the water, in itself offering a rather limited number of possibilities when it comes to transformation into something else, is overridden by God's speech. Essentialism is trumped by the greater determining reality of God's Word.

For Luther, however, this emphasis on words is not simply a philosophical commitment but one that carries deep moral implications precisely because it is God who speaks these words and this reality into existence. God's Word is not a morally neutral thing; it is the powerful speech of a holy and sovereign God. Thus, discussions of the creativity of that Word cannot be reduced to a metaphysical or logical game. God's Word establishes a relationship between Creator and creature that reflects the very character and status of God.

This is clear from Luther's account of the temptation and sin of Adam and Eve in the garden. Moses describes the events leading up to the fall as a struggle over the meaning and status of verbal statements that God made to Adam and Eve. It is indeed no coincidence in Luther's mind that the serpent chooses to attack God's Word as the means of assault upon Eden because, in so doing, he strikes at the character and power of God. Commenting on Genesis 3:1, Luther says:

---

[4] LW, 1:49.

Moses expresses himself very carefully and says: "The serpent said," that is, with a word it attacks the Word. The Word which the Lord had spoken to Adam was: "Do not eat from the tree of the knowledge of good and evil." For Adam this Word was Gospel and Law; it was his worship; it was his service and the obedience he could offer God in this state of innocence. These Satan attacks and tries to destroy. Nor is it only his intention, as those who lack knowledge think, to point out the tree and issue an invitation to pick its fruit. He points it out indeed; but then he adds another and a new statement, as he still does in the church.[5]

This passage offers a fascinating insight not only into Luther's understanding of the fall but also into his understanding of God's Word in general. Luther sees the serpent's attack on God's Word as attempting to create a new reality, an alternative to that established by God himself. This assault on God's Word and the meaning of that Word represents nothing less than an assault upon God's status as sovereign Creator and as determiner of reality. Thus, in casting doubt upon God's trustworthiness and upon the reality of the words he has spoken, the serpent casts doubt upon the character of God, the power of his Word, the normativity of his Word, and thereby the nature of the reality in which Adam and Eve find themselves. When Adam and Eve eat the fruit, they are accepting the serpent's word as the true account of reality. They are rejecting God and claiming that creatures can determine what is and is not real. They repudiate God's words and the reality he has established. The problem is, of course, that the reality they accept is no reality at all. It is an illusion, a falsehood, and an immoral one at that. What they have done is reject God and a true definition of themselves. They have attempted, in short, to make themselves into gods.

This passage from Luther's *Lectures on Genesis* shows that the linguistic philosophy of late medieval nominalism dovetails beautifully with his understanding of what the Bible says about the relationship between God and created reality. In addition, we can also see how the connection of this speech to God's person, and thus the rejection of this speech to a rejection of God himself, is not simply a matter of epistemological significance for Luther. It is also of serious moral significance as well. Adam and Eve accept the serpent's words not because they fail to understand what God has told them. They accept the serpent's narrative because they are acting wickedly.

Given all this, it becomes clear that Luther builds a dramatic theol-

---

[5] *LW*, 1:146.

ogy upon what is, at first glance, a rather arid philosophy of language. For Luther, the question of language is far more than a matter of meaning or predication; it connects directly to how God has chosen to relate to his creation. As he speaks it into existence, as he supports it by the Word of his power, so his words become the means whereby he deals with people in general, and his special people in particular.

This has significance for Luther's understanding of the church and its function. In short, the church is the place where God's Word is spoken. Therein lies the church's power, because the preached Word is how God is actively present. Luther roots this understanding in his view of the Old Testament, where, he notes, God's speech is indeed the primary mode of his presence. As we saw above, human beings can have to do with God only as he reveals himself to them; and that means they can have to do with him only as he chooses to speak to them. Thus, the absence of God's speech is, for Luther, the same as the absence of God, a very terrible situation to contemplate. Commenting on Amos 8:11, he observes:

> *I shall send a famine on the land.* This is the last blow. It is the worst, the most wretched, of all. All the rest of the blows would be bearable, but this is absolutely horrible. He is threatening to take away the genuine prophets and the true Word of God, so that there is no one to preach, even if men were most eager to wish to hear the Word and would run here and there to hear it. This happened to the Jews in the Assyrian captivity and in that last one.[6]

The absence of God's Word is the absence of God. More significantly, from the point of view of understanding pastoral ministry and the spiritual life of the Christian, the absence of the prophets who speak God's words is tantamount to the absence of God. This has acute and immediate practical significance. As Luther will make clear later in this same passage, the modern preacher is the successor of the ancient prophet and thus central to the notion of God's presence within the New Testament church. If the Christian is to live in the presence of God, then that presence is primarily mediated through the presence of God's Word. This points to the importance of the church as the gathering of God's people in Luther's theology of the Word, a point that occurs again and again in his thought.

With this basic foundation of Luther's theology of the Word in hand,

---

[6] *LW*, 18:182–83.

we are now able to return to the question asked at the start of this chapter: What kind of preaching arises out of this kind of theology?

The Content of Preaching: Law and Gospel

If the Word of God is creative, then it is important that the word preached contains the Word of God. For Luther, it is not that any old words based on the Bible will perform the task for which preaching has been appointed. Further, the preacher is not simply to convey information; still less is he there to entertain. His task is far too serious for either of these: he is exposing a current reality (the human tendency to seek to be right with God through self-righteousness) and creating a new reality (where we are clothed with the crucified Christ's righteousness). Thus, he is to show people that all their righteousness is as filthy rags and as reliable a leaning post as a spider's web; and that, counterintuitive and countercultural as it may be, true righteousness, mercy, and grace are to be found in the filthy and broken corpse of a man condemned as a criminal to hang on a cross. This is the preaching of law and gospel, and it carries with it transformative power.

Because God's Word addresses human beings in this way, it can never be a morally indifferent force. It challenges us at the most basic level of our being, in terms of our very identity. If Luther were alive today, he would no doubt see the passion aroused in the secular world by the Bible's teaching on homosexuality as an example of this: God's Word does not just tell us certain things are wrong; in so doing, it tells us that we are not who we like to think we are, the masters of our own self-created identities and destinies, but instead creatures subject to the Creator.

Luther brings out the moral power of the Word preached perhaps most nicely in *The Bondage of the Will*. Here, he uses the example of Moses confronting Pharaoh with the demand that the people of Israel be released. This message, of course, reminds Pharaoh that he is not the supreme king, that there is One to whom he himself will one day be accountable. That is not a message anybody could receive in a matter-of-fact way:

> It is thus that [God] hardens Pharaoh, when he presents to his ungodly and evil will a word and work which that will hates—owing of course to its inborn defect and natural corruption. And since God does not change it inwardly by his Spirit, but keeps on presenting and obtruding his words and works from without, while Pharaoh keeps his eye on his own

strength, wealth, and power, in which by the same natural defect he puts his trust, the result is that Pharaoh is puffed up and exalted by his own imagined greatness on the one hand, and moved to proud contempt on the other by the lowliness of Moses and the abject form in which the word of God comes, and is thus hardened and then more and more provoked and exasperated the more Moses presses and threatens him.[7]

The Word of God is intrinsically powerful. Pharaoh, like all fallen human beings, does not like to be reminded of his creatureliness and his obligation toward God. Therefore, if God chooses not to transform Pharaoh's mindset by the work of the Holy Spirit, Pharaoh naturally responds in a manner consistent with his sinful, would-be autonomous human nature. The same is true for all hearers of God's Word. If God does not free the hearer to believe the gospel, the hearer's fallen will causes him to be hardened and to deepen in his opposition to the God who confronts him in the Word. Thus, as Isaiah declares, the Word of God cannot return to him empty. For Luther, indifference to the Word is therefore impossible because it is a moral force that challenges us at the deepest level of our beings. It is not a simple redescription of reality.

This point is important for understanding why corporate worship plays such a large role in Luther's conception of the Christian life. In Luther's time, most people were illiterate and thus the corporate reading and preaching of the Word were the only ways in which the Word could come to them. Yet there is more to it than the question of literacy: the external Word—the Word mediated to me via another from outside and thus not immediately filtered through my own sinful mind—confronts me in a way that my own Bible reading can never do. The external Word preached is thus, for Luther, one of the major means of personal transformation.

This view of the Word is reflected in a term used in the Schmalkaldic Articles of 1537, composed by Luther as the initial confessional basis of the Schmalkaldic League, the political and military alliance of Lutheran princes in the Holy Roman Empire. Article 8.3 says, "We must hold firmly to the conviction that God gives no one his Spirit or grace except through or with the external Word."[8] Luther is writing in a context already shaped by reaction against the radical approach of the spiritualists and Anabaptists, who downplayed the significance of the Word, but the article is a consistent

---

[7] LW, 33:179.
[8] BC, 312.

application of his theology. The Word comes from God, it comes from out-side our reality, and it defines and transforms that reality. When it comes as a word of gospel or grace, then it brings God's Spirit and it saves.

This external Word must not be reduced to mere cognition. Transfor-mation of the individual comes not simply from understanding the Word's propositional and conceptual content, nor its practical intention. Pharaoh presumably understood the Word Moses preached to him; but it was not his simple comprehension of the content of that Word so much as his realiza-tion of the personal implications of that Word that made him so furious in response. The Word itself is a challenge to our identity. The Word binds and the Word liberates. The Word condemns and the Word forgives.

Luther categorizes this power as twofold, that of the law and that of the gospel. This basic structure is already present in the Heidelberg Disputa-tion. The distinction underlies much of the theology of the disputation but is explicit in thesis 26: "The law says, 'do this,' and it is never done. Grace says, 'believe in this,' and everything is already done."[9] Fundamental to Luther's understanding of salvation, and thus of the Christian life, is the antithesis between doing and believing, between trying to earn salvation and receiving salvation in Christ, between works and faith, between law and gospel. In fact, when Luther clashes with Erasmus in 1525 over the bondage of the human will, the fundamental flaw that he sees in Erasmus's somewhat vague and concessive position on the role of the human will in salvation is that it confuses the law and the gospel.[10]

In his work *How Christians Should Regard Moses* (1525), Luther draws this contrast by comparing the Lord's speech at Sinai in Exodus with Peter's speech at Pentecost: the one demands human works; the other declares the works that God has done.[11] This law-gospel distinction in Luther is not, however, a canonical one, in the sense that the Old Testament is the former and the New Testament the latter. In fact, the distinction refers to how the Bible is *applied*: when the Old Testament is read as offering the promise of Christ, it is gospel; when the New is read as demanding obedience as a basis for a relationship with God, it is law.[12]

---

[9] *LW*, 31:41.
[10] E.g., "Now, I ask you, what good will anyone do in a matter of theology or Holy Writ, who has not yet got as far as knowing what the law and what the gospel is, or if he knows, disdains to observe the distinction between them? Such a person is bound to confound everything—heaven and hell, life and death—and he will take no pains to know anything at all about Christ." *LW*, 33:132.
[11] *LW*, 35:162.
[12] E.g., Luther speaks of Moses's offering fine examples of faith and belief and of punishment of the faith-less (*LW*, 35:174). He also indicates that, for example, the point of the Sermon on the Mount is to preach

The task of the preacher, therefore, is to take the Bible and to do two things in every sermon: destroy self-righteousness and point hearers toward the alien, external righteousness of Christ. The preacher must therefore expound the Bible in such a way that the law crushes the sinful human tendency toward self-justification by works, and he must then point the congregation toward the unconditional grace of God manifested in the Lord Jesus Christ. Luther makes this work of the law clear in his preface to the Epistle to the Romans:

> It is right for a preacher of the gospel in the first place by revelation of the law and of sin to rebuke and to constitute as sin everything that is not the living fruit of the Spirit and of faith in Christ, in order that men should be led to know themselves and their own wretchedness, and to become humble and ask for help.[13]

Thus, as the law's function is to bind and to crush, so the first task of the minister is to preach the law in such a manner that it does this. He must hold before the congregation a vision of the transcendent glory and holiness of God, and force congregants to see just how catastrophically far short of that they all fall. His task is not that of the typical American televangelist: giving people a pep talk and helping them have a good self-image and more confidence in themselves. For Luther, those are the lies of Satan. The preacher's task is first and foremost to shatter self-confidence in his audience and to drive them to despair.

Once the preaching of the law has driven a person to despair, then the minister is to declare the gospel and point to Christ. That is what the gospel is: an account of the life, work, and significance of the Lord Jesus Christ, as Luther makes clear in his preface to the New Testament: "The gospel, then, is nothing but the preaching about Christ, Son of God and of David, true God and man, who by his death and resurrection has overcome for us the sin, death, and hell of all men who believe in him."[14] Thus, preaching represents dramatic movement from exposing the folly of self-righteousness and cultivating despair and humility to providing comfort in the Lord Jesus Christ, the promise of whom is grasped by faith.

A good example of how Luther himself demonstrated this approach to

---

the law in all its perfection and that, by making it into something that only applies to the spiritual elite, the Roman Catholic Church has evacuated it of its true meaning (*LW*, 21:3–4).
[13] *LW*, 35:372.
[14] *LW*, 35:360.

preaching is his sermon in Weimar on October 22, 1522. The text is Matthew 22:37–39: "And he said to him, 'You shall love the Lord your God with all your heart and with all your soul and with all your mind. This is the great and first commandment. And a second is like it: You shall love your neighbor as yourself.'"[15]

The sermon starts with the bad news: the law demands love to God and love to neighbor of a kind that is utterly impossible for fallen human beings. Luther makes it clear that typical acts of piety such as fasting and prayer are of no use if they do not arise out of perfect love for God; and as no one can have this perfect love, none of these works are of any use before God. Luther proceeds to point out that it was love to God that motivated Abraham's willing obedience to sacrifice his son, while the child sacrifices in which the children of Israel later indulged (Ps. 106:37–38) were an abomination because such acts arose from hatred of God and his Word. In typical Luther fashion, he then connects this critique to the contemporary scene, pointing out how the modern-day priests impose pilgrimages on people as a way of enhancing penance and earning God's favor. What drives such things is devotion to the pope, not to God. Indeed, the perfection of love to God that the law demands is impossible for anyone and thus places us all under condemnation. Along the way, Luther also lashes out against monasticism and argues that vows to an order are not binding, as they hinder the true pursuit of love to neighbor. Finally, Luther's concluding paragraphs offer a magnificent statement of the gospel:

> Therefore, this is what the law requires and says: You owe nothing except to love Christ and your neighbor; otherwise you are eternally condemned. But then afterwards Christ comes and says: I suffered, died, and rose again in order that I might fill you with the riches and grace of my Holy Spirit and thus strengthen you. So if you have the Spirit, then you are not an outward spirit; no, you have salvation. Then a person thinks this way: Now, Lord Jesus, I will serve you, die and live for you, and patiently suffer all that is disagreeable from you and from men; do with me as you will. That person will be washed of his sins by the blood of Christ.
>
> Hence, if I have the Holy Spirit, I have faith, by which I cling to God. And if I believe in God, then I also have his love and I love God, foe, and friend. That is why Paul says: I can do all things through the Spirit of God [Phil. 4:13]. The Spirit does not come through fasting, praying, pil-

---

[15] The text of the sermon is in *LW*, 51:104–11.

grimages, running to and fro around the country; no, only through faith.
So Christ bestows his gifts upon you without any merit whatsoever and
what he did for him [i.e., Paul], he does for you also. Here, of course, you
must guard against thinking that you are capable of faith; God must give
it to you.[16]

In Luther's subsequent sermon, preached on the same day, he sets forth the
demands of the law again but elaborates in greater detail upon the gospel,
particularly in terms of how the believer comes to have Christ as his possession and thus to enjoy the benefits of Christ's work. Here he emphasizes
that it is faith and baptism that make a person a Christian, not anything
they do outwardly. In other words, to be a Christian is to have a certain
status given by Christ, which is then the foundation for the Christian life;
the life is not the basis for the status, the Word of God and its reception by
faith are.[17]

Preaching the Word is, for Luther, the powerful center of the church,
the very foundation and instrument of reformation, individual and corporate. Perhaps he expressed this nowhere more dramatically than in Wittenberg in 1522. Luther returned to the town from the Wartburg at a time
when Karlstadt and Zwilling had unleashed the forces of iconoclasm upon
Wittenberg, aided and abetted by the Zwickau Prophets. Faced with scenes
of social chaos and abandoned by his supporters among the knights, Luther was far more vulnerable at this moment than he had ever been before
and possibly ever would be again. If the Reformation became a political
revolution, Frederick the Wise would have no choice but to withdraw his
support and close it down. In this situation, Luther literally preached the
Reformation back onto a steady course, winning over popular opinion and
putting the radical elements to flight.

In one of these sermons, he makes a most memorable statement about
the power of the Word:

> I will preach it, teach it, write it, but I will constrain no man by force, for
> faith must come freely without compulsion. Take myself as an example.
> I opposed indulgences and all the papists, but never with force. I simply
> taught, preached, and wrote God's Word; otherwise I did nothing. And
> while I slept [cf. Mark 4:26–29], or drank Wittenberg beer with my friends

---

[16] *LW*, 51:109–10.
[17] *LW*, 51:116–19.

Philip and Amsdorf, the Word so greatly weakened the papacy that no prince or emperor ever inflicted such losses upon it. I did nothing; the Word did everything.[18]

There is the Lutheran (and indeed Reformed) pastor's dream scenario: sitting in a pub, drinking beer, while the Word is outside on the rampage, putting devils to flight, bringing down to the dust the strongholds of evil, and ushering Christians into the kingdom of God. Of course, the statement is a classic example of Luther's ability to express his thought in a funny, shocking, or blasé way that grabs the attention while making a serious point. And that point is that the Word of God is powerful; both the theology of this paragraph and the sermon in which it occurs are classic examples of precisely that kind of power. As Luther said in one of his most famous hymns about the prince of darkness, "One little word shall fell him."[19]

Concluding Reflections

The pastor or Christian who reads Luther's sermons will immediately notice certain things. Luther, rather like Spurgeon, often seems to have a very loose approach to exegesis of passages, to the extent that Luther's commentaries and sermon series tended to disappear as sources for such very shortly after his death. Perhaps the one great exception was his second commentary on Galatians (and greatest commentary), which enjoyed many reprintings and appeared in numerous translations. Arguably, however, that is because this work was such an excellent statement of his doctrine of justification rather than because it was a definitive example of verse-by-verse exposition.

The modern reader of Luther's sermons will probably also notice that, after a while, the sermons all start to seem much the same. That is because the law-gospel pattern is reflected in them all. For Luther, the purpose of preaching was to crush the self-righteous and, having done so, to point them to the promise of God in Christ. That move from law to gospel, from wrath to grace, was the core of the Christian's daily life and was thus to be embodied in, and facilitated by, the preaching of the Word. Powerful as such drama is, it did tend to impose a certain form upon Luther's sermons.

These two observations might seem like criticisms, and to an extent

---

[18] *LW*, 51:77.
[19] Luther composed his most famous hymn, "A Mighty Fortress," around 1527.

they are. The preacher is to preach the Word in a manner as rich and as inflected as Scripture itself. That means eschewing a one-size-fits-all approach to sermon preparation. Nevertheless, I would suggest that Luther's approach does speak to an era like ours, in which the culture of individual uniqueness has such a deep hold even on the Christian mind.

From childhood upward, we are told that we are special. Sometimes this is even done in God's name. The televangelists and megachurch pastors who talk about having "your best life now" are essentially presenting a picture of God as one who panders to the particular needs and concerns of the individual. The danger is that preaching can start to do the same—even worse, that preaching becomes sidelined because each person has to have his or her particular needs and problems addressed in a specific fashion.

Luther's approach to preaching is a refreshing riposte to this kind of narcissistic nonsense in at least two ways. First, his application of the categories of law and gospel in his sermons captures one crucial truth: human beings, for all of their uniqueness, are not unique in terms of their status before God. There are only two ways of approaching God: by law or by gospel. And there are only two things one can say about any human being before God: a person is under wrath or under grace. While individuals have their own histories and circumstances, their own problems and challenges, the basic problem of where to find a gracious God is the same for all, as is the answer.

Thus, Luther's sermons first of all remind us of a very important truth: we are not the center of the universe; God is. And we are not so unique that we need tailor-made personal answers to our greatest problem. The answer is always the same: God's promise in Christ. Thus, preachers and congregants alike must understand that the most important thing one can hear on a Sunday is not some pep talk on how to have a good marriage or how to cultivate an appropriate self-image or how to raise one's children. The most important thing is to hear what God has done in Christ and then to grasp that message by faith. That is a great antidote to Christianity's capitulation to particularist conceits of the contemporary culture as evidenced in the dethroning of preaching by placing it on par with, or even below, one-to-one counseling.

Second, Luther's theology of preaching reminds us that the Word has power in itself because it is the Word of God. Luther understood both law and gospel as possessing moral force. They expose the heart of the theologian in everyone, of course, showing every human being to be a theologian either of glory or of the cross. In the Word, each person is confronted not simply by an idea but by God himself, either as the transcendent and holy God who demands perfection and terrifies us, or as the God who has made himself weak and died on the cross that death would not have the final word over us. When this is preached, the Spirit uses it to work mighty miracles. Technique becomes less important. Party tricks, stand-up comedy, and vaudeville antics are rendered unnecessary. In fact, Luther might well have considered them a confusion of categories, an attempt to improve upon God's work by making it into a work of our own. That in itself he would have seen as a confusion of law and gospel. Preaching is a means of grace. It is done by preachers, but only in a proximate sense. The real Word comes from God, via his servant of course—but it is not the servant who gives it its power. That is why Luther could declare the Reformation to have been nothing of his doing and simply the product of God's Word.

Thus, Luther's theology of the Word and preaching stands at the center of the Christian life. There in the sermon, in the move from law to gospel, the fundamental struggle of the Christian is played out every time the preacher ascends the pulpit. But this is no mere theatrical display: as the Word is preached, the Christian is torn down by the law and built up in the gospel. Preaching is a supernatural act, and that should give great confidence and assurance to every preacher tasked with the public exposition of God's Word. Luther's view of the Christian life, like his view of the success of the Reformation, was rooted first and foremost in the overwhelming power of the preached Word.

CHAPTER 4

THE LITURGY OF THE CHRISTIAN LIFE

If I could see the world,
Through the eyes of a child,
What a wonderful world this would be.

PATSY CLINE, "EYES OF A CHILD"

The Liturgical Life

If the Christian life is, for Luther, rooted in the corporate gathering of the church, especially in the preaching of the Word to the congregation, then the liturgy is also vitally important. This is one area of Luther's thinking that many modern evangelicals might find somewhat alien. Evangelicalism as it has developed under influences such as revivalism and the megachurch movement has not tended to be particularly self-conscious in its liturgical reflection.

Before I address Lutheran liturgy in particular, I should note as a truism that every church has a liturgy. Now, not every church has a *formal* liturgy as one might find in a traditional Anglican Church, which uses the Book of Common Prayer, for example; but every church has a way of structuring its service and a series of set forms (even if these are just the praise songs). That is liturgy. The question is thus not whether a particular church has a liturgy but what sort of liturgy it has. One might also press further and ask whether the liturgy has been consciously developed to embody a particular theology or represents rather an unconscious reflection of the church's theology (or lack thereof).

Even a moment's reflection will make clear that Luther's theological revolution—his discovery that the preached Word is central and that justification is by grace through faith in the promise of God in Christ—demanded a major liturgical change. In the medieval period, the liturgy was in Latin, and the sacrament of the Mass had been central. For Luther, the liturgy needed to be in the vernacular, and preaching had to be at the heart of the Christian life.

We have looked at the theology and nature of preaching, but what was the formal liturgical context within which the public declaration of the Word took place? Ironically, for all of his reputation as a man of action, Luther did not implement a full German liturgy in Wittenberg until 1525, nearly eight years after he first came to public attention. Indeed, his moves toward liturgical reform were gradual and hesitant. This is how he describes his approach in *An Order of Mass and Communion for the Church at Wittenberg*, a pamphlet of 1523:

> Until now I have only used books and sermons to wean the hearts of people from their godless regard for ceremonial; for I believed it would be a Christian and helpful thing if I could prompt a peaceful removal of the abomination which Satan set up in the holy place through the man of sin. Therefore, I have used neither authority nor pressure. Nor did I make any innovations. For I have been hesitant and fearful, partly because of the weak in faith, who cannot suddenly exchange an old and accustomed order of worship for a new and unusual one, and more so because of the fickle and fastidious spirits who rush in like unclean swine without faith or reason, and who delight only in novelty and tire of it as quickly, when it has worn off. Such people are a nuisance even in other affairs, but in spiritual matters, they are absolutely unbearable. Nonetheless, at the risk of bursting with anger, I must bear with them, unless I want to let the gospel itself be denied to the people.[1]

Here, Luther makes it clear that he is concerned to handle delicate consciences with care and also to give no ground to those who seek novelty or innovation for its own sake. He is also emphatic that it is not his intention to abolish liturgical worship but rather to correct it and purify it in light

---

[1] *LW*, 53:19.

of his theological reforms.[2] The liturgy he then describes in 1523 is itself very conservative, essentially a cleaned-up version of the traditional Mass, still in Latin except for the sermon and a few hymns. Indeed, Luther can hardly be described as being in the vanguard of the application of his own theological principles to liturgical reform: churches in Basel and Pforzhelm had vernacular liturgy before Wittenberg; and the one-time Luther ally and later deadliest of his enemies, Thomas Müntzer, produced a German Mass, matins (a service of morning prayer), and vespers (a service of evening prayer) in 1523, establishing himself as perhaps the most ambitious of the early Protestant liturgists.

Even in 1524, as he wrote against the radicals, Luther rejoiced that the Mass was now said in German, but also argued that such a practice should not be made compulsory, lest it become a new legalism. He was also not yet satisfied that the German liturgy captured the full beauty of what was going on.[3] It was not until October 29, 1525, that a full German Mass was celebrated in Wittenberg, and not until 1526 that the liturgy was published.

It is interesting to note that it took five years to move from the arguments of *The Babylonian Captivity* to a celebration of a Mass consistent with them; and, even in the preface to the 1526 German Mass, Luther stresses that the issue is not to be forced if it offends weak consciences.[4] In fact, he does not object to the Mass continuing in Latin, as long as the people who make up the congregation are conversant with the language. Indeed, he expresses the wish that all German Christians were fluent in Latin, Greek, Hebrew, and the vernacular, in which case he would gladly hold worship services in all four languages.[5]

This is important for understanding Luther's approach to the Christian life as one of a pastor to his people. He seems to have understood that proposed changes to aesthetics and things that are familiar often create the most challenges to any kind of reform within the church. Many pastors in the 1980s would no doubt have confirmed as much when seeking to move congregations from the King James Version to one of the newer transla-

---

[2] *LW*, 53:20.
[3] *Against the Heavenly Prophets*, in *LW*, 40:141.
[4] *The German Mass and Order of Service*, in *LW*, 53:61.
[5] *LW*, 53:63. On the matter of Luther's conservative aesthetics and the connection to his pastoral sensitivity, we should also note the persistence of the very word *Mass* in Lutheran theology and liturgy. Indeed, those familiar with the Book of Concord will know that the term enjoys confessional status among Lutherans down to the present. Article 24 of the Augsburg Confession in both the Latin and German texts uses the word and (in the German, at least) claims it is celebrated with more reverence and earnestness by Lutherans than by their Roman opponents.

tions. While the older version has a beauty unmatched by any later English translation, it is without doubt more difficult to understand today than other, clearer translations. Changing translations, however, often provokes serious resistance. While there are important scholarly discussions to be had about textual bases and translation philosophies, most resistance in the pews is ultimately motivated by a dislike of change. Human beings like the familiar. That is not in itself a bad thing; but it does make reformation a tricky matter when it comes to minimizing the human damage involved.

Luther lays out the pastoral principles for liturgical reform in his pamphlet *Concerning the Order for Public Worship* (1523). There he identifies three major errors in the medieval liturgical tradition. First, and worst, the Word has been silenced, by which Luther means that preaching has all but vanished, leaving only Bible reading and singing in its place. Second, the loss of the Word has meant that all kinds of nonsensical fables and hymns have crept into public worship. Third, the worship service itself has come to be regarded as a work offered to God.[6]

Luther's objection to the last point is worth emphasizing. Obviously, it is part of his typical polemic against the notion that human beings can offer anything to God as a means of earning his favor, a point that underlies his objection to the Roman notions of priesthood and sacrament. But there is also an interesting implication here: if worship is not something offered to God, then it must be understood within the context of God's own action. Worship is either a response to God's prior grace or itself a means of that grace. Given the theology of the Word that we have already explored, we can conclude that worship is itself in a deep sense an action of God: when the Word is preached, it is God who acts.[7]

This is why Luther stresses in this pamphlet that the congregation, as congregation, should never meet without the preaching of the Word and prayer.[8] He also argues for consistent public reading of the Bible in a manner that moves through the whole canon over a period of time. That might seem a tall order or an overly lengthy process, but Luther assumes that services will be daily affairs, probably at least twice every day. While he

---

[6] *LW*, 53:11.
[7] This point is also made in the Heidelberg Catechism, an irenic Reformed catechism produced in Heidelberg in 1563 in an attempt to promote unity between the Reformed and the moderate Lutherans, or Philippists. The Heidelberg is divided into three sections: misery, grace, and gratitude. Significantly, treatment of the church occurs in the section on grace. The catechism's structure thus highlights the fact that the church herself is an act of God's grace, not a human response to God's grace.
[8] *LW*, 53:11.

accepts that not everyone will be at every service, this idea surely reflects the fact that, in an illiterate age, it is only in such a context that people will come to know the Bible. And it also reflects the fact that, in Luther's theology, knowledge of the Word of God and regular exposure to it are absolutely basic to the Christian life.[9]

This points toward one of the striking aspects of Luther's approach to liturgy: there is a very real sense in which the church's gathered worship is a catechetical exercise, not in the sense of catechisms that operate by question and answer, but in the broader sense of the school of faith. Gathered worship is intended for the education of the people in sound theology upon which to build their lives.

A surprising element of this, yet one that demonstrates sound pedagogical sense, is the emphasis Luther places on music in the service. In fact, his conviction that the German Mass needed good and appropriate music was a major factor in his delaying its composition and implementation. He indicates this in his major critique of the radicals, *Against the Heavenly Prophets in the Matter of Images and Sacraments* (1525), where he makes the following comment:

> I would gladly have a German mass today. I am also occupied with it. But I would very much like it to have a true German character. For to translate the Latin text and retain the Latin tone or notes has my sanction, though it doesn't sound polished or well done. Both the text and notes, accent, melody, and manner of rendering ought to grow out of the true mother tongue and its inflection, otherwise all of it becomes an imitation, in the manner of the apes.[10]

This is a fascinating comment for a variety of reasons. First, it shows that Luther realizes that the aesthetics of worship are important. The form should match the content in a way that reinforces it and presses it on the congregation. As any music lover knows, music has an emotional and psychological power that is both mysterious, in that it often seems to operate at a subconscious level, and frequently overpowering. It also facilitates verbal memory, as my own facility for recalling lyrics from a myriad of trite rock songs demonstrates. And Luther understands all this and knows that it is not enough to deliver the drama of a Reformation Mass simply by

---

[9] *LW*, 53:12.
[10] *LW*, 40:141.

words; the music by which that drama is expressed is also of crucial importance, especially given the pedagogical intent of the whole.[11]

Given Luther's concern that worship fulfill a pedagogical/catechetical function, it is perhaps not surprising, though certainly impressive, that he sees the whole week as providing an opportunity for structured Christian education through the various liturgies of the church. Monday and Tuesday, the service is to focus on teaching about the Decalogue, the creed, the Lord's Prayer, baptism, and the Eucharist. These are the established elements of Christian catechesis from the Middle Ages, and Luther clearly assumes them as foundational to the Christian life. Wednesday is to be devoted to teaching from the Gospel of Matthew, as Saturday afternoon is to be devoted to the Gospel of John. Thursday and Friday are to focus on other New Testament writings. Sunday is the big day, with multiple services and three sermons devoted to the Gospels. The overall purpose is "to give the Word of God free course among us."[12]

The rather exhaustive liturgical structuring of the entire week might seem excessive to Christians today. It is rare these days to find Christians who attend the means of grace twice on a Sunday, and sometimes hard to find churches that have both a morning and evening service. Yet we must remember that Luther's people were for the most part illiterate, and so the church was the primary place, and perhaps for many the only place, where they could actually learn God's Word. It is, of course, doubtful that any but a tiny handful, if anyone at all, took advantage of every single service; but that is not the point. Luther regarded gathered worship as the central element in the Christian life from the perspectives of salvation, experience, and education.

Penance: The Almost Sacrament

One aspect of Lutheran liturgy that proved contentious among Luther's followers, even within his own lifetime, was confession and absolution. Luther's attitude toward confession—the acknowledgment of sin, whether in

---

[11] The concern for appropriate music also shows that Luther has what we might now call a certain cultural sensitivity: certain tunes and musical forms work well in particular cultures and not so well in others. To draw on an example from personal experience: on moving to the United States in 2001, I attended a psalm-singing church because I had belonged to a psalm-singing denomination back in Scotland. I was fascinated that here were two churches singing from the same hymn book—the Psalter—and yet the tunes were different and, even when not, were sung slightly faster in the United States than back home. Each culture influenced the aesthetics in subtle ways, not in this case so that the ultimate effect was different, but so that the effect might actually be the same, given the different contexts.

[12] LW, 53:68–69.

the public worship service or in a one-to-one pastoral context—was somewhat ambiguous in terms of its status as a sacrament.

Medieval theology held that confession and absolution pronounced by a priest were, together, one of the seven sacraments. Luther was not so sure. In 1519, in a short series of sermons on the sacraments, he was happy to refer to penance as sacramental and as very necessary for the calming of disturbed Christian consciences.[13] There are three elements to the sacrament, he declared: the words of the priest, the grace of God, and the faith of the Christian.[14] When he wrote his great manifesto for sacramental reform in 1520, *The Babylonian Captivity of the Church*, he was rather more ambivalent on its sacramental nature. Near the start of the work, he reduces the number of sacraments to three: baptism, the Mass, and penance.[15] Yet at the very end, he observes that the term *sacrament* should really be restricted to those things which have signs attached to them, by which definition penance is excluded.[16]

This ambivalence is arguably more semantic than theological. The basic points Luther wishes to make with regard to penance are clear. Polemically, he rejects the Roman Catholic practice of rooting the power of penance in the sacramental priesthood as leading to the abuse of power, the withholding of forgiveness, and the unnecessary disturbing of consciences.[17] Positively, he sees penance—the confession of sins to another and the specific declaration by that other of the forgiveness of the gospel—as basic to a healthy Christian life.[18] Indeed, in article 8.1 of the Schmalkaldic Articles, he stresses that penance and absolution are important, especially for those with tender and weak consciences.[19]

In terms of his own practice, Luther repudiated any notion that private confession should be enforced by church authorities.[20] As with so much of Luther's Reformation, however, he was acutely aware that changes in practice would have dramatic impact upon the lives of ordinary people. Thus his approach was that of gentle gradualism. In 1522, he returned to

---

[13] *LW*, 35:9.
[14] *LW*, 35:11.
[15] *LW*, 36:18.
[16] *LW*, 36:124.
[17] *LW*, 36:83–84, 123.
[18] *LW*, 35:10–11.
[19] "Since absolution or the power of the keys, which was instituted by Christ in the Gospel, is a consolation and help against sin and a bad conscience, confession and absolution should by no means be allowed to fall into disuse in the church, especially for the sake of timid consciences and for the sake of untrained young people who need to be examined and instructed in Christian doctrine." *BC*, 312.
[20] See Schmalkaldic Articles, 8.2, *BC*, 312.

Wittenberg from the Wartburg Castle in order to restore order in the town in the wake of the radical reforming moves made by Karlstadt and Zwilling during his absence. As part of his campaign to regain control of the Reformation, he preached a series of sermons and addressed the issue of confession in the so-called "Eighth Sermon" of March 16, 1522:

> I will allow no man to take private confession away from me, and I would not give it up for all the treasures in the world, since I know what comfort and strength it has given me. No one knows what it can do for him except one who has struggled often and long with the devil. Yea, the devil would have slain me long ago, if the confession had not sustained me. For there are many doubtful matters which a man cannot resolve or find the answer to by himself, and so he takes his brother aside and tells him his trouble. . . . We must have many absolutions, so that we may strengthen our timid consciences and despairing hearts against the devil and against God. Therefore, no man shall forbid the confession nor keep or draw any one away from it. And if any one is wrestling with his sins and wants to be rid of them and desires a sure word on the matter, let him go and confess to another in secret, and accept what he says to him as if God himself had spoken it through the mouth of this person.[21]

Here we see the power of private confession: it is the context in which that powerful, confrontational, and objective Word from outside can be applied specifically to the individual. While Luther did not believe that every sin had to be confessed individually to be forgiven, he nonetheless considered private confession to be most helpful and desirable. This was indeed the common opinion among Lutheran pastors.

The importance of this idea to Luther and his followers is evident from one of the lesser-known controversies within Lutheranism during the early years of the Reformation. Lutheran liturgy included an act of public, corporate confession and a declaration of absolution by the presiding minister. This was not to the taste of all Lutheran preachers. Andreas Osiander, the controversial Reformer of Nuremberg, was concerned that this corporate confession and absolution would undermine the importance of private confession. As a result, he excluded this element from the Brandenburg-Nuremberg Church Order of 1533, which he coauthored with Johannes Brenz. Evidence suggests that his fears were well grounded and that the good

---

[21] LW, 51:99.

citizens of Nuremberg were neglecting private confession and thus (as far as Osiander was concerned) forfeiting a valuable opportunity for assurance, along with robbing the ministers of a context for encouraging moral reform.

The story of the controversy is complicated. In short, the council appealed to Luther and Melanchthon for advice. In reply, they pointed out to the council that preaching was in itself a form of absolution, whether to crowds or to individuals; they also explained that few people would understand corporate absolution unless they experienced private confession, indicating Luther's and Melanchthon's preference for the latter. This did not satisfy Osiander, however, who regarded the both-and solution as compromising the sacramental significance of confession. Like baptism and the Lord's Supper, confession as a sacrament had to be received individually, and for confession, that meant one-to-one and in private. Further, Osiander regarded grace as actually conveyed by the sacrament and not simply offered. This *ex opere operato*[22] factor was, of course, denied by Luther: though the sacraments are not merely symbolic but do really offer Christ, the Christ they offer must be grasped by faith if they are to be of any salvific use. This point is clear in his 1530 treatise *The Keys*: God's Word never fails; if the result of God's Word is not salvation, that is no fault or weakness of the Word; it is because human beings reject it.[23]

One of the reasons this debate is important is that it indicates a basic assumption concerning Lutheran pastoral care and the Christian: the physical presence and availability of the pastor to the people is vital. In the preface to the *Instructions for the Visitors of Parish Pastors in Electoral Saxony* (1528), Luther makes it clear that he regards absenteeism, the distancing of the bishop from the day-to-day life of the parish and lives of the parishioners, as a sign of the current decay of the church:

> When things reached their lowest, the deputies themselves remained at home in a warm house and sent perchance some rascal or ne'er-do-well who wandered around the countryside and in towns, and what he heard from mean mouths or gossip among men and women in the taverns he reported to his superior who then exercised his fleecing office, scraping and skinning innocent people of their goods and leaving murder and misery where there had been honor and good name.[24]

---

[22] "By the work performed."
[23] *LW*, 40:367.
[24] *LW*, 40:270.

Instead of this, the minister's first calling is to be present with those for whom he has oversight. We might even borrow Lutheran terminology from elsewhere: the minister's presence in his parish is not to be merely symbolic; rather he is to be there as a real presence: in, with, and among his people. This will not only inform his preaching such that it speaks more directly to the particulars of his people's lives; it will also allow for cate-chizing, over which the minister has responsibility, and for the one-to-one confession and absolution that some delicate consciences require.

Absolution is connected in Luther's mind to the doctrine of the keys, the binding and the loosing of consciences by the Word of God through the church; and Luther's doctrine of the keys thereby makes ministerial pres-ence necessary. Luther's Reformation was from its inception an attempt to revise notions of ecclesiastical authority. At the heart of this debate was discussion about the identity of the keys given to Peter in Matthew 16:18–19. For Luther, the keys of the kingdom are the law and the gospel as preached by ministers in the context of the church. Indeed, in *On the Councils of the Church*, Luther makes possession of the keys the fourth mark of the church after preaching, baptism, and the Mass. It is added as a mark beyond preaching because it speaks directly to the discipline or the abso-lution that flows from the application of the Word to Christians in either a corporate or an individual setting.[25]

Two things about Luther's doctrine of the keys point toward the neces-sity of the pastor's presence in the congregation and thus in the life of the Christian. First, in his treatise *The Keys*, he makes the point that Catholic abuse of power was predicated on a top-down power structure that was often ignorant of whether a person had repented of the sin for which he was being excommunicated. In response, Luther asserts the need for con-gregational input into the exercise of church discipline. Only those in the local area could know if sins had been committed and, if so, whether the sinner had repented.[26] And if that applied to the congregation, it applied above all to the pastor.

Second, in *On the Councils of the Church*, he argues that some Christians had such tender consciences that they required personal, one-to-one abso-lution from the pastor himself. Such would scarcely be possible if the pas-tor did not live among his people and know them well. For the pastor to be

---

[25] *LW*, 41:153.
[26] *LW*, 40:371–72.

able to apply the gospel with full effect in such circumstances, he needed to meet with people, hear their confessions, and point them to the Christ who was the answer. Again, this is surely of a piece with Luther's underlying concern that the Reformation deal with the most tender of consciences in the most delicate of ways.[27] This is perhaps akin to what we might today call biblical counseling, though it is important to note that this is an explicitly ecclesiastical matter for Luther: it is the ordained pastor who is the counselor, although his concept of the priesthood of believers means that, in theory at least, all Christians have an obligation to apply the Word to others when need and opportunity arise.

The Catechetical Life

Returning to Luther's liturgical reformation, one of the striking things noted above is how he structured the week with a strongly catechetical aspect, whereby the key elements of traditional catechesis—the Decalogue, the Apostles' Creed, the Lord's Prayer, and the sacraments—were addressed. This points to a further aspect of Luther's framework for the way the Word, written and spoken, connected to the Christian life: formal catechisms and catechizing.

Catechesis—that is, basic Christian instruction—was a staple of the church from its earliest times. The rise of catechisms in the form with which we are now familiar—pedagogical tools structured by questions and answers to be learned by heart—arose in the Middle Ages, probably at the hands of one Bruno of Würzburg in the eleventh century. By Luther's day, both the question-and-answer structure and the elements of catechesis were standardized. Nevertheless, we should note that when Luther refers to "catechism," he is typically referring to teaching on the Decalogue, the Apostles' Creed, and the Lord's Prayer, rather than to any specific document involving questions and answers.

The production of question-and-answer catechisms in the sixteenth

---

[27] "Fourth, God's people or holy Christians are recognized by the office of the keys exercised publicly. That is, as Christ decrees in Matthew 18[:15–20], if a Christian sins, he should be reproved; and if he does not mend his ways, he should be bound in his sin and cast out. If he does mend his ways, he should be absolved. That is the office of the keys. Now the use of the keys is twofold, public and private. There are some people with consciences so tender and despairing that even if they have not been publicly condemned, they cannot find comfort until they have been individually absolved by the pastor. On the other hand, there are also some who are so obdurate that they neither recant in their heart and want their sins forgiven individually by the pastor, nor desist from their sins. Therefore the keys must be used differently, publicly and privately. Now where you see sins forgiven or reproved in some persons, be it publicly or privately, you may know that God's people are there." *LW*, 41:153.

century went from strength to strength. With the fracturing of Christendom, which the Reformation brought in its wake, there was need to make sure people knew what they believed and why they believed it. This need, of course, was more than simply pastoral: theology was intimately bound up with politics; as the Reformation advanced, confessional commitments came to determine territorial identities and alliances in the Holy Roman Empire and beyond. This political aspect of confessionalization need not concern us here; but it is important to note that the need for any group to write catechisms arose in part from opposing groups doing the same.

Luther wrote two catechisms, which continue to hold authoritative status within confessional Lutheran circles because of their inclusion in the Book of Concord. As we will see in chapter 7, he wrote them in part as a response to the pedagogical and, indeed, moral problems that were manifesting themselves in dramatic ways in the Lutheran church from the mid-1520s onward. The problem was that neither pastors nor people were properly connecting doctrine and piety in the way Luther had anticipated early on in his reforming career.

The two catechisms are quite different in scope. The Large Catechism is clearly not designed for memorization but is more akin to a collection of brief sermons or homilies on the elements of the catechism. It is important to remember, of course, that at the time of the Reformation, not only laypeople were ignorant of Protestant theology and frequently unlearned. The clergy too were often not particularly adept at preaching and teaching the new doctrines and thus required tools to facilitate their ministry. As with Eastern Europe in 1989, it was one thing in the Reformation to dethrone the princes of the Roman Church and quite another to supply every pulpit with a competent Protestant minister. Training took time, and so most pastors would have made the transition from being Roman Catholic to being Protestant without obtaining the requisite knowledge. For these men, the Large Catechism, rather like the Anglican Book of Homilies, functioned as a source of homiletic material. If they could not preach themselves, the catechism at least gave them a text they could read or upon which they could closely model their sermons.

The Small Catechism is very much what one might today expect from a catechetical work: brief questions and answers covering the major heads of Christian doctrine as framed by the classical elements of catechesis. It has a deceptively simple and warm feel to it, but we must remember that

Luther was the first author of a catechism in the history of the church who
came to the task as a father. Experience always shapes pedagogy. For some
years I assisted my wife in teaching children's Sunday school, and we could
always tell when the syllabus we were using had been written by somebody
with no experience of actually teaching children: the content was always
too complex and abstract. As any father knows, children's questions are
often very predictable and very concrete, and his answers therefore need
to be as simple and straightforward as possible. This is reflected in the tone
and approach of the catechism. Take, for example, the two first questions:

> *"You shall have no other gods."*
> What does this mean?
>
> Answer: We should fear, love, and trust in God above all things.
>
> *"You shall not take the name of the Lord your God in vain."*
> What does this mean?
>
> Answer: We should fear and love God, and so we should not use his name
> to curse, swear, practice magic, lie, or deceive, but in every time of need
> call upon him, pray to him, praise him, and give him thanks.[28]

The pattern is obvious, akin to: "That's a bird, son." "What's a bird,
daddy?" "A bird is a feathered animal which flies in the sky and makes its
nest in the trees." In addition, we should note that children fascinated Luther as examples of simple faith. In fact, he saw one of the Devil's most
lethal strategies to be the robbing of Christians of their childlikeness and
thus their faith.[29] By contrast, children's unquestioning approach to the
Bible's teaching and the simplicity with which they believe captures the essence of what it means to have Christian faith. That conviction is reflected
in the limpid pedagogic style of the Small Catechism.[30]

Luther's purpose in catechizing is connected to his theology: faith has
content. To understand law and gospel, one needs doctrinal knowledge.

---

[28] *BC*, 342.
[29] *LW*, 54:55–56.
[30] E.g., "Afterward, watching his son, he [Luther] praised the boy's ingenuousness and innocence: 'Children are better informed in the faith [than adults], for they believe very simply and without any question
in a gracious God and eternal life. Oh, how good it is for children to die while they're young. To be sure,
it would cause me great grief because part of my body and part of their mother's flesh and blood would
die. Such natural feelings don't cease in godly parents, no matter how hardened and calloused they think
they are, for feelings like these are a work of divine creation. Children live altogether in faith, without
reason. It's as Ambrose said. 'There is lack of reason but not of faith.'" *LW*, 54:335.

To understand Christ's work, one needs doctrinal knowledge. To have a "relationship" with God, one needs doctrinal knowledge. Indeed, the antithesis between doctrine and relationship that is a mark of certain strands of contemporary Christianity would have been incomprehensible to Luther. Theologically, the distinction between the two kinds of theologian, of glory and of the cross, points to the different doctrinal content: both types may use the same vocabulary, but they fill that vocabulary with content that stands in diametric opposition to that of the other. Thus, doctrinal instruction, of which catechizing is a key part, is essential to the Christian life. Luther even contends that those who refuse to be catechized should be refused the sacrament, denied food, and subject to banishment by the prince.[31]

One further important aspect of catechizing is its progressive, cumulative nature. The Small Catechism is really preparation for the more elaborate teaching of the Large Catechism: "After you have thus taught this brief catechism, take up a large catechism so that the people may have a richer and fuller understanding."[32] This pedagogy is significant in a number of ways. First, as with his caution over liturgical innovations, Luther stresses the need for catechesis to be conducted using the same words and formulas throughout. The order is to teach the form of sound words first, and then to teach the people what these words mean. Clearly, he regards it as important first to have a form of sound words into which sound content could then be set.[33] Second, this learning is to continue and to deepen as one moves from the Small to the Large Catechism.

This is an important point. For Luther, the Christian life is to be marked in part by a growth in knowledge. Again, although our era often seems obsessed with the relational at the expense of the dogmatic, there is no such opposition in Luther's thought. To learn doctrine is to learn about divine and human identity: who we are before God, who God has decided to be toward us. It is thus *revelational*, in that the cross is the lens through which this is to be understood; but it is also *relational*, because that basic distinction between the two kinds of theologian is not reducible simply

---

[31] "If any refuse to receive your instructions, tell them that they deny Christ and are no Christians. They should not be admitted to the sacrament, be accepted as sponsors in Baptism, or be allowed to participate in any Christian privileges. On the contrary, they should be turned over to the pope and his officials, and even to the devil himself. In addition, parents and employers should refuse to furnish them with food and drink and should notify them that the prince is disposed to banish such rude people from his land." Preface to the Small Catechism, *BC*, 339.
[32] *BC*, 340.
[33] *BC*, 339.

to doctrine. It connects to doctrine and to personal faith. It is actually the determining factor in who one is before God and thus before the world.

This also takes us back to the basic purpose of all Christian teaching, as exemplified in preaching: the Christian life is characterized by Christians' realizing that they are damned in themselves before God because of their self-righteousness, and thus repenting before him and turning to grasp Christ by faith. Every single element of this is doctrinal, requiring knowledge of who God is, what we were created to be, and how we can stand before him as righteous after the fall. Yet every element is also existential. The law terrifies; the gospel brings comfort. Law and gospel are objective truths, but they lay claim to human beings at the deepest level of their existence. The theologian of the cross knows Christ as a wife knows her husband: she does not simply recognize him when she sees him; her heart beats a little faster, her mind fills with beautiful memories and desires and longings; over the years, as her knowledge of him grows, so does her love. Her knowledge of him is never less than factual but it transcends notional knowledge and moves her at the deepest level of her being. So should be the church's love for Christ, her Bridegroom.

Concluding Reflections

Luther's understanding of the individual Christian life is in some ways refreshingly simple and straightforward. We live at a time when the church always seems to be looking for new and elaborate ways of winning converts, of discipling, of bringing people to maturity in the faith. Luther's approach is rather different. Building upon the objectivity of God's action in Christ as set forth in his Word, he sees the Christian life as one fueled by the reading and hearing of this Word, primarily in a corporate context.

This is a great antidote to a number of perennial problems for Christians. First, there is the "need" for something more than the Bible. The success of books that offer something spectacular—whether accounts of dying and coming back to the land of the living or low-key claims to special, extra words from God—shows that the Christian world loves something out of the ordinary.

Luther would respond that such things are absolutely unnecessary, for what we need is the Word of God in the humble, mundane form that he has given it to us. Why read a book on a child who claims to have died and come back when one can read the Gospels and find there God, clothed in frail human flesh, dying and rising again? Why desire further, special words from God when the great Word of God, Christ himself, is offered to every individual as the Bible is read, preached, and sometimes applied individually through the confessional? Luther would see the market for such books as a function of our striving to be theologians of glory, unsatisfied with how God has chosen to reveal himself to be toward us, and always craving to make God conform to our expectations of what we need.

Luther thus offers to pastors and to churches a model for Christian education. Pastors should focus their preaching and teaching on the basics of the Christian life because such truths are in a sense the whole of the Christian life. Churches should intentionally shape their liturgies to reflect their theological convictions. The feel-good factor or the cool-aesthetic or even the contextualization imperative are as nothing compared with the great truths of God's Word addressed to his people through Christ. All other factors are to be radically subordinated to this. For Luther, there was drama in the routines of worship, as the congregation was moved from law to gospel, from conviction and repentance to faith in Christ. Each service was a dramatic recapitulation of the story of the people of God, and thus a reminder, a reaffirmation, even a re-creation of identity. Of how many worship services can that be said today?

Luther also reminds us that the church's calling is to cultivate the Christian life as laid out in the doctrines of the catechism. The church does not exist to help people with their self-image, to learn how to be good parents, and to have happy marriages, still less to enjoy their best life now, when all of this is understood in terms of the mores of twenty-first-century America. The church is there to teach about God. Thus, it is far more important for the church to teach the catechism than to hold classes on parenting or personal financial management. Those things are worthy too and may well fall into the path of a pastor as he deals with individuals in his flock; but they are not the task of the church in the first instance and can indeed be addressed only within a context where the big things, the simple things, have been carefully taught.

Underlying Luther's teaching on the liturgical life, of course, is his abiding confidence in the Word to do all that God has tasked it to do. Therein lies much of the difference between the routines of the Christian life and church as Luther understood them and the liturgical confusion that often grips the church today. The theologian of the cross knows that the Word in its weakness can do all things. The theologian of glory thinks that this is foolishness, and he looks constantly to the world for tips on how to be more successful. In light of this sad fact, 1 Corinthians 1:25 seems a key text: "For the foolishness of God is wiser than men, and the weakness of God is stronger than men." For Luther, the theology of the cross determines the nature of the church, of worship, and of discipleship. Whatever the world says to the contrary, the church is to preach Christ and him crucified.

CHAPTER 5

LIVING BY THE WORD

One little word shall fell him.

MARTIN LUTHER, "A MIGHTY FORTRESS"

By this point in our discussion, we have laid out the theological foundations of Luther's approach to the Christian life in his understanding of how God acts to create and redeem through his Word. We have also noted how Luther saw that the Word needed to be impressed upon Christians through the preaching and teaching of the church. This teaching imposes a kind of liturgical and catechetical structure on life that is embodied in the rites of the church, the structure of Luther's catechism.

We now arrive at a point where we can ask: What is the "normal" day-to-day Christian life like? How do Word and sacrament function within the specific circumstances of the individual Christian's world? How would Luther advise the Christian struggling with some aspect of life or faith to use the means of God's grace at his disposal?

The astute reader will probably already have guessed that the more we examine Luther on the Christian life, the less he would seem to agree with the classic evangelical models. Yes, Luther had a high regard for the Bible, as we have seen, but he also placed a great premium on doctrine and, above all, the objectivity of the foundations of the Christian life.

The Practical Experience of the Word

Given Luther's theology of the Word and his ecclesiastical practice that flowed from it, what exactly did Luther expect a practical life in the Word to look like for a typical Christian believer?

Luther gives some insights into this in the preface to the 1539 edition of his German works. Here, he takes King David as the great example of the man who wrestled with God in prayer and the fruit of whose Christian experience was shown forth in his psalms. Luther's choice of David as such a paradigm is not surprising: scholarship on Luther has come to see his move toward his Reformation theology as connected to a hermeneutical shift he makes with regard to the Psalter.

Luther produced a major series of lectures on the Psalms, known as the *Dictata*, early in his career (1513–1515). The series began with Luther seeing the Psalms in an essentially christological light, rooted in a highly spiritualized interpretation. By the time he reached Psalm 119, however, he had come to see the Psalms as often being the voice of the faithful synagogue and thus as expressing the longing of the people of God for Christ and for redemption. Thus, the shifts taking place in Luther's exegetical understanding of the Old Testament both moved him toward his later Reformation theology and provided an experiential framework for understanding what it meant to be the people of God.[1]

So when Luther later seeks to find a paradigmatic Christian, David is the obvious candidate, for in the Psalms we have an outstanding and detailed expression of the experience of what it means to be one of God's people. Indeed, Luther argues that David exhibited three key elements of the Christian life with respect to the Word of God, which he names (in Latin) *oratio*, *meditatio*, and *tentatio*. We can translate the first as *speech* and the second as *meditation*. The third is typically translated by the German word *Anfechtungen*, which scarcely helps clarify the matter in English. We might perhaps translate it as "feelings of dread that take a toll upon the person," but for the sake of brevity and conformity with convention, I will use the German term.

For Luther, David's speech (*oratio*) refers to his constantly calling out to God. This is not a contentless cry—simply a shout of joy or a scream of

---

[1] *LW*, 11:414, where Luther claims that he is breaking with all previous commentators by taking the psalm at face value, as a prophetic utterance of the people of God and, by implication, not first and foremost a prayer offered by Christ. See also J. S. Preus, *From Shadow to Promise: Old Testament Interpretation from Augustine to the Young Luther* (Cambridge, MA: Belknap, 1969).

pain—but a cry focused on the Word of God. David needs understanding, and he calls constantly to his God to help him understand what is contained in God's Word. The cry has a specific object and a specific purpose. It should also be the personal cry of every believer, not simply something that one can trust the priest or the church to do on one's behalf. "Kneel down in your little room and pray to God with real humility and earnestness, that he through his dear Son may give you his Holy Spirit, who will enlighten you, lead you, and give you understanding."[2]

Yet the Christian life is not simply a matter of the passive reception of enlightenment from God. David also meditates upon the Word. He reads it, he speaks it out loud, he hears it read, and he even sings it.[3] It is interesting that meditation is thus nothing like what we find in the contemplative piety of the medieval mystics, nor does it have any resemblance to what is called meditation today. Meditation for Luther is active and practical. It is also oriented, once again, to the Word, a point that he emphasizes in order to distinguish his position from that of the radicals who stress the inner leading of the Spirit. For Luther, the Spirit is only given with the external Word.[4] Indeed, this emphasis on the external Word shows that, in Luther's mind, personal piety and corporate piety flow into each other: the Word must come from outside; sometimes that is by reading or reciting it to oneself; at other times, it comes from hearing it read and expounded in church.

Luther's convictions on this point shape his specific practical advice for specific parishioners. Perhaps the most famous example of this is his letter to Peter Beskendorf the Barber on the matter of prayer. Peter, one of Luther's oldest friends, had asked Luther how he might be able to pray more effectively and consistently, and Luther responded by writing him a little treatise on the matter.[5]

The opening paragraph of the treatise is worth quoting in full:

> First, when I feel that I have become cool and joyless in prayer because of other tasks or thoughts (for the flesh and the devil always impede and obstruct prayer), I take my little psalter, hurry to my room, or, if it be the day and hour for it, to the church where a congregation is assembled and,

---

[2] *LW*, 34:285–86.
[3] *LW*, 34:286.
[4] *LW*, 34:286.
[5] Peter was first mentioned by the Reformer in a letter to Christopher Scheurl in 1517 (*LW*, 43:189). At Easter 1535, tragedy overtook the barber: at a party (and presumably drunk) he stabbed and killed his son-in-law when the latter boasted that he was invulnerable to injury. Luther and Peter's friends interceded for him, and he was not executed but exiled for life.

as time permits, I say quietly to myself and word-for-word the Ten Commandments, the Creed, and, if I have time, some words of Christ or of Paul, or some psalms, just as a child might do.[6]

Several points are worthy of note here. First, there is the activity of the Devil. As noted before, in Luther's world the Devil and his minions are virtually physical presences. Luther does not use the Devil's presence as an excuse for sin or doubting of God's favor, but the Evil One is always there, waiting to capitalize on the weakness of the sinful flesh in order to destroy the saints. The Christian life is, in one sense, mortal combat with an external Enemy who has unusual access to the enemy that always lurks within.

Second, there is a certain prioritizing of public worship over private devotions. The latter are an important option but Luther sees that when it is the time of public worship, the troubled or lethargic soul would be better served in the context of the gathering of the saints. This is what one would expect from a theology that puts so much emphasis upon the Word coming from the outside. I can sit in my room and read my Psalter, which is fine; or I can go to hear the Word sung and proclaimed to me by others, which has a confrontational, external aspect to it over which I have no control and toward which I cannot be neutral but must respond either in unbelief or in faith.

This point cannot be stressed enough. In our own day, biblical counseling has become a very trendy and attractive movement within the church, particularly in cultures where there is a strong emphasis on secular counseling and psychology. Luther's equivalent of this was the practice of private confession and absolution, a practice (we have noted) that he maintained himself and commended to others. Yet Luther would never have regarded such private dealings as having equal importance to what happened in church or as being a replacement for regular attendance at the corporate means of grace. One could imagine a person seeking Luther's advice for, say, struggles with assurance. Luther's first question of him would almost certainly be, Are you going to church to hear the Word and receive the sacrament? If the answer came back in the negative, it is safe to assume that Luther would send the person away to attend church for a few weeks before he would consider giving him individual counsel. If the person had excluded himself from the objective means of grace, not only would spiri-

[6] LW, 43:193.

tual problems be expected, but also Luther could really offer nothing else to help him.

In his treatise on prayer, Luther also brings out the usefulness of recitation. Prayer is to be the believer's priority at the start and end of each day, but the Devil, as Luther notes, is assiduous in attempting to undermine this. Thus, the Christian often does not feel like praying. This is no excuse but rather grounds for proper preparatory work. Prayer is not an option dependent on how one feels; it is a vital part of the Christian life, as eating is to the body. Thus, Luther advises his friend Peter to recite to himself some words of Christ or the Decalogue as a means of fueling the desire to pray. Evangelical sensibilities shaped by an emphasis on conversion and (for want of a better term) *feeling* the faith as a hallmark of authenticity in the avoidance of formalism might well react against something that looks like idle repetition. But again, for Luther this is all part of the externality and objectivity of the Word. One cannot always be under the sound of the Word read or preached, and in such circumstances one can speak the Word to oneself.[7] The Word has power independent of how we feel about it. Its presence, even through our own rote repetition, can be used by God to achieve his purpose in our lives.

Luther then presents the Lord's Prayer as the model prayer for the Christian, offering explanatory comments on the various petitions.[8] This is then followed by the Decalogue,[9] and then the Apostles' Creed.[10] In other words, his personal advice to Peter is very much in line with the structure and content of his Small Catechism. The Christian life has a shape—a catechetical shape—that moves from law to gospel, from Decalogue to Apostles' Creed. Again, although Luther stresses the advantages of repeating key phrases to oneself, he also indicates that it is the conceptual content, not the precise wording, that is important. To allow the wording to become a mere form is indeed a real danger to guard against.[11] He also points out that prayer ought not be long and elaborate so much as frequent and fervent.[12] In the glosses he provides on each of the major texts he recommends, he stresses the need for the individual to sorrow over sin and rejoice over the gospel. This is to be no mere rote learning; to learn the Lord's Prayer, the Decalogue, and the

---

[7] *LW*, 43:194.
[8] *LW*, 43:194ff.
[9] *LW*, 43:200ff.
[10] *LW*, 43:209ff.
[11] *LW*, 43:198.
[12] *LW*, 43:209.

Apostles' Creed is to know God, to know oneself, and to understand the relationship between those two in a better and deeper way.

Throughout the treatise, Scripture is the bedrock on which Luther sees the life of prayer as being built. He speaks of the Decalogue as "a school text, song book, penitential book, and prayer book," and recommends that the Christian alternate meditation on the commandments with reflection upon a psalm or another chapter of Scripture day by day.[13] For Luther, it is not the desire for reading Scripture that fuels prayer; it is reading Scripture that fuels the desire for prayer. That the Christian may not *feel* like praying is one of the Devil's tricks played on weak and sinful flesh; the answer is the discipline of reading and meditation, both corporate and individual. One might draw an analogy with marital love: the husband is commanded by God's Word to love his wife. That command is independent of how the husband feels at any given moment. He is to act in a loving way toward her, and as he does so, his love for her will itself deepen and grow. So it is to be with prayer: reading Scripture shapes people in such a way that their prayer life will deepen and grow as a result.

What is perhaps most noteworthy in all this, of course, is the *routine* nature of the practice of the Christian life. Nothing Luther proposes is in itself particularly exciting or novel. We live in an age mesmerized both by technique and by the extraordinary. Modern evangelicalism, particularly in America, has been shaped by the kind of revivalism pioneered by Charles Finney in the nineteenth century. Find the right techniques and one will achieve the desired spiritual results; and typically those techniques involve something unusual or impressive. For Luther, this would all have been alien and obnoxious: the Word is powerful in and of itself; and the ways in which the Word works are ordinary and routine. Liturgies with a catechetical structure, a focus on the Word read and the Word preached, and a constant meditation upon that Word—those were the major elements of personal spiritual growth and discipleship.

Anfechtungen

Yet there is more to Luther's appropriation of the Word than meditation. In medieval theology, the third element of the Christian devotional life was contemplation. It is here that Luther makes a stark break with medieval

---

[13] *LW*, 43:209.

piety and introduces something new and dynamic to the subject. For him, the life of the believer is also to be understood as one marked by peculiar existential struggle, a kind of seesaw between despair and hope. The Word addressed the whole person, gripped the whole person, permeated the experience of the whole person.

Like many pastors before and since, Luther was no stranger to what we would now call depression. Indeed, given what could be characterized as his extreme personality prone to exuberance, anger, joy, and despair, he looks like a classic case of a depressive. Luther, of course, had no medical or psychological categories for thinking about these things. For him, all things were spiritual in origin and essence. Thus, he approached his *Anfechtungen* as elements of his experience that were susceptible to spiritual explanation.

Indeed, when we come to the matter of *Anfechtungen*, we arrive at the existential and experiential heart of Luther's understanding of the Christian life. These *Anfechtungen* were the fears, terrors, and moments of despair that, for example, he describes as marking his encounter with Romans 1:17 prior to his "breakthrough" in understanding God's righteousness in the gospel. Yet they did not cease to haunt him subsequent to that and, indeed, may quite possibly have grown worse. As I will argue below, Luther had no dramatic "conversion experience" that freed him from fear but rather a view of the Christian life as constantly swinging back and forth between despair and assured faith.

The origins of *Anfechtungen* lie in the human tragedy. As fallen creatures, human beings are subject to the curse and thus to pain and frustration here on earth. We cannot attain to who we were intended to be. Indeed, we are ultimately doomed to physical death. Luther makes it clear in his lecture on Genesis 4:10 that sinners have guilty consciences and that, when these are active, they change the whole of reality:

> And those whom sadness of spirit seizes experience similar sensations, for to them all creatures appear changed. Even when they speak with people whom they know and in turn hear them, the very sound of their speech seems different, their looks appear changed, and everything becomes black and horrible wherever they turn their eyes. Such a fierce and savage beast is an evil conscience. And so, unless God comforts them, they must end their own life because of their despair, their distress, and their inability to bear their grief.[14]

---

[14] *LW*, 1:287.

Human guilt is such that it generates fear and loathing within the heart of the individual. Even friends appear strange and repellent. It would seem that this passage, saturated as it is in experiential/existential language, is an autobiographical statement of Luther's own religious experiences.

Anfechtungen can also derive from an overattachment to the material world. Hence, in commenting on Psalm 118:1, Luther mentions that the stirring of a leaf or a pain in the leg can cause us to fill heaven and earth with curses and recriminations. We are, he says,

> like a king who becomes frantic because he loses one pfennig [one-hundredth of a German mark]. Though he owns half the world, with countless money and possessions, he plays the martyr, throws a tantrum, curses, denounces God, and fulminates against Him with other blasphemous language, as today cursing troopers show their manliness by resorting to profanity.[15]

Here one can see the similarities between Luther and Augustine: misguided love for or reliance upon the material world leaves humanity in an unstable and indeed immoral state subject to disturbance and chaos at the merest sign that the world is a fickle and uncertain place. Further, like the later Augustinian Pascal, we can also discern that Luther sees clearly the psychological rationale behind such attachment to the material universe: it makes men and women think of themselves as gods; when reality hints that this is not the case, *Anfechtungen* follow, as Luther proceeds to say in his comment on Psalm 118:

> The good God permits such small evils to befall us merely in order to arouse us snorers from our deep sleep and to make us recognize, on the other hand, the incomparable and innumerable benefits we still have. He wants us to consider what would happen if He were to withdraw His goodness from us completely. We also are to look at our misfortunes in no other way than that with them God gives us a light by which we may see and understand His goodness and kindness in countless other ways. Then we conclude that such small misfortunes are barely a drop of water on a big fire or a little spark in the ocean.[16]

This passage indicates that *Anfechtungen* are the existential aspect of the deeper foundations of Luther's theology. Indeed, these fruits of

---

[15] *LW*, 14:49.
[16] *LW*, 14:49–50.

the dark contradictions of the human predicament are connected to a number of Luther's antithetical distinctions. For example the distinction between the two kinds of theologian rests upon the counterintuitive, counterempirical nature of God's revelation and truth. This has a twofold significance for *Anfechtungen*. The theologian of glory is always doomed in the end to despair because death is unavoidable and deep down inside he knows that. All of his glorious aspirations for himself must ultimately end in the dust. That basic contradiction between self-understanding and actual experience is bound to manifest itself in *Anfechtungen* at points. Indeed, we might make a contemporary observation that levels of anxiety and depression are higher in the West now than they have ever been, at the very moment in history when we are more affluent and, in terms of our control over the natural world, have never been more powerful. Our godlike self-understanding, however, keeps colliding with the facts of death and of the fallen finiteness of this world. Truly, ours is an era where *Anfechtungen* have the character of a social affliction of pandemic proportions.

Second, the very essence of being a theologian of the cross is that one sees God's strength as manifested in weakness. The primary significance of that is the incarnation and the cross. God's means for overcoming sin and crushing death are the humiliation of his Son, hidden in human flesh. Nevertheless, the cross also has a certain paradigmatic aspect to it, for it indicates that God does his proper work through his alien work. That can be rephrased: God does what he intends by doing the opposite of what we humanly expect. Luther expands on this relative to our own sufferings in the 1520 *Treatise on Good Works*:

> Therefore, to destroy such works of ours as well as the old Adam in us, God overwhelms us with those things which move us to anger, with many sufferings which rouse us to impatience, and last of all, even with death and the abuse of the world. By means of these he seeks nothing else but to drive out of us anger, impatience, and unrest, and to perfect his own work in us, that is, his peace. Thus Isaiah 28[:21] says, "He takes upon himself an alien work, that he may do his own proper work." What does that mean? He sends us suffering and unrest to teach us to have patience and peace. He bids us die that he may make us live. He does this as long as and until a man, thoroughly trained, reaches such a pitch of peace and poise that he is no longer upset whether things go

well or ill with him, whether he dies or lives, whether he is honored or dishonored.[17]

Sufferings shape our character into that which God wishes it to be. These are not what we would desire, for they are painful and unwelcome; but they are the way God has chosen to work, and they reflect, of course, the logic of the cross. Thus, the theologian of the cross has the right lens for understanding God's purpose in misfortune and, indeed, in the constant presence of *Anfechtungen*.

The Devil and Doctor Martin

There is a further element in Luther's view of *Anfechtungen*, however, and that is the role of the Devil. I noted in the introduction that Luther's world was very different from the one we live in today. Even conservative Christians who believe in a personal Devil generally regard him as something quite remote, even a little abstract. For Luther, the Devil was always close at hand, hiding in the cupboard or under the bed or in the woods, whispering in his ear, bringing tangible temptations to him and terrifying accusations against him. In fact, his *Table Talk* is full of anecdotes about the Devil's doings, both in general and against Luther in particular.[18] The Devil and his demonic minions are everywhere, constantly looking for ways to destroy God's people.[19] Indeed, Luther even sees the Devil as operating at times like an actual hit man. Thus, when he and Katie are almost killed by the collapse of a wall, he thinks that the failure to keep the wall in a good state of repair handed the Devil an opportunity for an assassination attempt.[20] The Devil also knocks over fences in an attempt to kill people, and in his role as the one who brings death, he is the author and cause of all illness and disease.[21]

Luther certainly regards the cultivation of despair as one of the primary tasks of the Devil. Thus, in contradiction to traditional medieval teaching,

---

[17] *LW*, 44:77.
[18] The editors of Luther's *Table Talk* use his dialogues with the Devil as evidence that Luther is obviously not always quoting people directly (*LW*, 54:26). Their apparent assumption is that he could not have intended to mean that he did actually engage the Devil himself in conversation. That view is possible; but we should not thereby underestimate Luther's belief in the actual presence of the Devil in his life. Even the idiom of putting words in the Devil's mouth indicates a very different world from that in which we now live.
[19] *LW*, 54:172.
[20] *LW*, 54:46.
[21] *LW*, 54:53–54, 102, 145–46.

he argues that suicides are not necessarily damned, because they are often simply weak people who have been overcome by the Devil.[22] Doubt of God's favor is the Devil's stock-in-trade. Thus, he will constantly accuse Luther of not being truly called to the ministry.[23] The Devil will fix on a single sin of Luther's and use it to disturb his conscience, as he does with all believers when given the opportunity.[24] Such an attack on Luther is typical satanic strategy, whereby he confronts Christians with the law and their sins in order to shatter their confidence.[25] Indeed, the Devil, by his very nature, must continually attack the gospel and try to overthrow it.[26] He steals God's Word away from the Christian by turning the gospel into the law.[27] Thus, he also hates preaching and does his best to suppress it, as through the Spirit-focused theology of the radicals.[28] He also tends to attack Christians when they are on their own, and Luther himself comments that he is particularly afflicted by the Devil when in bed at night.[29]

This satanic strategy reflects the heart of Luther's theology: the Christian life is built upon the assurance of God's free grace given in Christ. Everything hangs on this, from confidence before God to ethical conduct before neighbors, to the ability to look death in the face and not despair. If the Devil can undermine assurance or push the Christian back to relying upon his own works—if the Devil can, we might say, turn the theologian of the cross back into a theologian of glory—then his job is done. In his lectures on Galatians, Luther also notes that the Devil at times does not entirely steal away the Word of God but seeks to make sure that the Word is distorted in such a way that the Christian sees only a part of Christ, or sees him in a very defective way. The Evil One will cite Scriptures to us, which he takes out of context, and inflate the law while reducing Christ in such a way that the former seems to overwhelm the latter. This too leads to despair and is particularly effective at a time when the Christian might also be suffering or afflicted in some way.[30]

Luther's advice on how to deal with the Devil in such circumstances

---

[22] *LW*, 54:29.
[23] *LW*, 54:73–74, 95.
[24] *LW*, 54:34, 275–76.
[25] Commenting on the argument of Galatians, Luther says, "In affliction and in the conflict of conscience it is the devil's habit to frighten us with the Law and to set against us the consciousness of sin, our wicked past, the wrath and judgment of God, hell and eternal death, so that thus he may drive us into despair, subject us to himself, and pluck us from Christ." *LW*, 26:10; cf. 26:35.
[26] *LW*, 26:13.
[27] *LW*, 54:105–7.
[28] *LW*, 54:186.
[29] *LW*, 54:83, 89–90.
[30] *LW*, 26:38–39.

varies. Perhaps the most appropriate advice he gives is to use the Word of God against him, as this is something he fears. When the Devil scares Luther at night and makes him break into a terrible sweat, Luther looks to the Word, which easily overcomes any terrors the Evil One can conjure up.[31] In fact, the Devil fears the spoken Word above all things, as he also does the sacraments because the power they derive is the incarnate Christ and the Word of promise.[32] Luther does, however, make note of a slightly less conventional strategy, which involved breaking wind at him, a technique that not only he himself employed but also a woman in Magdeburg found successful. Nevertheless, he regards this technique as dangerous because the Devil is not easily mocked.[33] A far better strategy is to point the Devil toward one's baptism and the Word, as these are the safest means of warding off his assaults.[34]

Yet, for all of Luther's talk of the direct attacks of the Devil, he regards him as typically working through means. These are usually not as physically solid as the badly maintained wall or the lopsided fence but are more often spiritual. Indeed, at the heart of the Devil's strategy lies his ability to create confusion between law and gospel, indicating that this distinction also plays into the whole matter of *Anfechtungen*.

Anfechtungen and the Law-Gospel Dialectic

In chapter 2, we noted the law-gospel dialectic as a basic element of Luther's theology: the law proves to us that we cannot stand before God in our own righteousness, and that drives us to the gospel. What is key to grasp, however, is that this is not simply a theological distinction but one carrying deep implications for human experience.[35]

The classic New Testament text for the law-gospel dialectic is Paul's letter to the Galatians. Luther expounded this letter in two separate sets of lectures at two different points in his reforming career. In 1519, as the Reformation was beginning to gather pace in Wittenberg but while Luther was still clarifying his thought, he lectured on the letter and thereby set

---

[31] *LW*, 54:89–90.
[32] *LW*, 54:197.
[33] *LW*, 54:16, 280–81.
[34] *LW*, 54:86.
[35] One of my concerns with the current trendiness of Luther's law-gospel distinction in certain evangelical circles is that it seems to have been stripped of its existential significance. The dialectic was an agonizing one for Luther, involving a certain seesawing between despair and hope. As we shall see in the next chapter, Luther himself was concerned that some law-gospel preaching in his own day was in fact merely gospel preaching, and that this did not constitute an appropriately biblical approach to the Christian life.

out his emerging theology of justification. In 1531 he returned to the letter, this time with a finely tooled and matured Reformation theology. These lectures were then published as his great commentary on the letter in 1535.

In these lectures, Luther offers perhaps a more acute analysis of Christian freedom in the context of the Christian life than anywhere else in his work. Central to his argument is the matter of *Anfechtungen*. Fear and terror are the products of the law, the inevitable result of that tendency within all of us to be theologians of glory, who wish to approach God on our own terms and thus find ourselves confronted with the terrifying God of perfect righteousness and holiness.

Commenting on Galatians 1:3, Luther brings out powerfully the need for the Christian to contemplate God only in the incarnate Christ. To seek for him elsewhere is to court despair, for in that God, the God of transcendence, we can only meet with one who is terrifying and incomprehensible.[36] Only Christ can give peace in such a circumstance. He does not do so as the apostles did (and by implication, as future generations of Christian preachers do) by preaching the Word; Christ himself is that Word and thus embodies, in himself and his actions, peace.[37]

For this reason, Luther regards doctrine, particularly christology, as absolutely vital to the practical Christian life. When the Devil comes and makes our sins so huge and Christ so small in our minds that they threaten to overwhelm us and bury the gospel, Luther declares that the answer is to have a good understanding of who Christ is:

> This is why I am so earnest in my plea to you to learn the true and correct definition of Christ on the basis of these words of Paul: "who gave Himself for our sins." If He gave Himself into death for our sins, then undoubtedly He is not a tormentor. He is not One who will cast down the troubled, but One who will raise up the fallen and bring propitiation and consolation to the terrified. Otherwise Paul would be lying when he says "who gave Himself for our sins." If I define Christ this way, I define Him correctly, grasp the authentic Christ, and truly make Him my own. I avoid all speculations about the Divine Majesty and take my stand in the humanity of Christ. There is no fear here; there is sheer sweetness, joy, and the like. This kindles a light that shows me the true knowledge of God, of myself, of all creatures, and of all the wickedness of the kingdom of the devil.[38]

---

[36] *LW*, 26:28–29.
[37] *LW*, 26:31.
[38] *LW*, 26:39.

This is truly magnificent teaching, rising up from the rich christology of Luther's thought and, indeed, his own experience. One has to say that it is very countercultural in our own day: we tend to look for techniques, things we can do, in order to solve our problems. Thus, the woman whose marriage is falling apart might well think that she needs to go to a church where the sermon series is on "putting your marriage back together." Luther would disagree: the person whose life is falling apart and who is thus tempted to despair needs to know Christ, and knowing Christ requires knowing who he is and what he has done. In other words, it is simple, catechetical doctrine. The sources of despair are ultimately found in an overestimation of the powers of the Christian's enemies—the world, the flesh, death, and the Devil. The answer to despair is thus an appropriate understanding of the overwhelming power of the God who made himself weak by taking human flesh and dying upon the cross.

On paper, of course, this looks very straightforward. But the human soul is a battlefield where the theologian of glory struggles constantly to overcome the theologian of the cross. To quote A. E. Housman's great poem *The Welsh Marches*:

> They cease not fighting, east and west,
> On the marches of my breast.

> Here the truceless armies yet
> Trample, rolled in blood and sweat,
> They kill and kill and never die;
> And I think that each is I.[39]

Christians are, in a sense, divided against themselves, and this division is both exacerbated and resolved by the preaching of law and gospel. These drive us in two different directions, one to ourselves, which is a fool's errand, destined to end in failure, and one to Christ. Yet we run to Christ only when we have first been brought to despair by the law. As Luther comments on Galatians 1:3, the human conscience knows it cannot stand on its own before God, and yet this knowledge does not in itself produce repentance. What it does is drive people to more and greater acts of self-righteousness, as exemplified by the religious orders of Luther's day. Yet all this activity can ultimately lead only to deeper and deeper

---

[39] http://www.bartleby.com/123/28.html.

despair.[40] Then, at the moment when the law has come and driven the individual to total despair, Christ comes into view and declares forgiveness and freedom.[41] This is the logic of the cross applied to the salvation of individuals: God exalts whom he humbles, makes strong the weak, makes clean the filthy, makes rich the poor.[42]

It is worth noting that this is not, for Luther, the equivalent of a one-time conversion experience. The law-gospel dialectic in the life of the believer is not primarily a chronological matter, whereby the individual labors under the condemnation of the law, finally despairs, and then turns to Christ and subsequently enjoys, to borrow a phrase, "your best life now." That is not how it works at all. As Luther describes it:

> [The gospel] knocks out the teeth of the Law, blunts its sting and all its weapons, and utterly disables it. Yet it remains a Law for the wicked and unbelieving; it remains also for us who are weak, to the extent that we do not believe. Here it still has its sharpness and its teeth. But if I believe in Christ, regardless of how sin may trouble me to the point of despair, I shall rely on the liberty I have in Christ and say: "I admit that I have sinned. But my sin (which is a sin that is damned) is in Christ (who is a sin that damns). This sin that damns is stronger than the sin that is damned; for it is justifying grace, righteousness, life, and salvation." And so when I feel the terrors of death, I say: "Death, you have nothing on me. For I have another death, one that kills you, my death. And the death that kills is stronger than the death that is killed."[43]

This reality—that the Christian is, in effect, a war zone between the law and the gospel—pushes us once again to the acknowledgment that the preached Word is vital. That external Word of which the Schmalkaldic Articles speak is important as the means by which the battle is conducted.

For example, the Christian, tending naturally always to be a theologian of glory, might well overestimate the power of his own righteousness and underestimate the glory of God's holiness. In such a case, he needs the law to shatter his self-righteousness and to drive him to despair. Once he despairs, then he needs the gospel to build him up once more. Alternatively, the Devil can so blind the believer with the extent of her sin and with lies

---

[40] *LW*, 26:27, 232–33.
[41] *LW*, 26:131–32.
[42] *LW*, 26:314.
[43] *LW*, 26:161–62.

about the inadequacy of Christ, that she is tempted to despair. At this point, she needs to be shown Christ and brought back to faith and hope. This takes place primarily in the corporate gathering of the church, where the preacher declares the law and proclaims the gospel and trusts the Spirit to apply it to individuals as needed. It also takes place in the sacraments, where, attached to the Word, the elements bring with them Christ and press him on the troubled soul of the recipient, as we shall see in more detail in chapter 6. The individual's Christian life finds its fuel in the corporate acts of the church.

Concluding Reflections

Given the role of *Anfechtungen* in making the Christian truly understand Scripture, it is worth reflecting on Luther's understanding of Christian experience. Here we enter complicated territory, not because Luther's thinking is particularly arcane but because we inevitably look back to Luther through the lens of later experiential strands of Protestantism. Luther had a powerful influence on both John Bunyan and John Wesley. Thus, his thinking was put to the service of, in the case of Bunyan, an occasionally very introspective Puritanism and, in the case of Wesley, a type of revivalist conversionism. Neither of these categories really reflects Luther's own position: his introspection was always a stepping-stone to looking at the outward and objective in Word and sacrament; and he would not really have understood revivalist conversionism, given that he would have regarded his baptism as his moment of entry into the church.

Thus, it is interesting that despair in Luther is not the result of a quest for signs of election or salvation. While later generations of pietists, Puritans, and evangelicals might be tempted to look inward to see if there are signs of the regenerative work of the Spirit, introspection in Luther is actually the work of the flesh or the Devil and a function of human self-righteousness. Indeed, he warns against looking for assurance of salvation anywhere other than in the revelation of God in Christ. Thus, in *The Bondage of the Will*, he declares that God's predestining of human beings to salvation is a matter of his hiddenness. It is not revealed to us and is thus not susceptible to our scrutiny. More than that, it is imperative that we not seek to penetrate the darkness in order to understand. Rather, we are to deal solely with God as he has revealed himself. In this context, Luther refers to this revealed God as "God preached." Thus, he is speaking of the

God of the external Word, the God who comes in his revelation from outside. We might expand that by saying that he is here speaking of a person, the incarnate Christ, and the preaching that brings that incarnate Christ to the congregation and to individual Christians.[44]

In fact, as Luther comments in the same work, despair is health giving when connected to the gospel because it highlights weakness.[45] Thus, while certain strands of Christian thinking see despair as an evil, a dead end, the result of a failed quest to find signs of salvation when looking within, Luther sees it as a good thing because it drives Christians to look outside themselves, to the Word and the sacrament, in order to be assured.

Such a view of despair will inevitably shape the pastoral response. The first thing that must be done is to diagnose the depth of despair and its cause. If it is the result of an introspective examination of one's soul for signs of election, Luther's answer is going to be that one needs to look outward to Christ for such assurance. If the despair is because the individual is overwhelmed by the magnitude and number of his sins, Luther is going to point him outward to Christ and emphasize the full sufficiency and power of Christ in the utter destruction of sin in his body on the cross. Either way, the answer to introspective despair is to look out to God as he offers himself to us in the flesh of Christ, now found in Word and sacrament. Despair and *Anfechtungen* have no value in themselves other than as they push us to Christ. This is the logic of the theologian of the cross: God brings to heaven by casting to hell.

On the issue of conversionism, readers of Luther have often had their imaginations captured by his description of the so-called tower experience, his account of the dramatic breakthrough he made in his understanding of "righteousness" in Romans 1:17. Luther gives a number of versions of this in his *Table Talk*,[46] but the most famous account appears in the preface to the 1545 edition of his Latin works.[47] There he describes being crushed by the law of God and then further devastated when reading in Romans 1:17 that the gospel reveals the righteousness of God as well. He understood this to mean that the gospel too was a kind of law, a standard of God's righteousness to which the Christian must conform. Only when he realized

---

[44] *LW*, 33:139–41.
[45] "I myself was offended more than once, and brought to the very depth and abyss of despair, so that I wished I had never been created a man, before I realized how salutary that despair was, and how near to grace." *LW*, 33:190.
[46] *LW*, 54:193–94, 308–9, 442–43.
[47] *LW*, 34:336–38.

that the righteousness of which Paul was speaking is that by which God declares us righteous did he come to a true appreciation of the good news.

Interpreting the tower experience presents numerous problems, not least the chronology. In the preface to his Latin works, Luther dates the breakthrough to 1519, which seems in some ways rather late, as Luther's other writings indicate that the specific change on righteousness was in motion some time earlier. Further, studying Luther's writings between 1515 and 1521 reveals no sudden, dramatic change but rather a steady development over time.

The chronological issues, however, are somewhat irrelevant to the question of whether the event Luther describes can be called a conversion experience. Several factors militate against this. First, as should already be clear, what he is describing is an exegetical breakthrough that had experiential implications for him, in that it lifted the burden of guilt from his shoulders. There is no hint in Luther's narrative that he became a Christian at this point or that he looked back on his life before the breakthrough as being that of a non-Christian.

Second, we should note that Luther never cites the tower experience as a means of validating that he is a Christian. Some strands of modern evangelicalism place great stock in particular conversion experiences as major grounds for assurance. The person knows he is a Christian because he recalls a moment or perhaps a period of time when he passed from darkness to light. At one point in his life he did not worship Jesus Christ or trust him for salvation, but now he does. In some very attenuated evangelical traditions, the recollection of a moment of decision, though not necessarily followed by any particular change of life or moral improvement, is sufficient to give assurance.

For Luther, as we shall see in the next chapter, if any event gave assurance, it was his baptism. That was not from some magical power inherent in the water, but from the Word to which the element of water was attached, which he grasped by faith. Importantly, this view of the Christian life does not require a crisis experience. Further, it is decidedly objective and external in its orientation: once again, as we noted above with the matter of despair and *Anfechtungen*, the terminus is on something outside and independent of us: Jesus Christ offered to us in his Word and sacrament.

We might also add that this external, objective emphasis promotes a different narrative of the Christian life than one typically finds in conversionist and revivalist evangelic circles. Here is a view of the Christian life that eschews the dramatic for the ordinary (at least as the world, or perhaps better, the theologian of glory, understands those categories). This narrative of the Christian life draws its strength from where Christ is to be found, and that is simply in Word and sacrament. Such a life is thus one of steady and careful nurture, of being baptized, of continually learning and relearning the catechetical faith, of being driven out of oneself by the law and being offered Christ in the gospel, and of being fed by the Mass.

And it is to this sacramental dimension that we now turn.

CHAPTER 6

FREED FROM BABYLON

BAPTISM AND THE MASS

It is taught among us that Baptism is necessary and that grace is offered through it.

THE BOOK OF CONCORD

If Luther is often cited as a great hero of modern evangelical Protestantism, that is typically on two grounds: his formulation of justification by grace through faith is something that evangelicals see as a major breakthrough, theologically and pastorally; and his stand against the Roman Church, particularly as captured in the proverbial "Here I stand!" moment at the Diet of Worms, makes him one of the closest things to a romantic hero figure that the Protestant church has ever produced. We might also add that even his bombast, his rudeness, and his extremity of language make him a more human, and somehow more appealing, figure than the comparatively colorless and dour Calvin.

Nevertheless, the rather embarrassing fact for evangelical admirers of Dr. Martin is that he would not have regarded any of them as actually being faithful to the biblical teaching on the Supper. Luther, after all, was a highly sacramental theologian. More than that, he saw his sacramentalism as a hallmark of true Christianity. When he famously declared during the Marburg Colloquy that Huldrych Zwingli was "of a different spirit," he was not commenting on Zwingli's temperament; rather, he was declaring that Zwingli was simply not a true believer, that whatever spirit motivated him, it was not the Holy Spirit. The reason? Zwingli understood the Lord's Supper as a symbolic action that did not actually involve the whole Christ, divine and human, in the elements of bread and wine.

For Luther, it was axiomatic that God could only be approached as gracious through the weak and frail humanity of the incarnate Christ. This had wide-ranging implications for Luther, not the least of which was his conviction that God gave himself to Christians in tangible, weak forms under which he was hidden from all but the eyes of faith. That was one reason why he retained Christian artwork depicting Christ: such was not a breach of the Decalogue, as the Reformed thought, but rather a legitimate expression of precisely how God had hidden himself in weakness in the incarnation.[1] And this idea was also very important to him when it came to the sacraments. There, in water, bread, and wine, Christ was offered. The world might mock. The theologian of glory would look on with incomprehension. But the theologian of the cross, with a simple, childlike faith, discerned in these things the presence of the gracious Christ who saves.

Given that most evangelical Protestants hold to a purely symbolic view of the Lord's Supper, and given that even the Reformed position, taking its cue from Calvin, does not involve an objective presence of the whole Christ in the elements, it is safe to conclude that Luther would not regard evangelicalism as properly Christian. With that in mind, we can now proceed to look at how Luther understood the sacraments of baptism and the Lord's Supper (or, to use Luther's preferred terminology, the Mass).

Luther and Baptism

Baptism is perhaps the most basic element of the Christian life for the simple reason that it is the rite of initiation. All Christians agree that baptism is what brings one into the church, even as they disagree about its subjects, mode, and precise significance.

Luther's understanding of baptism is, along with his view of the real

---

[1] For a statement of the Reformed position, see Heidelberg Catechism questions 96–98: "96. What does God require in the second commandment? A. That we in no wise represent God by images, nor worship him in any other way than he has commanded in his word. 97. Are images then not at all to be made? A. God neither can, nor may be represented by any means: but as to creatures; though they may be represented, yet God forbids to make, or have any resemblance of them, either in order to worship them or to serve God by them. 98. But may not images be tolerated in the churches, as books to the laity? A. No: for we must not pretend to be wiser than God, who will have his people taught, not by dumb images, but by the lively preaching of his word."

presence in the Mass, one that modern evangelical Protestants find most alien. Most evangelicals are probably Baptist, either by conviction or by default. Thus, Luther's militant attachment to infant baptism is alien. Yet it is not simply Baptists who find Luther's thinking in this area perplexing: Presbyterians and Reformed who have no disagreement with his belief that infants should be baptized find themselves at odds with his realist view of the sacrament's significance. If they baptize children because of their understanding of the scope of the covenant of grace, Luther does so because he sees baptism as a regenerative act by which the child is made into a Christian. To the evangelical mind, this seems to stand in contradiction to his emphasis on justification by faith.

To understand Luther sympathetically, we must first understand how his thinking on this matter develops over time. Thus, his autobiography is vital. By the time he arrives at his Reformation convictions in the years 1518 and following, he has moved significantly beyond the teaching he received from his medieval masters. They had taught that baptism was primarily a cleansing or a dampening down of a tinder-like tendency. Luther has become convinced that the human predicament is not that humans have a weakness or a wound. It is that they are dead. The dead do not require help or assistance or cleansing. Nothing short of resurrection will save them; and baptism has to be understood in light of this.

The Meaning and Efficacy of Baptism

The issue of baptism was to prove almost as contentious in the Reformation as that of the Mass. With the rise of Anabaptist movements in the 1520s, the literature on baptism rapidly became highly polemical. Prior to that, though, Luther had been able to forge his own position on the matter in relation to medieval teaching rather than the excesses of radical Protestantism. Indeed, his two finest expositions of the matter came early in his career, before the rise of the Anabaptists. First, there was his 1519 treatise *The Holy and Blessed Sacrament of Baptism*, dedicated to Duchess Margaret of Brunswick.[2] In this work, Luther lays out the three basic elements of baptism: the sign, the thing signified, and the faith that grasps the thing signified. Then, in the following year, baptism occupies a significant section of his Reformation sacramental manifesto *The Babylonian Captivity of the Church*.[3]

---

[2] *LW*, 35:29–43.
[3] *LW*, 36:57ff.

The sign is water, applied to the subject in the name of Father, Son, and Holy Spirit, and there must be both a placing under and a drawing out in order to capture fully that which baptism signifies.[4] Interestingly enough, Luther has a strong preference for full immersion of the infant to be baptized because submersion most conforms to what is signified: the death of the old sinful nature as well as the destruction of its sinfulness, and the rising up to newness of life.[5] Nevertheless, Luther does not make immersion a necessity so much as a preference, because it is not the sign but the thing signified that is important.

Luther is clear that the death of sin and the rising to newness of life are never fully completed in this life. Baptism thus has an eschatological significance, pointing toward the perfecting of the saints in glory. For this reason, Luther is able to describe life itself as one continual spiritual baptism whereby the Christian is always dying to self and rising to Christ: "Therefore this whole life is nothing else than a spiritual baptism which does not cease till death, and he who is baptized is condemned to die."[6] This echoes the very first of Luther's *Ninety-Five Theses against Indulgences*, that the whole of the Christian life is to be one of repentance. Water baptism signifies this at a single point in time, the very initiation of the Christian life; and the rest of the Christian life is to be constituted out of the substance of the sacrament.

Nevertheless, the Christian knows from experience that sins and sinfulness do not disappear with baptism. For all of the realist language Luther uses with regard to the sacrament, he knows it is no magical fix that works in and of itself. In *The Holy and Blessed Sacrament*, Luther emphasizes the activity of God in working within the Christian to bring about the steady (albeit imperfect) destruction of sin in this life. He even goes as far as to use conditional language, such that God's grace continues to be given to the baptized as long as they continue to strive to slay sin.[7] We perhaps see here vestiges of his medieval background, with its accent on the *pactum* as the means for connecting God and sinners in a relationship of grace. Just one year later, however, in *The Babylonian Captivity*, Luther places a much greater accent on the promise attached to baptism as that which baptism signifies. Indeed, the promise is the first thing the Christian is to think of in relation to baptism.[8]

---

[4] *LW*, 35:30.
[5] *LW*, 35:29; cf. 36:64.
[6] *LW*, 35:30.
[7] *LW*, 35:34.
[8] *LW*, 36:58.

Underlying Luther's high view of the importance of baptism is his conviction that God is the agent in the sacrament. That is why it is effective for salvation. God is the one who has made the promise; God is the one who has confirmed that promise in Christ; God is now the one who impresses that promise upon the Christian in baptism. In baptism, God truly engrafts the subject into Christ, truly offers him Christ. The reality of this is why Luther believes that children should be baptized. In a table talk, he draws an analogy between baptism and preaching. To the objection that children should not be baptized because they do not believe, Luther responds that the same would therefore apply to preaching. That we do preach to unbelievers indicates that we do not regard the reality of the Word, and of the Christ who comes in the Word, to be dependent upon the subjective faith of the hearer. Christ truly preached is truly there in an objective sense, in the same way that the promise is there in baptism. Further, to be baptized because of faith is to make the Christian, and not God, the decisive agent in the sacrament.[9]

This also bears on the role of the priest: the priest performs the outward rite, but it is still God who acts.[10] Thus, in line with established Christian teaching that the Word and sacraments depend for their efficacy not upon the moral condition of the priest but upon the Word and action of God, Luther counsels people not to be overly concerned about the technical minutiae either of the ceremony or of who is, humanly speaking, doing the baptism. Indeed, in his *Explanation of the Ninety-Five Theses*, he recounts the incident of an actor who was baptized in jest by his fellow pagan thespians and was thereby converted and apparently martyred without delay.[11]

For Luther, as someone not gifted in the matter of understatement, Anabaptists were allies of the Antichrist, another point of undoubted discomfort for modern evangelical appropriations of his theology. Not only was he a militant, unrepentant paedobaptist; he also ascribed rather negative eschatological significance to his opponents on this score.[12]

We should note, however, that despite his great emphasis on the objectivity of the sacrament and the reality of what is offered there, it is faith in the promise that ultimately brings the benefits of baptism to the Christian: "Thus it is not baptism that justifies or benefits anyone, but it is faith in that

---

[9] *LW*, 54:98–99.
[10] *LW*, 36:62–63.
[11] *LW*, 31:105.
[12] E.g., *LW*, 40:233.

word of promise to which baptism is added. This faith justifies, and fulfils that which baptism signifies. For faith is the submersion of the old man and the emerging of the new."[13]

Baptism and the Christian Life

For Luther, baptism is crucial for the Christian life. As noted above, it is the entry into that life and therefore has continuing relevance for the Christian. In *The Babylonian Captivity*, Luther laments that so few call to mind their baptism or glory in it in any way. This has an immediate and catastrophic effect: because such people do not consider their baptism and all that it means, they start to look elsewhere for their security before God—religious vows, penance, works righteousness.[14] In other words, we might say that Luther regards the primary error of the medieval church as a mistaken understanding and use of baptism.

This also points back to the promise as constituting the substance of the sacrament. For Luther, the failure of the priests constantly to press the promise upon the people has led to a failure to use baptism as a means of personal comfort and assurance. In a beautiful passage, Luther declares:

> This message should have been impressed upon the people untiringly, and this promise should have been dinned into their ears without ceasing. Their baptism should have been called to their minds again and again, and their faith constantly awakened and nourished. For just as the truth of this divine promise, once pronounced over us, continues until death, so our faith in it ought never to cease, but to be nourished and strengthened until death by the continual remembrance of this promise made to us in baptism. Therefore, when we rise from our sins or repent, we are merely returning to the power and the faith of baptism from which we fell, and finding our way back to the promise then made to us, which we deserted when we sinned. For the truth of the promise once made remains steadfast, always ready to receive us back with open arms when we return.[15]

What is noteworthy in this, and often neglected, is the importance of memory. Luther sees the remembrance of God's great acts of grace in the

---

[13] *LW*, 36:66.
[14] *LW*, 36:57–58.
[15] *LW*, 36:59.

past as crucial to the Christian's knowledge of God in the present. Luther, however, is not a nostalgic pietist or mystic in the sense of looking back over his life and seeing God's grace in this or that provision or experience. Baptism is the single great act of grace in the Christian's life that provides secure knowledge of God's grace in the present. In *The Babylonian Captivity* he draws a comparison to the function of the exodus in the collective memory of the children of Israel. The exodus constantly brought to mind in later generations who God's people were and, more importantly, who God was in relation to them. The Christian's baptism is her personal exodus from Egypt and thus something to constantly bring to mind: baptism means I am a Christian and therefore the Devil cannot have me. Alongside the Mass, baptism is one of the great acts of God's deliverance of individual Christians.

No conversion experience, no particular act of providence, can provide the kind of assurance of who God is toward the Christian that these objective sacramental actions can. Luther even cites an anecdote of an unnamed virgin who used her baptism as her sole defense at every moment of temptation, to great effect.[16] This was, in fact, a strategy he himself pressed upon members of his flock who were struggling with *Anfechtungen* brought about by the activity of the Devil.[17] Sometimes, however, an empty and idolatrous reliance on baptism can have deadly consequence: Luther tells the story of one man who, confronted by the Devil, did this and was immediately slain by the Evil One.[18]

To the obvious objection that the one baptized as a baby cannot possibly have any recollection of her baptism, Luther has an almost dismissive response in *Concerning Rebaptism*:

> I might reply, "My friend, how do you know that this man is your father, this woman is your mother? You cannot trust people, you must be sure of your own birth." In this manner all children would forthwith be free from obedience to the commandment of God, "Thou shalt honor thy father and

---

[16] *LW*, 36:60.

[17] Cf. this anecdote from the *Table Talk* recorded by Veit Dietrich: "I asked him [Luther] about a certain man who, when he had a stomachache for several days and as a consequence had pain in his head and was confused in his thoughts, got the notion and was afraid that he was falling into a state of melancholy. He disclosed his anxiety to me and asked that I notify the doctor, whereupon he [Luther] responded with these words: 'When the devil can bring this about, it means that imagination has produced the effect. On this account his thoughts ought to be changed. He ought to think about Christ. You should say to him, "Christ lives. You have been baptized. God is not a God of sadness, death, etc., but the devil is. Christ is a God of joy, and so the Scriptures often say that we should rejoice, be glad, etc. This is Christ. Because you have a gracious God, he won't take you by the throat."'" *LW*, 54:95–96.

[18] *LW*, 54:280–81.

thy mother." For I could retort, "How do I know who is my father and mother? I can't believe people. So I will have to be born again by them in order to see for myself, else I will not obey them." By acting in this way God's command would indeed be made altogether null and void.[19]

In fact, were we to reject Luther's understanding of the objectivity of baptism and root its efficacy instead in the faith of the person at the moment of baptism, a similar pastoral problem would emerge: how does one know that one's memories of faith at the moment of baptism are accurate? And if we cannot be sure of that, how can we do justice to the powerful, real function that Paul ascribes to baptism in the New Testament? Indeed, is this problem not potentially all the more dangerous precisely because it builds everything upon our own subjectivity?[20] For Luther, the facts that God is the agent and baptism has an objective reality serve a powerful function in the Christian life: they are the basis of Christian assurance because its substance is the promise God has made to be gracious toward us in Christ, a promise to be grasped by faith. Thus, when the Devil comes to tempt you, Luther would advise you merely to remind him that you have been baptized.

Luther and the Mass

Luther's understanding of the Mass can be divided into three broad phases. First, there is his revision of medieval eucharistic theology, which takes place in the years 1519–1520. Then comes the stage in which he is in conflict with his former friend and colleague Andreas Bodenstein von Karlstadt, a conflict that defines the fundamental contours of the Wittenberg Reformation in 1522 and the years immediately following. Finally, there is the conflict with Zwingli, which culminates in the Marburg Colloquy of 1529 but continues to shape Lutheran identity down to the present day. Indeed, in the struggle for control of Lutheranism in the years immediately after his death in 1546, the issue of the Mass is central, as it is to the

---

[19] LW, 40:234.

[20] Luther actually makes this precise point in his debate with Anabaptists: "I would compare the man who lets himself be rebaptized with the man who broods and has scruples because perhaps he did not believe as a child. So when next day the devil comes, his heart is filled with scruples and he says, Ah, now for the first time I feel I have the right faith, yesterday I don't think I truly believed. So I need to be baptized a third time, the second baptism not being of any avail. You think the devil can't do such things? You had better get to know him better. He can do worse than that, dear friend. He can go on and cast doubt on the third, and the fourth and so on incessantly (as he indeed has in mind to do), just as he has done with me and many in the matter of confession." LW, 40:240.

Formula of Concord in 1577. This latter document made Luther's position confessionally normative.[21]

Before looking at Luther's thought in detail, we should remember the role of the Mass in Luther's own Christian life prior to his emergence as a Reformer. As a priest, and not simply a monk, he was responsible for sacramental duties in the parish. His first Mass, that moment when he pronounced the words of institution and, according to medieval theology, the bread and the wine turned into the body and blood of Christ, was a traumatic moment for him, not eased by the presence of his father, who did not approve at all of his son's religious vocation. Thus, the Mass played into Luther's pre-Reformation despair and fear: how could he, a sinful human being, make and handle God with his filthy, immoral hands? Whether evangelical Protestants like it or not, Luther's high medieval sacramentalism was one of the factors that pushed him toward his Reformation.

The Mass and the Promise

In 1519–1520, as Luther's mind was turning toward the wider implications of his developing theology, he wrote three significant works on the Mass. In 1519, he penned the first of these, *The Blessed Sacrament of the Holy and True Body of Christ and the Brotherhoods*.[22] Here Luther argues that the sacrament has three aspects: sign, significance, and faith.[23] The sign is the bread and wine, and in highlighting this, Luther takes the opportunity to argue that a general council should decree that the laity be given the sacrament in both kinds. Late medieval practice withheld the cup from the laity, ostensibly on the grounds that the whole Christ was contained in the bread anyway; withholding the cup therefore prevented any risk of a theologically disastrous spillage of Christ onto the floor. No doubt such withholding also enhanced the image of the authority of the priests.[24]

The significance of the sacrament lies in the fellowship that all the saints have through their union with Christ. This is thus not merely sym-

---

[21] Philipp Melanchthon had attempted to attenuate, or at least make more ambiguous, the Lutheran churches' position on the Mass in 1540 when he had altered article 10 of the Augsburg Confession to make it vaguer on the nature of Christ's presence and to accommodate the views of John Calvin. This version of the confession, the so-called *variata*, became a major cause of tension within the Lutheran communion and was regarded by Melanchthon's opponents as a betrayal of the fundamental teachings of Luther.

[22] *LW*, 35:45–73.

[23] *LW*, 35:49.

[24] *LW*, 35:50. For the same reason, Luther here expresses a preference for immersion of babies in baptism as a more satisfactory sign than pouring or sprinkling.

bolic but an actual, real thing.[25] Nevertheless, it is perhaps worth noting here that the emphasis on fellowship will become muted during the conflict with Karlstadt and then with Zwingli as the objectivity of Christ's presence comes to the fore in the polemical discussion. Here, Luther is concerned with the certainty of the sign: the reception of the elements is actually a means by which God assures the individual of his participation in Christ. Thus, there is a realism that mere symbolism could not capture.

> To receive this sacrament in bread and wine, then, is nothing else than to receive a sure sign of this fellowship and incorporation with Christ and all saints. It is as if a citizen were given a sign, a document, or some other token to assure him that he is a citizen of the city, a member of that particular community.[26]

The Mass is in a sense analogous to a birth certificate or a passport. Such things do not merely symbolize that one was born or is the citizen of a certain nation but actually have a legal status that both reflects reality and influences and shapes how the individual interacts with that reality. The Mass does the same for the Christian. It assures him of his status rather than being a mere outward reflection of that status. Indeed, in this text Luther presents the Mass as a cure for *Anfechtungen*. The person burdened with fear and despair and woes needs to flee to the sacrament of the altar where she will find freedom and joy for her soul: "The immeasurable grace and mercy of God are given us in this sacrament to the end that we might put from us all misery and tribulation [*Anfechtung*] and lay it upon the community [of saints], and especially on Christ."[27]

This is why the Mass is repeated, as opposed to the unique event of baptism. The Mass is food for the Christian, a means of being strengthened against the attacks of the world, the flesh, and indeed the Devil. This is why it should be taken frequently.[28] Luther even goes so far as to declare that it is of little use or benefit to those not suffering from *Anfechtungen*, as they have little or no idea of what the Mass is supposed to be helping against.[29]

---

[25] *LW*, 35:50–51.
[26] *LW*, 35:51.
[27] *LW*, 35:54.
[28] *LW*, 35:56.
[29] "For this reason it even happens that this holy sacrament is of little or no benefit to those who have no misfortune or anxiety, or who do not sense their adversity. For it is given only to those who need strength and comfort, who have timid hearts and terrified consciences, and who are assailed by sin, or have even fallen into sin. How could it do anything for untroubled and secure spirits, who neither need nor desire it?" *LW*, 35:55.

Underlying all this is the idea that in the Mass, God is doing something for humanity, not the other way around. As medieval liturgical practice had focused on the sacrificial aspects of the sacrament and its offering up to God, so Luther is turning the matter on its head and making the Mass something God does for the believer.

Luther starts to work out the implications of this in his *Treatise on the New Testament, That Is, the Holy Mass* (1520). Here he emphasizes that the foundation of the Mass is the Word, specifically the Word of God's promise. Dismissing all the pomp and ceremony that has grown up around the Mass, Luther declares:

> If we desire to observe mass properly and to understand it, then we must surrender everything that the eyes behold and that the senses suggest—be it vestments, bells, songs, ornaments, prayers, processions, elevations, prostrations, or whatever happens in the mass—until we first grasp and thoroughly ponder the words of Christ, by which he performed and instituted the mass and commanded us to perform it. For therein lies the whole mass, its nature, work, profit, and benefit. Without the words nothing is derived from the mass.[30]

Here we see how the Mass connects to Luther's wider theological concerns: it is first and foremost a linguistic event, constituted by the words of institution. Those words will, of course, become a major source of controversy as Luther deals first with Karlstadt and then with Zwingli. In 1520, however, Luther is not concerned with their metaphysical implications for the presence of Christ so much as with their connection to God's action in Christ and thus to his promise. The words give the elements their significance and, as they are grasped by faith, make the sacrament effective.[31] This effect is experiential, for in the sacrament Christ declares that he bequeaths forgiveness and life to his people. Thus, it serves to combat the temptations of the Devil and his minions, and to strengthen our faith and increase our love.[32]

The most significant exposition of the Mass in Luther's early Reformation career occurs in the 1520 treatise *The Babylonian Captivity of the*

---

[30] *LW*, 35:82.

[31] "The best and greatest part of all sacraments and of the mass is the words and promise of God, without which the sacraments are dead and are nothing at all, like a body without a soul, a cask without wine, a purse without money, a type without a fulfilment, a letter without the spirit, a sheath without a knife, and the like." *LW*, 35:91.

[32] *LW*, 35:85–86.

Church. That was the year in which Luther laid out his positive manifesto for the Reformation; *The Freedom of the Christian Man* set forth his new ethics, rooted in his emerging understanding of justification. *An Appeal to the German Nobility* redefined the relationship between church and state. *The Babylonian Captivity* was his sacramental manifesto. For Luther, the Christian life was saturated in sacraments, and thus it was vital to establish clear thinking in this area if the church was to thrive.

In this work, Luther reiterates and extends earlier criticisms. In true dramatic style, he presents the Mass as being in captivity in various ways. The first captivity is the withholding of the cup from the laity.[33] The second captivity is the insistence on transubstantiation. Luther regards this as an error, rather than a heresy, because it maintains the vital truth of Christ's real presence according to both natures in the elements. The problem he has with transubstantiation is, ironically, the very opposite that a modern evangelical Protestant would have: it is the absence of the substance of bread and wine (which he sees as exegetically indefensible and the result of the intrusion of Aristotelian metaphysics into theology) rather than the presence of Christ.[34] The third captivity, the most heinous of all, is that the Mass has been turned into a sacrifice, something Christians do for God, rather than received as something that God does for Christians.[35]

This last point is where Luther brings out the positive meaning of the sacrament. Again, he uses language of promise and testament, connecting the two by stating that the latter is a form of promise delivered upon the death of the testator.[36] Because of this, worthy reception of the sacrament consists simply of grasping the promise attached to the elements by faith.[37] Luther anchors this in what he sees as God's standard way of dealing with humanity since the fall of Adam: a series of promises culminating in the great promise embodied in Christ. Further, while the Old Testament promise to Moses was earthly, not spiritual but connected to possession of the land, even there the Day of Atonement and the sacrificial system pointed forward to the substance of the gospel promise in Christ.[38]

---

[33] *LW*, 36:27. Luther notes here that it is not sinful to take the Mass in one element; rather, those sin who forbid it to be taken in both elements.

[34] *LW*, 36:28–35. In fact, Luther's criticism of Aristotelianism at this point is misplaced. Aristotle would have regarded the idea of something having the substance of one thing and the unrelated accidents of another as being incoherent.

[35] *LW*, 36:35.

[36] *LW*, 36:38.

[37] *LW*, 36:38–39, 43–44.

[38] *LW*, 36:39–40.

The promise aspect of the Mass also leads Luther to demand a vernacular liturgy. He will not achieve such a liturgy until 1525–1526, as we noted earlier. But if the Mass is to be a comfort, it must have a comprehensible (and that means audible and vernacular) linguistic context. Nothing so speaks of the captivity of the Mass, of the way the people have been deprived of all its real benefits, as the fact the words of institution are mumbled by a priest in Latin (a tongue unknown to most laypeople) with his back turned to the congregation.[39] Bringing his linguistic theology to bear on the Mass, Luther declares that God has only ever worked the gospel through the word (literally) of promise.[40] Further, Luther berates the medieval theologian Peter Lombard, whose *Four Books of Sentences* was the standard university textbook in theology throughout the Middle Ages, for completely neglecting the central matter of the Mass, the promise, and diverting attention instead toward the metaphysics of Christ's presence and the working of the sacrament in an autonomous, mechanical manner isolated from faith.[41]

What is striking in Luther's treatment of the Mass in *The Babylonian Captivity* is the rich language of emotion that he uses to describe what should be the Christian's appropriate response to the Mass. Of course, the Christian must have some faith when he comes to the altar. The reception of the elements as Christ's testament is crucial. Further, the emphasis Luther places on *believing* Christ's words of institution is a note that will become louder with the rise and influence of the Zwinglian Reformation. Yet here in 1520, it is the emotional response, fueled by the Holy Spirit, that is so noteworthy:

> From this you will see that nothing else is needed for a worthy holding of mass than a faith that relies confidently on this promise, believes Christ to be true in these words of his, and does not doubt that these infinite blessings have been bestowed upon it. Hard on this faith there follows, of itself, a most sweet stirring of the heart, whereby the spirit of man is enlarged and enriched (that is love, given by the Holy Spirit through faith in Christ), so that he is drawn to Christ, that gracious and bounteous testator, and made a thoroughly new and different man. Who would not shed tears of gladness, indeed, almost faint for joy in Christ, if he believed with

---

[39] *LW*, 36:41–42.
[40] "For God does not deal, nor has he ever dealt, with man otherwise than through a word of promise, as I have said. We in turn cannot deal with God otherwise than through faith in the Word of his promise." *LW*, 36:42.
[41] *LW*, 36:44–45.

unshaken faith that this inestimable promise of Christ belonged to him? How could he help loving so great a benefactor, who of his own accord offers, promises, and grants such great riches and this eternal inheritance to one who is unworthy and deserving of something far different?[42]

From this statement we see just how important the Mass is for Luther's conception of the Christian life. It is not a memorial. It is not a moment in the liturgical service when the Christian simply has an opportunity to think back to Christ's death or look forward to Christ's second coming. It presents the Christian with the promise of Christ, exhibited in his broken body and shed blood, and as these are grasped by faith and in a sense made more real because of their immediate physicality, the Holy Spirit stirs up joy and love within the recipient. In short, the Mass has a profound importance for the Christian life because it makes Christ and his promise more real, more present, to the Christian.

In light of this, we can perhaps begin to understand Luther's viscerally negative reaction to the teaching of Zwingli and company: by taking Christ from the sacrament, they turned it into something ironically similar to the Mass: something the Christian does (remember Christ; express faith and solidarity with the church in a public fashion) rather than something Christ does for the Christian. To use Luther's own terminology, it becomes a matter of law, not gospel.

Luther and the Real Presence

If Luther's early Reformation writings on the Mass focused on its significance as a promise and a testament, his later works (from 1522 onward) were increasingly preoccupied with maintaining the real presence of Christ in the elements. This is perhaps the most troubling area for evangelical Protestants, given that most of them hold to a purely symbolic view of the Lord's Supper (akin to that of Luther's nemesis Zwingli), and also that Luther's notion of the Supper seems to stand, like Luther's view of baptism, in considerable tension with his understanding of justification by faith.

These developments in Luther's thinking on the Mass were fueled, as was so much in his theology, by his autobiography. If the Mass was of perennial significance to him in part because of the trauma of the very first

---

[42] LW, 36:40–41.

time he officiated, so his increasing focus on the real presence was driven by a number of personal factors.

First, we must remember how Luther's existential quest for the gracious God was solved. The answer to the question, where can I find a gracious God? is in Christ and in Christ alone. This principle shaped all aspects of his theology. For example, he rejected the book of James partly because it does not appear to teach justification by grace through faith and thus stands at odds with Paul. More importantly, however, it does not push (*treibt*) Christ. If Christ, the enfleshed, incarnate God, is not there, then it is not gospel but law.[43] Thus, a personal theological imperative lay behind his insistence on the presence of the whole Christ in the elements: if the flesh is not there, then this sacrament yields no comfort to anyone who receives it.

The second autobiographical factor shaping Luther's view of the real presence was his experience with Karlstadt. While Luther was in the Wartburg, Karlstadt, Zwilling, and Melanchthon led the Reformation in Wittenberg. Karlstadt and Zwilling were both radical in tendency, and their model of reformation was both iconoclastic and revolutionary in terms of its view of the role of the church in society. Hence Karlstadt's sporting of peasant clothing as a political gesture of identification with the poor and oppressed. Luther noted two particular aspects of the theology of Karlstadt reformation that disturbed him: a prioritizing of Spirit over Word, and an understanding of the Mass as symbolic. This combination fixed in Luther's mind the idea that the language of symbolism and spiritual presence, when applied to the Mass, signified an underlying theological and political radicalism. Thus, when Zwingli entered the stage, with his view of the elements as symbolic and his refusal to speak of presence in anything other than spiritual terms, Luther smelled a radical rat. Zwingli was merely the polite face of the kind of revolutionary chaos that had brought Luther back to Wittenberg in 1522 and had nearly led to the termination of the

---

[43] It is worth noting that, in his preface to James, Luther praises the book as an excellent exposition of the law of God. *LW*, 35:395. The christological problem he describes as follows: "He [i.e., James] names Christ several times; however he teaches nothing about him, but only speaks of general faith in God. Now it is the office of a true apostle to preach of the Passion and resurrection and office of Christ, and to lay the foundation for faith in him, as Christ himself says in John 15[:27], 'You shall bear witness to me.' All the genuine sacred books agree in this, that all of them preach and inculcate [*treiben*] Christ. And that is the true test by which to judge all books, when we see whether or not they inculcate Christ. For all the Scriptures show us Christ, Romans 3[:21–22]; and St. Paul will know nothing but Christ, I Corinthians 2[:2]. Whatever does not teach Christ is not yet apostolic, even though St. Peter or St. Paul does the teaching. Again, whatever preaches Christ would be apostolic, even if Judas, Annas, Pilate, and Herod were doing it." *LW*, 35:396.

Wittenberg Reformation. Luther labeled as *Schwärmerei* Karlstadt and other advocates of a symbolic Eucharist and a spiritual presence. The term meant "swarms" and conjured up the image of a plague of bees. These people were, in his view, dangerous and crazy.[44]

By the time Luther and Zwingli met in person at Marburg in 1529, the pamphlet war between the two had been going on for some years. Indeed, the language by which Luther described his position was beginning to stabilize. In the Small Catechism 6.1, the body and blood are described as being given "under the bread and wine." This is elaborated in the Augsburg Confession 10, where the body and blood are described as "really present . . . under the form of bread and wine." Later Lutheranism would describe the presence as being *in, with, and under* the bread and wine, presumably so as to close any linguistic loopholes the earlier language might have left.

The detailed arguments between the Lutherans and the Zwinglians on the nature of Christ's presence are beyond the scope of this book, but some basic principles of Luther's thinking on the matter can help us develop a sympathetic understanding of why he thought the way he did.

His primary concern was to do justice to the ways in which the Bible says that Christ is given to us. In one of the accounts of the debates at Marburg, these words are ascribed to Luther in response to Zwingli's claims that spiritual eating removes the need for physical eating:

> Christ gives himself to us in many ways: first, in preaching; second, in baptism; [third,] in brotherly consolation; fourth, in the sacrament, as often as the body of Christ is eaten, because he himself commands us to do so. If he should command me to eat dung, I would do it. The servant should not inquire about the will of his lord. We ought to close our eyes.[45]

Luther articulates two important principles here: first, the question of the Mass is part of the general question of how and where God now gives himself to us in Christ; second, the guiding principle of theological discussion is always to be what God has said, not what human reason deems possible or plausible. This is why Lutherans do not find compelling those arguments against the presence of Christ's humanity in, with, and under the

---

[44] Luther would often link Zwingli to Thomas Müntzer, the radical spiritualist theologian who died a violent death in the Peasants' War of 1525, and claim that both of them were deceived into their sacramental errors by the Devil himself (e.g., *LW*, 26:192).

[45] *LW*, 38:19.

bread and wine which are based on the local circumscription of a human body. That would be a rational premise that must give way before the Word of God.

Underlying this principle, of course, is the fundamental irrationality (from a human perspective) of the incarnation and of Christ's work, in keeping with Luther's notion of the theologian of the cross: the theologian of the cross takes God as he offers himself in his revelation; he does not force God to conform to a preconceived Procrustean bed of human rationality and expectations of what he must be like. As the terrifying God of law yet makes himself small and weak and vulnerable in the incarnation, so the Christian is to come to where Christ is, not with querulous demands but with a humble, believing acceptance. This is where the real presence connects to Luther's understanding of justification: faith is trusting God and taking him at his Word; when Christ says, "This is my body which is broken for you," the Christian believes that by faith and does not stand in judgment on what is declared. Indeed, near the start of Luther's 1526 work *The Sacrament of the Body and Blood of Christ—Against the Fanatics*, he declares that God "delights to do what is foolish and useless in the eyes of the world."[46]

One further point regarding Luther's mature eucharistic thought is that this presence of Christ is truly objective. In other words, Christ is really present under the bread and the wine in such a way that even the unbeliever who eats the elements does in fact truly receive the body and blood of Christ. She does it to her damnation, but she still receives it. Faith is still necessary for the sacrament to be of benefit; but the presence of Christ in the sacrament is not dependent on the faith of the recipient, much less that of the priest.[47]

The Mass as Pastoral Tool: The Lutheran Way of Death

The pastoral importance of the Mass is made clear in a most dramatic way in one of Luther's earliest and most popular Reformation writings, *A Sermon*

---

[46] *LW*, 36:336. Luther clearly points in a number of passages to the idea of the ubiquity of Christ's flesh, which has sometimes been seen as relativizing his presence in the Mass. Luther himself does not see it this way, insisting that, though Christ is indeed present everywhere, he is not present everywhere as attached to his Word of promise. That presence is only in the gospel as set forth in the Word preached and in the sacraments duly administered (*LW*, 36:342).

[47] This is a key difference between the Lutherans and the Calvinist position. Calvin had a rich doctrine of the Lord's Supper that rejected Zwinglian memorialism and emphasized a real feeding upon Christ; but that feeding takes place in the context of the believer's spiritual union with Christ and is thus not something the unbeliever enjoys.

on Preparing to Die.[48] The work went through twenty-two printings in three years, and then two more by 1525, making it a very popular little tract.

The popularity of the work speaks to a time very different from that in which we find ourselves. Death has, on the whole, been marginalized and sanitized in our society. With the exception of medical professionals, many people in the West under the age of forty have never seen a dead body. Churches are no longer built adjacent to graveyards. While this is no doubt the result of zoning regulation and pressure of space, it serves to reinforce the sense that death is something very distant from us. In Luther's day, this was not the case. Infant mortality rates were high, so almost all families would know what bereavement was like. Life expectancy was not great. That life was nasty, brutish, and short was not an insight unique to Hobbes. It would have been the typical experience of most people at the time.

Given this, it is perhaps not surprising that by the late Middle Ages, the *Ars Moriendi* (literally, the art of dying) genre of writing was a staple of European culture and would have been a necessary part of any pastor's arsenal. Death would have been a constant presence in the life of pastor and people alike, and the ability to address the issue would have been vital.

The immediate context for the tract was that a certain Mark Sehart—a friend of George Spalatin's, who was Frederick the Wise's secretary and his contact with Luther—was suffering from anxiety about death, that greatest and most unavoidable of all *Anfechtungen*. Spalatin wrote to Luther in May 1519, asking him for help. Of course, Luther was very busy at that point, preparing for his debate at Leipzig with his indefatigable opponent John Eck. As with the little book on prayer for Peter the Barber, Luther again showed what an admirable pastor he was, making time in his intense schedule to produce something to help a struggling brother.

While written during Luther's early Reformation career, before he had reached complete clarity on issues of authority and justification, and before he had responded to the challenges of Karlstadt and Zwingli, it is still a remarkable treatise. Further, given what we will see is its strong sacramental focus, we should remember that the fundamental concerns of Luther's mature theology of the Mass—that it is a promise and truly presents the Christian with the whole Christ under the forms of bread and wine—were already part of his thinking at this point.

For Luther, preparing for death has a number of parts. Ever the practical

---
[48] *LW*, 42:99–117.

pastor, he first advises that worldly affairs be set in order and forgiveness be extended toward any against whom we hold longstanding grievances.[49] Then we should look toward God. What is striking about the Godward aspect of this advice is that Luther uses the language of vision and sight to characterize it. We must "turn our eyes towards God."[50] We are warned that death looms large before us because it has etched its image upon our nature and we constantly gaze upon this, encouraged to do so largely by the Devil himself.[51] Luther believes we should constantly have before our eyes the images of death, sin, and hell, though not as the Devil would like—as sources of despair—but as a means of understanding the brevity of life and our need of grace.[52] Fear of death is also the result of the Devil's greatest trick: encouraging Christians to try to see into God's hidden plans and discern whether they are of the elect.[53]

In fact, there is but one thing for the Christian to gaze upon: Christ on the cross. This helps explain Luther's approval of crucifixes: the sight of Christ hanging on the cross is the lens through which the Christian is to understand death, to see how his sin has been taken away, and to perceive how the final enemy, death itself, has been decisively overcome in and through the incarnate Son of God.[54]

What is fascinating is what frames Luther's extended advice on the images that the Christian needs to hold in mind to face death in an appropriate manner: sacramental discussion. The sacraments, particularly the Mass, are of significance at the hour of death.[55] This offers great insight into how important the sacraments are to Luther and how closely attached they are to the Word. He stresses that the Lord's Supper is preeminent in this context: the one who fears death is to receive the Mass as the first and most powerful means of fixing his gaze upon God. This is not something superstitious, as if the mere consumption of the elements would suffice, but is connected to that which the Mass shows forth and which must be grasped by faith: Christ himself.[56] The Christian is thus to be much preoc-

---

[49] *LW*, 42:99.
[50] *LW*, 42:99.
[51] *LW*, 42:101.
[52] *LW*, 42:102.
[53] *LW*, 42:102–3.
[54] *LW*, 42:105–7.
[55] It should be noted that Luther included Holy Unction (the practice of anointing someone about to die) in this text as part of the sacramental approach to death. In *The Babylonian Captivity*, Luther rejects extreme unction as a sacrament but allows that, in accordance with New Testament teaching and practice, the anointing of the sick and dying is certainly not wrong and may be beneficial (*LW*, 36:121).
[56] *LW*, 42:100.

cupied with the efficacy of the sacraments as these will counterbalance and ultimately distract from an overestimation of the power of our spiritual enemies.[57]

After a long section elaborating on the wiles of the Devil and the power of Christ, Luther returns to speaking about the sacraments, describing them as things upon which the Christian must rely, given that they contain nothing but God's Word, promises, and signs.[58] Indeed, connected to the Word of God and spoken and administered by a priest, they are "a truly great comfort and at the same time a visible sign of divine intent."[59] Indeed, there is nothing better, nothing more suitable for strengthening faith, than the sacraments. While many look for spectacular signs that indicate God's favor toward them, Luther points out that the sacraments, connected to the Word, are precisely such signs. Not only are the spectacular and extraordinary weak in comparison; they are rendered entirely unnecessary.[60]

Again, in this context, Luther stresses the objectivity of the sacraments. The strategy of the Devil, he declares, is to sow doubts in the Christian's mind as to whether he has received them worthily or not, thus promoting introspection and fear.[61] Luther responds that human worthiness is not an issue, for God gives nothing to anyone on the grounds of their worthiness. The Christian is simply to accept what God offers in the sacraments—his promise in Christ.[62] As with the external Word, we might say that the sacraments come to the Christian from the outside, freeing him from the *Anfechtungen* that assail him and drawing him out to Christ, who is grasped through the sacramental signs by faith.

Concluding Reflections

Luther's high sacramentalism is likely the most alien and perhaps even most confusing area of his positive theological thought to modern evangelical Protestants. Their church world is not a sacramental world. That is indeed one of the great ironies, as I have already noted a number of times: Luther, the great Protestant hero, would probably not recognize most Protestants today as Christian. That is not in line with the spirit of our age, in

---

[57] *LW*, 42:100–101.
[58] *LW*, 42:109.
[59] *LW*, 42:108.
[60] *LW*, 42:111.
[61] *LW*, 42:110.
[62] *LW*, 42:110.

which a desire for evangelical unity often focuses on a handful of distinctives, such as scriptural authority, the exclusivity of the gospel, and justification by faith, while marginalizing or ignoring other areas of difference, such as baptism. That Luther would rupture Protestantism over the nature of Christ's presence in the Lord's Supper seems an act of perverse pedantry to the denizens of this present age.

In fact, however, Luther's stand is quite comprehensible within the context of his theology as a whole. In answer to that basic theological/existential question, where can I find a gracious God?, Luther directs us to the incarnate Christ, offered to us by God in Word and sacrament. Salvation comes from the outside. Salvation has objectivity. Luther was surely as preoccupied with his own religious experience as anyone; yet his theology was remarkably objective, and the answer to the crises of his experience was always an external one—Christ—grasped by faith.

Can non-Lutheran Protestants profit from Luther's high sacramentalism? I would argue strongly in the affirmative. First, Luther's sacramentalism actually points to his confidence in the power of the gospel. For him, confidence does not come from a religious experience; it comes from the fact that God has given himself to be gracious to sinful humanity in the flesh of Christ. Christ is God's great act of salvation and Luther roots his confidence in that act and nothing else. The sacraments, like the Word, are the means whereby the story of Christ penetrates the story of individual Christians. Thus, when tempted, Luther thinks of his baptism. When fearing death, Luther takes the bread and wine in the Mass. These are the moments when, to use popular parlance, the Christian's story is taken up in Christ's—and thus God's—story. That foundation of assurance in the action of God in Christ is something all Christians need to understand.

Second, while Luther is often decried as an individualist (particularly when understood through a Bultmannian lens), his sacramentalism points toward the fundamental importance of the church in his understanding of the Christian life. The externality of the sacraments, as of the Word, demands that the Christian be part of an institution where these things can come to him from the outside. Baptism is a corporate rite, as is the Mass. The great saving acts of God in Christ are personalized and individualized in a context where Christians are gathered together and where the priest ministers to them as a congregation. Protestantism started as a corporate, churchly movement, founded on churchly actions.

This points to a further implication of Luther's sacramentalism: the nature of the ministry. We saw in the last chapter that the ministry is a ministry of the Word, that God acts through the Word read and proclaimed in the church. To this we must now add that the ministry is also one of sacraments. As the minister preaches each week, so he also administers baptism and the Lord's Supper. It is important to understand that in all this, Luther regards God as the agent. The popular phrase of "doing church" is thus entirely inappropriate within a Lutheran framework: Christians do not "do" church in any ultimate or definitive way. God "does" church. The minister—preaching, baptizing, and officiating at communion—is merely an instrument by which God achieves what he intends.

This is surely an antidote to the evangelical church's perennial obsession with the big, the spectacular, the extraordinary, and the impressive. The quest for the next big thing that allows the church to ride the cultural wave, or the technical silver bullet that makes outreach and discipleship so much more effective, would be entirely alien to Luther's way of thinking. Preach the Word and administer the sacraments: that is the minister's calling; these are the tools of his trade and the means by which he is to address pastoral problems. That they seem weak and ineffective from a technical perspective is irrelevant: their power and effectiveness come from the agent, God himself.

If the definition of ministry is set by Word and sacrament, so is the substance of the Christian's life. Luther's emphasis on Word, baptism, and the Lord's Supper should surely point believers toward how they should understand their lives: the church service is fundamental to Christian discipleship. The answer to spiritual weariness, fear, and those dreaded *Anfechtungen* that afflict the Christian is found not in anything special or extraordinary as the world understands it. That is what the theologian of glory desires. Further, every theologian of glory probably thinks of himself as unique and thus as having special problems that require special solutions. The theologian of the cross, however, while acknowledging that every Christian is unique in that every Christian is a specific individual, also understands that the answer to every unique Christian's problem is actually very general, and the means are very ordinary. The answer is always Christ crucified for me, and that Christ is found in Word and sacrament.

CHAPTER 7

LUTHER AND CHRISTIAN RIGHTEOUSNESS

O God, the protector of all that trust in thee, without whom nothing is strong, nothing is holy; Increase and multiply upon us thy mercy; that thou being our ruler and guide, we may so pass through things temporal, that we finally lose not the things eternal.

BOOK OF COMMON PRAYER

One of the most vexed questions among those who seek to appropriate Luther's theology of the Christian life is the extent to which personal holiness matters. In more popular Christian parlance, does Luther's theology have a place for sanctification? This is a very important question because it touches on precisely what it means, in practical terms, to be a Christian. Should the Christian expect to grow in holiness, and to what extent (if any) should she be able to discern such growth? What constitutes growth in holiness? And how does the law of God play into this? Does it fulfill a purely negative role, reminding us of our unrighteousness before God? Or does it have more positive things to say about the ethical behavior of the Christian? These are not abstract issues but rather points of concern for every Christian.

The temptation in addressing these matters is to turn immediately to the works of Luther and to mine them for any statements that might touch on the issue. That has often been the approach to great theologians of the past. In this present age, when such vacuous phenomena as Twitter have persuaded vast tracts of the human race that no idea is so profound as to require more than 140 characters, such a method may have even more appeal than in times past.

In this chapter, however, I am going to argue that this kind of proof texting is to be eschewed on an issue such as this. Luther's position is nuanced, complicated, and deeply embedded in his life and times. Thus, we must first address the context before we will be in any position to assess his thinking.

The Reformation: A Work in Progress

One of the most striking things about the popular evangelical reception of Luther today is its rather truncated view of his life and works. One might almost say that if Luther had perished of an aneurysm on his wedding night in 1525, not only would he have perished happy, but the way in which his theology is typically understood would be entirely unaffected. The key texts for the popular evangelical understanding of Luther were all in place by then: *The Ninety-Five Theses*, *The Heidelberg Disputation*, *The Freedom of the Christian Man*, and *The Bondage of the Will*. One or two great texts were yet to be written (the great commentary on Galatians being the obvious example), but on the whole these four titles cover the working canon through which most Protestant evangelicals approach Luther. They also contain most of the exciting sound bites and Tweetable phrases with which we are familiar: "theologians of glory and of the cross," "the whole of life as repentance," "the hidden God and the revealed God," and so forth. In addition, the 1525 date is also helpful because it avoids our having to address the writings in the Zwingli controversy, which, with their high sacramentalism and their blistering rejection of symbolic views of the Eucharist, are simply embarrassing, extreme, and incomprehensible from the perspective of an incredulous evangelicalism.

Yet there is an obvious problem: Luther lived on until 1546; and he also continued to write, teach, and preach as if words were in danger of going out of style. By 1525, he had lived just eight years as a Reformer and had only just arrived at the point where he was introducing vernacular liturgy to Wittenberg. He had another twenty-one years of active theological life before him.

This leads to a second point that is rarely noted: Luther's Reformation theology was a work in progress. When he started moving toward reformation, he changed the nature of the pastoral task and the tools of the pastoral trade. As he did so, his new theology itself generated new questions—pastoral, theological, and social. These new questions caused him to refine, revise, and in some places rethink his theology. To imagine this process somehow stopping or dramatically slowing down in 1525 would be both an arbitrary judgment and inherently implausible.

Thus, we need to bear in mind that Luther's declaration of Christian freedom in 1520 was a dramatic break with, indeed an inversion of, previous Christian thinking and also, therefore, would have generated unforeseen consequences for those who received the new teaching. Some of these consequences would most likely have required Luther to reflect upon his 1520 statements at some point and possibly to nuance or change them where necessary. Of course, we may find that he did not do so; but we cannot simply assume that 1520 remains normative in either expression or content for Luther over the next twenty-six years.

Knowing the Times

Another part of reading Luther correctly is knowing how he himself understood the times in which he was living. We noted in chapter 1 that Luther experienced a violent and extreme change of mind on the matter of the Jews. In 1523, he argued that they should be treated well by Christian neighbors, to open opportunities for the gospel. In 1543, however, he argued that they should be subject to persecution and, where possible, genocide. The change in mind is significant, not simply for exemplifying the bitter anger of a man reaching the end of his life but also for illustrating his transformed understanding of the times.

The change actually reflects in part Luther's eschatological frustration. He was heir of the late medieval view that the world was coming to an end and that Christ would soon return. In the early years of the Reformation, the spectacular and unlikely successes of the Reformation seemed to indicate that this was indeed happening. When Luther began to be identified with figures in the book of Revelation after the Diet of Worms, the eschatological expectation took on a heightened and concrete form. Yet by the late 1520s, matters were taking a darker turn: the conflict with the radicals and then with Zwingli had fragmented the Reformation movement. Squabbling and petty rivalries among the Lutherans were weakening the cause. The nobles had shown themselves to be more interested in secular power than in true reform. All of this implied that perhaps the end was not as near as expected and that the Reformation might not be setting the stage for the imminent return of Christ.

How does this impinge upon the question before us? It is significant because there is a world of difference between how one preaches when convinced that God is moving with eschatological decisiveness and is bringing history to its close and how one preaches when bracing for the long haul. In 1522, Luther was able to boast from the pulpit that the Reformation succeeded because he, Melanchthon, and Amsdorf sat in the pub drinking beer while the Word of God did all the work. That is the kind of bravura statement a man can make who is supremely confident that history is flowing precisely his way. But by 1527–1528, the picture looked somewhat different. By then, it was becoming clear to Luther that the preaching of the Word was not in itself enough to achieve all the things he wished to see done. There was need for nuance, organization, and a clarification and even recalibration of certain doctrines and emphases.

In summary, we can now see the problem with the "evangelical Luther canon." The texts were all written at a time when Luther was very confident of the Reformation outcome and very confident that the simple preaching of the Word could do it all. Given his altered understanding of the times after 1525, we cannot automatically assume that statements before that date are normative or that they proved unproblematic even within Luther's own lifetime.

The Motive for Good Works in the Early Reformation Luther

Luther's basic position on righteousness is set forth in his 1519 sermon "Two Kinds of Righteousness." There he distinguishes between alien and proper righteousness. *Alien righteousness* is that which the Christian obtains when he receives Christ by faith. This is an infinite righteousness that swallows up all sins and renders the believer perfect before God.[1] There is progression in this righteousness, but it is progression gauged by growth in faith and knowledge of Christ, and thus should not be confused with growth in what we might term actual righteousness.[2] *Proper righteousness* involves the

---

[1] *LW*, 31:298–99.
[2] *LW*, 31:299.

slaying of the flesh and the crucifying of wicked desires, coupled with the performance of good works for our neighbors.[3] This is akin to what we might typically call the work of sanctification, and it has an outward manifestation.

The crucial matter is the relationship between these two kinds of righteousness. Luther is very clear that such a relationship does exist. The alien and the proper are not unconnected and independent. But the alien righteousness has the logical priority: proper righteousness builds directly upon the relationship with Christ that is constituted by the believer's possessing Christ and thus his alien righteousness. Indeed, Luther says that proper righteousness is the result of the Christian's working with his alien righteousness and, indeed, is the fruit and consequence of alien righteousness.[4] He describes it as follows:

> This [proper] righteousness goes on to complete the first [i.e., alien righteousness] for it ever strives to do away with the old Adam and to destroy the body of sin. Therefore it hates itself and loves its neighbor; it does not seek its own good, but that of another, and in this its whole way of living consists. For in that it hates itself and does not seek its own, it crucifies the flesh. Because it seeks the good of another, it works love. Thus in each sphere it does God's will, living soberly with self, justly with neighbor, devoutly toward God.[5]

The motive for this righteousness is rooted in christology. Luther sets forth Christ as the great example to follow, but does not do so in a short-circuited manner such as "Christ helped the poor; go out and help the poor!" Rather, he takes his cue from Philippians 2: "Let this mind be in you." Thus, he sees the motivation of Christ as shaping the ethics of his practical conduct. Christ humbled himself in the incarnation, and thus all Christians who understand what it is to be clothed in alien righteousness will, or at least should, start to act as servants toward their neighbors.[6] We might say that Luther regards proper righteousness as the natural outgrowth of the cognitive realization of the significance of being justified by the alien righteousness we receive in Christ. Love is both the motive for works and that which shapes them.[7]

---

[3] *LW*, 31:299–300.
[4] *LW*, 31:299, 300.
[5] *LW*, 31:300.
[6] *LW*, 31:302–3.
[7] Cf. Luther's teaching on works in *The Freedom of the Christian Man*, in *LW*, 31:371.

We should, however, note two potential problems. The first is the assumption that alien righteousness will cause proper righteousness. One might infer that simply preaching alien righteousness will be enough to effect the practical consequences Luther sees as desirable in a Christian. The second is the ethic of servanthood, which Luther also characterizes as an ethic of love. This sounds most admirable, but we must remember that love and servanthood are themselves concepts that need to be filled out with more precise ethical content. The Mafia boss who wants an opponent killed may well ask one of his underbosses to do it for him. That underboss may well oblige. But such would not be an act of servanthood and love. The serial killer who thinks slaying victims is a way of serving them by releasing them from their bodily cages is not acting in a loving manner. Further, in our day when the word *love* has been evacuated of any meaning beyond cheap sentimentality or a disposition that allows people to do anything they want, the weakness of a love-based ethic, taken in isolation, should be evident.

In short, we might ask: What does love look like? What does servanthood look like? And how are these to be cultivated among Christians? These questions were to be raised in an acute form for Luther in 1527.

The Parish Visitation

By 1526, the Lutheran Reformation had entered its consolidation phase. Theological lines were being clearly drawn between the evangelical churches and the Roman Catholics.[8] The nobles had seized much church property—monasteries, chantries, and more—and had thus shattered much of the financial base of Rome's power in Saxony. Further, the preaching of the gospel, as outlined above, had been going on for some years. It was at this point that Luther felt it time to take stock of developments.

Those who are really only interested in Luther's ideas might easily forget that the problems the Reformers faced were often strikingly material. It was one thing to proclaim that a territory had moved into the evangelical camp, but quite another to make sure that every pulpit within the area had a priest competent to preach evangelical doctrine. Training preachers took time, time that the Reformation did not allow as it spread rapidly across

---

[8] I am using the term "evangelical" here to mean "Lutheran Protestant," and not to make a simple equation between the Lutherans and later evangelicalism.

the land. Thus, from late 1525 onward, Luther was urging Elector John of Saxony to allow for a visitation of the parishes. He was concerned, among other things, that the nobility had used money from the seizure of church property to make themselves richer and not to build schools and other institutions for the common good. He also wanted to see how the Reformation was helping ordinary people at parish level.

Initially, the impact was negligible, and so in November 1526 Luther complained to Elector John about the greediness of the nobles in keeping Reformation revenues to themselves. As a result, in February 1527 the elector established the parish visitation. Each visitation team consisted of four members, two to look at economic and social conditions in each parish and two to address theological and spiritual matters. The visitation lacked direction and coherence, however, and so gradually Luther, Melanchthon, and a number of others began to formulate basic guidelines for the visitors, which in late 1527 Melanchthon made into a formal document, the *Visitation Articles*. This document triggered a controversy between the gentle Greek scholar and Johannes Agricola of Eisleben. The point at issue was the role of the law. Agricola thought that Melanchthon conceded too much to the papists on certain issues.

The result of the visitation controversy was interesting: the elector requested that Luther provide a preface to the articles in early 1528, which he did. Thus, although the articles were formally the work of Melanchthon, they had Luther's clear imprimatur, and inasmuch as he himself revised them over coming years, they are typically included in his works as representing his own convictions relative to the visitation.

The visitation was most significant in that it provided Luther with detailed information about what parish life was like under Lutheran preaching, allowing him to assess how evangelical emphases were being worked out in the everyday lives of Christian men and women. The results neither impressed nor encouraged him. This precipitated his production of his two catechisms. Perhaps most significantly, the argument between Melanchthon and Agricola foreshadowed in its principles the conflict that was to break out between them in 1537. Hints of what was to be the substance of the later conflict appear in the opening section of the *Visitation Articles*:

> Many now talk only about the forgiveness of sins and say little or nothing about repentance. There neither is forgiveness of sins without repentance nor can forgiveness of sins be understood without repentance. It follows

that if we preach the forgiveness of sins without repentance that the people imagine that they have already obtained the forgiveness of sins, becoming thereby secure and without compunction of conscience. This would be a greater error and sin than all the errors hitherto prevailing. Surely we need to be concerned lest, as Christ says in Matt. 12[:45] the last state becomes worse than the first.[9]

This is a most significant statement because it highlights a vital balance in Luther's teaching: for all his emphasis on the decisive and all-sufficiency of God in Christ, Luther did not wish to see a unilateral emphasis on that grace which would then result in swallowing up the power of the law, eclipsing the holiness of God and effectively underplaying the perilous state in which fallen men and women existed. This was the issue that would explode again in the later 1530s, as we will see below. In the meantime, we should note how Luther addressed the matter in 1528: through the production of his catechisms.

The Catechisms

The opening paragraphs of Luther's preface to the Small Catechism capture beautifully the indignation and horror Luther felt at what he had witnessed in the parishes:

Grace, mercy, and peace in Jesus Christ, our Lord, from Martin Luther to all faithful, godly pastors and preachers.

The deplorable conditions which I recently encountered when I was a visitor constrained me to prepare this brief and simple catechism or statement of Christian teaching.

Good God, what wretchedness I beheld! The common people, especially those who live in the country, have no knowledge whatever of Christian teaching, and unfortunately many pastors are quite incompetent and unfitted for teaching.

Although the people are supposed to be Christian, are baptized, and receive the holy sacrament, they do not know the Lord's Prayer, the Creed, or the Ten Commandments, they live as if they were pigs and irrational beasts, and now that the Gospel has been restored they have mastered the fine art of abusing liberty.[10]

---

[9] LW, 40:274.
[10] BC, 338.

The phrase "they live as if they were pigs" is eloquent. The problem in the parishes is both pedagogical and moral: the people do not know what they should know; and they live like swine. From what we have seen so far in this book, the two are, of course, related: a failure to understand God as he has given himself in Christ to us in his objective Word and sacrament must inevitably mean that the Christian life is built on sand. What is also obvious is that the mere preaching of the gospel is not enough to achieve what Luther wishes to see: a true, godly reformation of parish life. Luther needs to think much more carefully about how to achieve this. No longer can he simply sit in the pub and drink beer while God's Word does it all.[11]

If we then turn to the content of the Small Catechism, we note the typical Lutheran order—the Decalogue comes before the Apostles' Creed, and thus the law comes before the gospel. What is interesting, however, is the practical detail that the catechism offers. Indeed, in the preface, Luther instructs preachers to focus in particular on those sins to which their congregations might be most prone. Thus, a focus on stealing is good among peasants and laborers, as something to which they are most likely to be tempted, and on obedience to parents when there are many children present.[12]

Also of interest is that the responses to questions about the Decalogue are rooted in the notion of love to God. We noted above that love to God and neighbor is the formal basis of the proper righteousness that flows from possession of alien righteousness by faith, but we also observed that this love in itself is a somewhat empty category. The Bible's teaching on love always has a specific content: God loves Israel by bringing her out of Egypt. He loves the church by sending his Son to die for her.

Christian love is not reducible to an aesthetic or a sentiment but requires content. That is provided in the Decalogue section of the Small Catechism. For example, on the eighth commandment, the Small Catechism says:

> *"You shall not bear false witness against your neighbor."*
> What does this mean?

---

[11] Of course, this comment from 1522 was itself a hyperbole; Luther was always doing more than simply sitting around. But by 1527–1528, it was obvious that far more intentional organization and planning were required since preaching in itself would not do everything.

[12] *BC*, 340.

Answer: We should fear and love God, and so we should not tell lies about our neighbor, nor betray, slander, or defame him, but should apologize for him, speak well of him, and interpret charitably all that he does. [13]

One way to interpret this, and Luther's prefatory comments, is simply in terms of the standard law-gospel dialectic: for the preacher to make an impact, he needs to be very specific in his applications of the law. Yet, it is hard not to read the comment about living like pigs as implying Luther's extreme distress at the failure of those who hear the gospel to live as Christians. In this context, the exposition of the law seems to have implications beyond the ideas of exposing imperfection and driving sinners to despair as preparation for turning to Christ.

We see this in the catechism's exposition of the second petition of the Lord's Prayer:

"Thy kingdom come."
What does this mean?

Answer: To be sure, the kingdom of God comes of itself, without our prayer, but we pray in this petition that it may also come to us.

How is this done?

Answer: When the heavenly Father gives us his Holy Spirit so that by his grace we may believe his holy Word and live a godly life, both here in time and hereafter forever. [14]

Here the Holy Spirit is given so that the believer might live a godly life. There is no reason why this concept of a holy life should be reduced to an increasing sense of dependence upon alien righteousness to the exclusion of any other category of activity.

What is true of the Small Catechism is even more true of the Large Catechism. In this work, Luther's exposition of the Decalogue goes far beyond highlighting the requirements of each commandment; it also points to the need for certain patterns of behavior to be taught and cultivated. Thus, Christian parents are to teach their children to show respect, defer-

---

[13] *BC*, 343; remember, of course, that the numbering of commandments in the Decalogue is counted differently in Lutheranism.
[14] *BC*, 346.

ence, and care for their parents. They are to instruct them on how to honor them with their property and their money, as well as in appropriate forms of address.[15] Even more explicit are Luther's instructions with regard to the seventh commandment: the people are to be taught the commandment so that they might be restrained from committing acts of fraud and theft. Thus, the purpose of expounding the law is not simply to terrify consciences; it is also to shape the social mores of Christians. The teaching of the catechisms clearly implies that a way of life is to be taught and fostered ("this is what love looks like in action"), and not simply a theological principle ("God is holy; you as a sinner can never measure up"). This message is of a piece with what Luther taught earlier, in his first series of lectures on Galatians in 1519:

> The Commandments are necessary, not in order that we may be justified by doing the works they enjoin, but in order that as persons who are already righteous we may know how our spirit should crucify the flesh and direct us in the affairs of this life, lest the flesh become haughty, break its bridle, and shake off its rider, the spirit of faith. One must have a bridle for the horse, not for the rider.[16]

Here the commandments of God fulfill a positive function. They do not create justifying righteousness, but they do provide a guide to how the Christian is to keep his flesh under control and thus shape his outward life. We might characterize Luther as saying here, as in the catechisms later, that for the Christian united to Christ by faith and motivated by love to God and neighbor, the law provides the idiom (refracted through the lens of love) by which the practical Christian life is to be expressed.

What is clear from the *Visitation Articles* is that there were serious weaknesses in the effects of Reformation preaching stemming from imbalances in the way Luther's teachings were being received and transmitted by parish priests. The tendency noted in the articles to preach gospel without law and to try to cultivate faith without repentance had led to behavior that could in no way be considered Christian. Jesus plus nothing was proving to be problematic, and Luther and his colleagues understood that and wished to address it. The law needed to be given its place as that which drives one to repentance. In a subtle way it also needed to be given a role in shaping exactly what the Christian response of love to God and neighbor should

---

[15] *BC*, 379–81.
[16] *LW*, 27:232.

look like. As the return of Jesus seemed to slip further away, the need for a more careful and precise moral pedagogy became more obvious.

The Antinomian Controversy

The Antinomian Controversy of the late 1530s was the largest major theological conflict within the bounds of Lutheranism during Luther's lifetime. The details are somewhat complex, and only a brief outline of events can be offered here. The theological significance of the controversy, however, should not be underestimated, because it offers insights into how Luther's teaching was received and developed by certain of his followers, and how he himself regarded these developments.[17]

The key antagonist in the conflict was Johannes Agricola, the man who had clashed with Melanchthon over the visitation of 1527. In early 1537, Agricola supplied Luther's pulpit while the latter was away on business. During that time, some of Agricola's distinctive views started to emerge, particularly the notion that God's wrath was revealed not through the law but through the gospel. One can perhaps see how this might be regarded as a radical application of the theology of the cross, and certainly the cross does reveal God's wrath. But to reduce the revelation of God's wrath to the cross does not do justice to scriptural teaching; and to say that the gospel, not the law, reveals God's wrath raises obvious questions about the status and necessity of the law itself. As the conflict developed, it became clear that this peculiarity of Agricola's teaching was structurally and theologically of crucial importance: the law simply played no practical role in Christian teaching. Agricola's concern was perhaps admirable—to avoid anything that smacked of works righteousness or legalism—but the results were disastrous.

Luther's major response came in the relatively brief treatise *Against the Antinomians* (1539). The work opens with a disparaging reference to those who seek to exclude the Decalogue from the church and confine it to, we might say, city hall—that is, the secular sphere.[18] He then underlines how much time he has spent expounding and applying the Ten Commandments in print.[19] Of course, Luther is too good a theologian to argue that one cannot preach God's wrath by focusing on the cross, and he cites his own prac-

[17] For the narrative of the controversy, see Martin Brecht, *Martin Luther: The Preservation of the Church 1532–1546* (Minneapolis: Fortress, 1999), 156–71.
[18] LW, 47:107.
[19] LW, 47:109.

tice in this regard, with Bernard of Clairvaux as his precedent.[20] Yet he still insists that the law is the basic way to rouse sinners to repentance and that this was the apostle Paul's approach, set forth in Romans, which is to be paradigmatic for modern preachers.[21] Indeed, Luther rejects outright the new approach of preaching grace before wrath.[22]

What the antinomians have forgotten, and what it is crucial for us to remember at this point, is the basic Lutheran principle that all human beings are both righteous and sinners. Specifically, we need to remember that Luther does not view the Christian life through the kind of conversionist lens that later evangelical Christians would regard as basic to their understanding. Law preaching does not precipitate a once-in-a-lifetime crisis experience that helps to translate a person from wrath to grace and thereby negates the need for any further reference to the law. Rather, the Christian is an ongoing battlefield with a mind that seesaws between the blandishments of works righteousness and the gift of God in Christ. Given that this war will rage until death puts an end to it, the law remains of perennial significance.

We can also connect this to Luther's observation of 1528 that the people live like pigs. The law is there to crush self-righteousness; but it is also clear that Luther sees it as providing the content of what love in action toward God and neighbor looks like.

As a final postscript to this, it is worth noting Luther's comments on the marks of the church in his 1539 treatise *On the Councils of the Church*:

> For Christian holiness, or the holiness common to Christendom, is found where the Holy Spirit gives people faith in Christ and thus sanctifies them, Acts 15[:8–9], that is, he renews heart, soul, body, work, and conduct, inscribing the commandments of God not on tables of stone, but in hearts of flesh, II Corinthians 3[:3].[23]

He goes on to excoriate those who seem to teach that grace is everything, presumably having in mind Agricola and his acolytes:

> For they, having rejected and being unable to understand the Ten Commandments, preach much about the grace of Christ, yet they strengthen

[20] *LW*, 47:110.
[21] *LW*, 47:111, 114.
[22] *LW*, 47:114.
[23] *LW*, 41:145.

and comfort only those who remain in their sins, telling them not to fear and be terrified by sins, since they are all removed by Christ. They see and yet they let the people go on in their public sins, without any renewal or reformation of their lives. Thus it becomes quite evident that they truly fail to understand the faith and Christ, and thereby abrogate both when they preach about it. How can he speak lightly about the works of the Holy Spirit in the first table—about comfort, grace, forgiveness of sins—who does not heed or practice the works of the Holy Spirit in the second table, which he can understand and experience, while he has never attempted or experienced those of the first table?[24]

The first few lines are devastating for any who argue that all you need is grace in the Christian life. Luther could not make it clearer that an imbalanced emphasis on grace and on "Jesus only" leads to false assurance and immoral license. Clearly Luther, at least by the late 1530s, regards a transformation of behavior as a sign that the gospel is truly preached. This brings us back, of course, to the question of what such behavior should look like, to which his catechisms have already provided the answer: it looks rather like the Decalogue, motivated by and interpreted through the lens of love.

Typically, Melanchthon is the one credited with developing the so-called third use of the law, its use as a guide for the practical daily life of the Christian. In fact, I would argue that the basic concept, if not the actual terminology, is there in Martin Luther (especially after 1525). How do I love my neighbor? By not murdering him, by not stealing from him, by not fornicating with his wife, by not coveting what is his. Should I do these as a Christian? Yes. Will I do these as a Christian? The paragraph quoted above seems to leave little room for doubt on that score. Thus, we need to press beyond Luther's rhetoric on the law to what he thought of as being the practical content of love. It is true that Luther himself generally eschewed positive language about the law in the context of salvation, making it very clear that law fulfilled the functions only of guiding civic morality and driving individuals to despair in themselves. But when one moves behind what he says and looks to what he actually envisages as the content of love, it looks like the ethical principles of the Decalogue.[25]

---

[24] LW, 41:147.
[25] Luther gives a clear and dramatic statement of the limits of the law's purpose while commenting on Gal. 3:19 in the second series of Galatians lectures (LW, 26:315–16).

Concluding Reflections

I have included this chapter for the simple reason that Luther's status as the fountainhead of that most important of all Protestant doctrines, justification by grace through faith, means that he has—and will continue to have—an important role in discussions of this and closely related doctrines in the contemporary evangelical church. While we Protestants are Bible people and like to anchor all arguments in the text of Scripture, we also know that invoking the name of a past hero does carry significant rhetorical weight. And rightly so: we stand as debtors to those who have gone before; and when it comes to men of the stature of Luther, we do well to think long and hard before we dismiss their views on any given matter.

In the current climate, the unilateral emphasis on grace in some quarters carries huge weight. The all-sufficiency of Christ, the nature of justification as being by faith, and the freedom that such brings are all matters dear to the heart of good evangelical Protestants. And Luther certainly lends himself to appeal in support of this, given his own insights on the issues.

Yet we must remember the points I made at the start of this chapter: Luther's theology was itself a work in progress and developed over time as the pastoral results of Lutheran preaching required changes in emphasis and nuance. Further, the eschatological disappointments of the post-1525 Reformation gave Luther a much more sober view of how his vision of the Christian life could be implemented and how much more intentional and clear Protestant pedagogy needed to be.

The later Luther is acutely aware that the nature of the reception of grace teaching is closely connected to the outlook of those receiving it. To the one who has been told that he is under the damning wrath of God because of his failure to fulfill God's law, grace comes as a serious thing, with serious consequences. He receives it with joy and gladness and revels in his subsequent freedom, a freedom shaped at a deep level by his understanding of God's holiness. To the one who has *not* been told that he is first of all damned in God's sight because God is holy and he is filthy, grace breeds presumption and a lack of concern for a truly Christian response.

It should be redundant to say this, but I will say it anyway: we live in an age where the fear of a holy and righteous God is not something that one finds in the wider world. Western culture, particularly affluent Western culture, is self-absorbed and overindulged. To preach grace before or even without law and wrath to such a generation will have the obvious outcome: complacency, antinomianism, and, to quote Luther, living like pigs. Luther's doctrine of justification depends upon two things: the constant preaching of the wrath of God in the face of sin; and the realization that every Christian is at once righteous and a sinner, thus needing the hammer of the law to terrify and break the sinful conscience.

This also takes us back to the point I made in chapter 2: Luther spoke of theologians of the cross, not of the theology of the cross. The latter can be an intellectual system or lens through which we simply make the necessary inversions of meaning and expectation with words like *strength* and *weakness*. The former, however, demands the existential engagement of the individual, and that at the deepest level possible. The theologian of the cross simply cannot talk glibly, with an easygoing smile and a cocksure wink, about the theology of the cross. Indeed, to do so would be a sure sign that one is actually dealing with a theologian of glory. There was, after all, a crucial difference in Luther's mind between preaching the cross and preaching about the cross. Anybody can do the latter; only the theologian of the cross can do the former.

Finally, we should note that Luther himself felt the need to refine and elaborate his talk of love as the motive and content of good works. Had Christ returned before 1525, maybe that would have been adequate as an ethic. By 1527–1528, however, it was becoming clear that something with a little more clarity and precision was needed. The catechisms indicate that this basic content was provided by the moral substance of the Decalogue.

Again, this is important today. Love has become almost the only transcendent moral imperative in our society. It is used to justify abortion, euthanasia, same-sex marriage, and adultery. This list in itself should indicate that it has become a virtually contentless term and, like its opposite, hate, can be used to justify anything and silence all objections. The result is that Christians who wish to develop a Christian ethic need more than the word *love* at their disposal. Love needs content if it is to be anything more than empty sentiment or an aesthetic. Again, a study of Luther's personal development, rather than the isolated cherry-picking of selected texts, can be very helpful. As Luther reminds us, the Bible shows that love has a specific form, that it involves the cultivation and encouragement of some patterns of behavior and the rejection of others, and that the need for this transformation of behavior is an important part of Christian preaching, teaching, and discipleship.

CHAPTER 8

LIFE AND DEATH IN THIS EARTHLY REALM

GOVERNMENT, CALLING, AND FAMILY

An excellent wife who can find?
She is far more precious than jewels.

PROVERBS 31:10

One of the most pressing questions for Christians of any age and any society concerns civic behavior. The Christian belongs to the church, but the church is typically not coterminous with society as a whole. This then raises the question of how the Christian should relate to the world outside the church. If Christ is King but there are also earthly kings and rulers, how should the Christian connect the two? Christ himself spoke of rendering unto Caesar what belonged to Caesar (Matt. 22:21), and Paul called for obedience toward the civil magistrate (Rom. 13:1–7). And yet these too raise questions: What exactly is the property of Caesar? And what should one do as a Christian if the civil magistrate is, say, Adolf Hitler, and is commanding that one slay the innocent?

The end of church and state as coterminous entities is itself the result of the theological and social revolution of which Luther was such a major part in the sixteenth century. In medieval Europe, everyone was baptized as an infant into the one church, and therefore a material identity connected the realm of the church and the realm of the state. Jews, of course, were not baptized; that is one of the major reasons why they were persecuted, for that meant that they were basically unassimilable, given the structure of society at the time.

Protestant theology shattered the model of medieval Christendom. It did so, first, by creating confessional communities that were alternatives to what Rome offered. Thus, in the sixteenth century, the confessional state was born where, under the terms of the Peace of Augsburg (1555), a territory's confessional identity was determined by the religion of its prince. Even fifty years before this, such a settlement would have been inconceivable. In the world in which Luther grew up, the idea that church would not be one, but many, would have been unimaginable.

The tension that Luther's theology created for understanding the nature of society, and of the church's place in society, surfaced early in Luther's reforming career. If 1520 was the year in which Luther laid out his ethical manifesto (*The Freedom of the Christian Man*) and his sacramental manifesto (*The Babylonian Captivity of the Church*), it was also the year in which he set forth a proposal concerning the future relationship of church and state. Indeed, his *Appeal to the German Nobility* was a strategic treatise of great importance. Faced not simply with the church's refusal to implement Luther's suggested reforms but also with its efforts to silence him, the Reformer turned to the only other people with the power to bring about reformation: the nobility. And in so doing, he started to draw out the implications of his understanding of salvation for the nature of Christian life in the civic sphere. The world was about to change in unforeseen and, in retrospect, uncontrollable ways.

Redefining Spiritual and Temporal

In 1520, captivity was much on Luther's mind, as the very title of his sacramental manifesto indicates. The image of shackles ran throughout *The Babylonian Captivity*, highlighting Luther's view that the institutional church had placed the people in bondage. This concern was evident in the other two treatises: he chose the language of freedom in *The Freedom of the Christian Man* with a specific purpose; and when he came to addressing the relationship between the church and the civil magistrate in *An Appeal*, he was particularly concerned to expose the means by which the church had bolstered its power.

Before looking at this appeal in more detail, it is worth remembering that these concerns flow from Luther's theological conviction that the cross is the lens through which the Christian life, and therefore all Christian ministry and institutions, must be seen. As we noted in chapter 2, the theologian of the cross revises and indeed inverts all his expectations in light of the fact that the transcendent God of life made himself human and died an ignominious death on a cross. The ethical impact of the cross event upon the church and upon notions of church power is that suffering and servanthood are to mark her life. Thus, a large part of the Reformer's task was to critique the church and her claims in light of God's revelation in the crucified Christ.

In *An Appeal*, Luther assumes this basic approach and declares that the papacy has built three walls to defend itself against reformation at the hands of the secular authorities: first, it makes a distinction between temporal (or secular) power and spiritual (or sacred) power that places the former below the latter; second, it claims a monopoly on the true interpretation and application of Scriptures, thus immunizing itself against being held to account; third, it claims that only the pope can call a general council.[1] Of these, it is the first, the hierarchical distinction between the sacred and secular, that concerns us here.

The medieval church assumed this distinction and concluded therefrom that certain callings were intrinsically holier than others. Luther's own life bears witness to this: his move to the monastic cloister, while not meeting with his father's approval, took him out of a secular calling and placed him in one that carried much more spiritual prestige and much more meritorious potential in matters of salvation.

In *An Appeal*, Luther begins his polemic by denying this basic distinction:

> It is pure invention that pope, bishop, priests, and monks are called the spiritual estate while princes, lords, artisans, and farmers are called the temporal estate. This is indeed a piece of deceit and hypocrisy. Yet no one need be intimidated by it, and for this reason: all Christians are truly of the spiritual estate, and there is no difference among them except that of office.[2]

Underlying this statement is the basic contrast between the inward and the outward that Luther has been making since at least the *Disputation against*

---

[1] *LW*, 44:126.
[2] *LW*, 44:127.

Scholastic Theology of September 1517, and which stands at the heart of *The Freedom of the Christian Man*.[3] What makes someone righteous is not the intrinsic value of the external works they do but the relationship of the person to the Word of God.[4]

This has clear implications for the relationship of the church to the secular sphere. The one who believes the Word is the one who is spiritual. It is not her outward behavior or job description that does this. Luther further underscores this point by raising the matter of priesthood: it is by baptism that the person is placed into Christ and therefore becomes a priest through Christ's own priesthood. That not only demands that the church revise its understanding of ordination and priesthood but also points again to the fundamentally fallacious nature of the hierarchical distinction by which the Roman church defends her power.[5]

The need to reconstruct the relationship between the spiritual and the secular is clear from the fact that all are members of both. The civil magistrate is, by virtue of baptism and justification, a priest, a truth that the Roman church has all but destroyed.[6] Thus, as all Christians are priests, the question of outward earthly calling cannot be understood in terms of spiritual versus nonspiritual. In a key passage, Luther summarizes his view as follows:

> Therefore, just as those who are now called "spiritual," that is, priests, bishops, or popes, are neither different from other Christians nor superior to them, except that they are charged with the administration of the word of God and the sacraments, which is their work and office, so it is with the temporal authorities. They bear the sword and rod in their hand to punish the wicked and protect the good. A cobbler, a smith, a peasant—each has the work and office of his trade, and yet they are all alike consecrated priests and bishops. Further, everyone must benefit and serve every other by means of his own work or office so that in this way many kinds of work may be done for the bodily and spiritual welfare of the community, just as all the members of the body serve one another.[7]

---

[3] E.g., *LW*, 31:11, 362.

[4] *LW*, 31:344–45.

[5] *LW*, 44:127–28. Luther declares that, in ordination, the bishop acts on behalf of the whole community, and that he is set aside for the ministry not because of any spiritual superiority but because good governance requires such delegation of power.

[6] *LW*, 44:128.

[7] *LW*, 44:130.

Luther expresses a number of key ideas here. First, we should note that the Christian ministry derives its significance closely from the fact that the men involved are set apart for the administration of Word and sacrament. There is nothing intrinsically holy about the men themselves, nor anything meritorious about the calling. They are instruments in God's work.

Second, Luther parallels the ministry with the calling of the secular magistrate and offers a point of clear distinction with significant implications: as the minister's tools are Word and sacrament, so the secular magistrate's tools are rod and sword.

This is a most important distinction because it also points to the underlying difference between spiritual or ecclesiastical power and rule, on the one hand, and that of the secular world, on the other. The church has power in the form of Word and sacrament. We have noted this in earlier chapters, and this is a good reminder that the church is not to conceive of her power in earthly terms involving worldly strength, ambitions, and coercion. Hers is a cross-shaped power, rooted in that which the world finds despicable and weak: a crucified God who now works through the weakness of the Word preached and the sacraments administered. In a world where the pope was typically immersed in the chicanery of earthly politics and sometimes even in military conflict, this was radical teaching.

The civil magistrate, by way of contrast, has the rod and the sword. His power is coercive and established in order that the wicked might be punished and the good protected. Thus, we see here the foundations of what will later come to be called Luther's idea of the two kingdoms: that the spiritual and the secular spheres are two different categories of reality in which all human beings are placed and which are governed using different tools and different rules.

Although Luther will elaborate and defend this idea in greater detail, it is clear even in this early passage that he sees its implications: all earthly callings become legitimately spiritual when done in faith. Here he cites the examples of the cobbler, the smith, and the peasant who works the land: as kings and priests in Christ, they are holy; their earthy callings are a legitimate part of the overall structure of earthly society, and they perform their tasks in a way that facilitates the well-being of the whole community.

The Civil Magistrate

In 1523, Luther produced a work that formed a sequel to his earlier *Appeal*, the latter titled *Temporal Authority, to What Extent It Should Be Obeyed*. Much of significance had happened between 1520 and 1523, not least Luther's own act of defiance, arguably a piece of civil disobedience, at the imperial Diet of Worms. Thus, in this second treatise, he set himself the task of a more rigorous defense of secular authority and more precise reflection upon the nature and extent of its power.

The treatise has proved highly controversial over the years, primarily for the way it can be used to deny any right of resistance to the civil magistrate. Given Germany's subsequent history and the apparent passivity of many churches in the face of Nazi atrocities, this has placed Luther's political thought in a somewhat negative light. It is beyond the scope of this study to examine all the aspects of this issue, but a number of salient points are of relevance to our argument.

First, Luther regards the civil magistrate as established by God. The office thus has divine sanction and carries significant authority in its appointed sphere. Luther's basic text is Romans 13:1: "Let every person be subject to the governing authorities. For there is no authority except from God, and those that exist have been instituted by God." This makes it clear that the magistracy is divinely ordained.[8] Further, the laws that the magistrate is to enforce, or at least the general laws on which societies are to build their specific case laws, have existed from the beginning, as is clear from Cain's guilt and punishment after he slew Abel (Gen. 4:9–16).[9] Now, while Luther believes that Christians as Christians require no external law because they will live as true Christians, he is also aware that very few of the baptized fall into this category. That is why the civil magistrate is necessary: for the maintenance and appropriate application of the law to punish the guilty and protect the innocent.[10] Further, the civil magistrate can carry out his task, even that of capital punishment of the wicked, confident that he does so with God's approval. Indeed, in one comment recorded in the *Table Talk*, Luther mocks a story he heard in which, under the papacy, hangmen used to ask forgiveness of those they were about to execute, as if they were committing some sort of sin.[11]

---

[8] *LW*, 45:85–86.
[9] *LW*, 45:86.
[10] *LW*, 45:90–92.
[11] *LW*, 54:179–80.

Because the magistrate is established by God, the Christian owes him obedience. The Christian life is not lived in separation from the earthly political sphere, as if joining the church required repudiation of society at large. Yet Christianity does make a difference, since the Christian's obedience to the state is not limitless but is rather confined within the boundaries of the magistrate's own sphere of authority over the secular kingdom. Indeed, while some have argued that Luther's view of the magistrate's authority gives no ground for any resistance at all, this is too simplistic a view. In *Temporal Authority*, he offers a fascinating example that repays thoughtful reflection:

> If your prince or temporal ruler commands you to side with the pope, to believe thus and so, or to get rid of certain books, you should say, "It is not fitting that Lucifer should sit at the side of God. Gracious sir, I owe you obedience in body and property; command me within the limits of your authority on earth, and I will obey. But if you command me to believe or to get rid of certain books, I will not obey; for then you are a tyrant and overreach yourself, commanding where you have neither the right nor the authority," etc. Should he seize your property on account of this and punish such disobedience, then blessed are you; thank God that you are worthy to suffer for the sake of the divine word. Let him rage, fool that he is; he will meet his judge. For I tell you, if you fail to withstand him, if you give in to him and let him take away your faith and your books, you have truly denied God.[12]

Clearly, Luther here teaches that the Christian can refuse to comply with a command from the civil magistrate if that command falls outside his sphere of authority. The magistrate cannot demand that the people side with the papacy, throw away their Lutheran books, or believe certain things. These matters pertain to the Word of God and to the spiritual kingdom over which the magistrate has no jurisdiction.

What is critical to see here, however, is that Luther does not view this overstepping of the bounds of power as destroying the legitimacy of the magistrate. If, as a result of the Christian's refusal to comply with the command, the magistrate then strips him of his goods or, to push further than Luther in this passage, even his life, the Christian is to rejoice and accept

---

[12] *LW*, 45:111–12. When the emperor failed to subscribe to the Augsburg Confession in 1530, Luther's thinking on resistance did shift a little in that he came to allow that lesser magistrates (the electors) might resist the emperor because the emperor's power is ultimately derived from them.

it, not to rebel. Here, we might say, the Christian truly acts as a theologian of the cross, seeing in the earthly suffering he then experiences a sign of God's work in his life and of the ultimate blessing to come.[13]

The Christian and Calling

If the civil magistrate is ordained by God and thus legitimate, the sphere over which the magistrate presides also has its own legitimacy and integrity. We noted above how Luther mentioned cobblers, smiths, and peasants as those who contributed by their work to the well-being of society as a whole. This points toward Luther's notion of calling, an important concept in his understanding of society.

Luther's thinking in this matter is elaborated in his 1526 treatise *Whether Soldiers, Too, Can Be Saved*. The immediate pretext for the work was a conversation between Luther and a professional soldier, Assa von Kram, in July 1525. Von Kram was increasingly uneasy about how to reconcile his Christian faith with his earthly calling, and Luther eventually wrote this treatise in order to salve his tender conscience. Luther's conclusion is that military service is certainly a legitimate calling for the Christian because it is part of the civil magistrate's bearing the sword for the protection of the innocent and the punishment of the wicked.

This specific conclusion, however, is based on some more general conceptual distinctions that Luther makes. First, he distinguishes professions from the people who hold them. It is possible, he says, for a wicked man to have a legitimate profession and to pursue it in such a way that he does it very wickedly. Thus, the office of judge is a good one but it can be held by a corrupt man who uses the position to do evil, and the same principle applies to that of soldiering.[14]

Second, Luther makes his typical distinction between inward and outward righteousness, or perhaps we might say in this context, between spiritual righteousness and civic righteousness. The specific issue before him is battlefield slaughter: can the kind of butchery of other human

---

[13] When teaching on Luther, I am often asked, "What would Luther say to a doctor instructed by his employer to perform an abortion?" My answer is that he would tell the doctor he should not perform the abortion—the hospital authorities have no right to order the killing of an innocent but rather have an obligation to protect such. But then the hospital would have the perfect right to dismiss the doctor for disobeying instructions, and the doctor should respond not by suing but by rejoicing in his suffering for righteousness' sake. The wicked ruler is still put in place by God and has God-given authority, even if he chooses to abuse it.

[14] *LW*, 46:94–95.

beings that warfare demands be consistent with Christian righteousness? Luther's answer is that it can be if it is connected to the civic duty of the magistrate, that is, protection of the innocent and punishment of wrong-doers.[15]

The general principle underlying this specific application is that all earthly callings that feed into the well-being of society are legitimate. This is important. For example, if we were to read Luther's comments from his polemic against the Roman clergy to the effect that the Word is what makes a calling spiritual, we might perhaps conclude that anything goes in the civic sphere: one could be a prostitute or a freelance hit man as long as one grasped the Word by faith. In fact, those would be just two examples of callings that are not legitimate because they do not conform to the principle of advancing the well-being of society through love to neighbor.

If not all callings are legitimate because some fail to help the civic good, those which are legitimate are made spiritual for the Christian when they are performed in faith. The godless soldier who strikes and kills a rebel on the battlefield performs an outwardly righteous task, albeit in an inwardly unrighteous manner. The Christian who does exactly the same outwardly righteous task does it righteously because, living by faith, he does all things for the love of God and not just the love of neighbor, and does them to God's glory.

It is hard to underestimate the significance of this for Western culture in general and for approaches to the Christian life in particular. One thinks of the paintings of the Dutch Golden Age. Jan Vermeer may have been a Roman Catholic, but only someone with a Protestant sensibility could have painted a subject as mundane as a milkmaid going about her daily business and yet imbued the scene with something of the sacred. Further, only this sort of thinking can infuse a kind of dignity into even the most humble and menial of human tasks. Done in faith and for the love and the glory of God, even carrying a milk pail becomes something beautifully spiritual.

We might also add that this provides an interesting angle on discussions of what constitutes the Christian worldview. Is it an epistemology? A particular approach to the arts or to politics? Can it be formulated in terms of a series of policy proposals or specific beliefs about some matter or other? For Luther, the Christian worldview is not about "transforming the culture" or about developing specifically Christian philosophies or tech-

---

[15] *LW*, 46:95.

niques. It is about pursuing legitimate earthly callings in faith, in love to God and neighbor, and to the glory of God.[16]

Marriage

The Christian's civic life, of course, does not simply consist in his relationship to the civil magistrate and his means of earthly employment. Family is important too, as Luther's example demonstrates.

Luther understands marriage as something that predated the fall and was thus part of the good structure of creation itself. In his *Lectures on Genesis*, Luther sees the creation of the woman as necessary in order to allow for the procreation of the human race. Thus, he understands the "good" in Genesis 2:18 as referring not to any loneliness Adam might feel because of the lack of a partner but to the common good of procreation and thus of society in general.[17] For this reason, he berates the contemporary age because of couples, particular among the nobility, who do not wish to have children. Their lack of descendants and thus the oblivion that awaits their family name is an appropriate reward for such behavior.[18]

He regards the fall as expanding the need for women quite considerably: they are vital for household management, companionship, mutual protection, and a legitimate outlet for sexual desire. Household management seems to have been particularly crucial in the Luther marriage, to the extent that one wonders whether Luther's exegesis of Genesis 2 is perhaps shaped more by his own experience than he might have realized. He comments in the *Table Talk* that Katie's organization of the household is crucial in allowing him to do his own pastoral work.[19]

Luther does believe that sex was originally intended for procreation—joyous and pleasurable procreation—but that the fall has led to an expansion of sexual needs and desires. He believes that animals need to copulate only once a year for purely procreative purposes; the lack of control that human beings exhibit is a result of their sin.[20] Further, that

---

[16] I also find it hard to imagine that Luther would have regarded as "Christian" any view of the world that denied that the whole Christ is present in the elements of bread and wine in the Lord's Supper. This, in turn, points to another problem with contemporary discussions of a Christian worldview: they tend to assume it is a singular, not a plural, phenomenon and then build it on an attenuated, minimalist doctrinal account of what Christianity actually is. That is a discussion for another time and another place; suffice it to note here that Luther would have been most impatient with such a view.

[17] *LW*, 1:115–16.

[18] *LW*, 1:118.

[19] *LW*, 54:23. Elsewhere, he indicates that she was in charge of the basic household finances (*LW*, 54:153).

[20] *LW*, 1:116. Luther can, however, refer to marriage as being for the fulfillment of the natural desire for sex (*LW*, 54:25).

married couples feel the need to hide themselves away and have sexual relations in private indicates that the activity now has a shameful quality because it is tainted by sin and lust. Before the fall, however, no activity was as glorious and God-honoring as sexual intercourse between man and wife.[21] Further, the cohabitation of man and wife, their cooperation in running the household, and their joint task of rearing children are, for Luther, faith shadows or echoes of what life before the fall in Eden was intended to be.[22] In other words, we might say that for Luther, the family is the most basic unit of human society. The magistrate is necessary as a result of the fall; the family was God's intention for humanity before sin entered the scene.

As a monk and priest, Luther did not consider marriage an option for him. Later, he came to regard the restoration of marriage to a place of honor in the Reformation as a sign of the great advance of God's kingdom.[23] Yet, by the time the Reformation was established and, with it, the rule of celibacy for the clergy had ended, Luther was well into what would have been considered middle age and a confirmed bachelor. Nevertheless, his unexpected marriage to his Katie proved to be delightful, loving, and fruitful. Today, visitors to the Augustinian cloister in Wittenberg (a gift from the elector to the Luthers on their wedding day) will see that the door frame has a little stool built into it on each side. The door frame was a present from Katie to her husband, made at a time when she felt they were not spending enough time talking to each other. Thus, at the end of a busy day, Martin and Katie could sit on either side of the door and talk to each other. Inside and upstairs, there is a window frame with a similar arrangement, presumably for when the Saxon weather made an outdoor tryst somewhat wet and cold. This in itself speaks eloquently of the love and the happiness that marriage brought to the life of the Reformer.

That Luther always regarded love as central to marriage is evident long before matrimony became even a theoretical possibility for him. Years prior to his own nuptials and long before he repudiated his vow of celibacy, Luther declared in a sermon of 1519, *On the Estate of Marriage*, that marriage is given of God to provide man with a special helpmeet in companionship and in procreation. It is a uniquely human institution, finding no equivalent anywhere else in the animal kingdom. While it is now damaged

---

[21] *LW*, 1:117–18.
[22] *LW*, 1:133.
[23] *LW*, 54:177.

by the ravages of sin, which have led to adultery and lust, it continues for the purpose of providing loving friendship and children.[24]

In this sermon, Luther talks about three different kinds of love: false love, natural love, and married love. False love is self-seeking, such as that exemplified in fornication, theft, and ruthless worldly ambition. We might say that this is the classic expression of what Luther sees as the human predicament: that human nature is turned in on itself. Natural love is that which holds between family members and friends.[25] Married love, however, is different. In a beautiful paragraph that is quite remarkable coming from a celibate monk with no experience of married love, Luther describes it this way:

> But over and above all these is married love, that is, a bride's love, which glows like a fire and desires nothing but the husband. She says, "It is you I want, not what is yours: I want neither your silver nor your gold; I want neither. I want only you. I want you in your entirety, or not at all." All other kinds of love seek something other than the loved one: this kind wants only to have the beloved's own self completely.[26]

Certainly, Luther's own marriage appears to have been a happy one, a context where true emotional and physical love was a hallmark of everyday life.

While Luther's sermon on marriage comes from a time when he was a celibate, marriage introduced him to the experience of sex, which appears to have been a most welcome discovery, as his brood of six children testifies.[27] Luther regarded sex as a great good. Indeed, when he wrote to the newly married George Spalatin in late 1525, he commented that he intended to guess when the Spalatins would receive the letter so that he might make sure he and Katie were engaged in lovemaking at the same time as the newlyweds. Perhaps it is my English sensibility, but if I had been Spalatin or, perhaps even more so, Mrs. Spalatin or Mrs. Luther, I

---

[24] LW, 44:7–8.
[25] LW, 44:8–9.
[26] LW, 44:9.
[27] The consummation of the Luthers' marriage was, of course, witnessed, a fact that seems a little odd to our more squeamish age. We need to remember, however, that such was standard practice among nobles, given the desire for evidence of virginity, and not uncommon even in recent time in many peasant societies. For Luther, the need of a witness was perhaps even more significant: as the most notorious heretic in Europe and one who had taken solemn vows of celibacy that he was about to break, it was useful for him to have a witness on hand to confirm that nothing supernatural or evil happened. It is hard for us today to imagine the controversial nature of Luther's marriage, but the axiomatic nature of clerical celibacy and the standard Roman propaganda about the Reformation being motivated by a desire for sex both made the marriage a highly contentious event.

would have found that thought somewhat off-putting. It does, however, speak eloquently of Luther's enjoyment of lovemaking, despite all the theological rhetoric about sex being an outlet for lust.

Marriage required quite a bit of readjustment for Luther, given his status as a middle-aged confirmed bachelor at the time of his nuptials. Indeed, he wittily describes the change in a table talk:

> Man has strange thoughts the first year of marriage. When sitting at table he thinks, "Before I was alone; now there are two." Or in bed, when he wakes up, he sees a pair of pigtails lying beside him which he hadn't seen there before. On the other hand, wives bring to their husbands, no matter how busy they may be, a multitude of trivial matters. So my Katy used to sit next to me at first while I was studying hard and would spin and ask, "Doctor, is the grandmaster the margrave's brother?"[28]

The humor in references such as this points to the affection between the two. Luther cherished his wife. *Table Talk* is full of references to Katie, as are his letters. Often he adds "my Lord Katie sends her greetings" at the ends of letters or refers to her as his "rib." He also plays on the similarity of the name Katherine with the Latin word *catena*, meaning "chain." The two clearly shared much in common, including a love for German beer. In fact, in Luther's last letter to his wife, he praised a particular type of beer from Naumburg for giving him "three bowel movements in three hours," an indication that perhaps wives and therefore love letters were made of earthier, sterner stuff than later generations.[29] Nevertheless, as Luther understood marriage as a profound expression of human love, he also warned that the Devil would therefore seek to disrupt it at every opportunity, and that hatred was never so powerful as when it existed between two spouses.[30]

Given the timing of the marriage at the height of the Peasants' War, it seems likely that Katie was crucial to his mental health over the next two years. Luther's violent reaction to the rebellion and his call for the butchering of peasants brought his reputation and standing to an all-time low in Germany. Prone as he always was to depression, to attacks of the Devil, and to *Anfechtungen*, the presence of Katie as a sane and stabilizing

---

[28] *LW*, 54:191.
[29] *LW*, 50:291. Beer features elsewhere in his correspondence with Katie too: cf. *LW*, 50:81. She also appears to have been a competent home brewer herself, undoubtedly making her the archetypal, ideal Lutheran pastor's wife (*LW*, 50:94).
[30] *LW*, 54:25.

influence was crucial. Later, during times of necessary separation when Luther was on the road preaching or because of the political situation, he would write to her frequently. They were clearly close and Luther felt her absence deeply. Thus, while sequestered in the castle at Coburg, awaiting news from Augsburg regarding the emperor's response to Melanchthon's confessional statement, he took the opportunity of a passing messenger to write a brief note to Katie.[31] Other letters contain joyful references to the birth of children. Yet even when there was nothing special to report, mention of Katie is frequent and constant. His love for her is evident, as in this comment from the *Table Talk*:

> I wouldn't give up my Katy for France or for Venice—first, because God gave her to me and gave me to her; second, because I have often observed that other women have more shortcomings than my Katy (although she, too, has some shortcomings, they are outweighed by many great virtues); and third, because she keeps faith in marriage, that is, fidelity and respect. A wife ought to think the same way about her husband.[32]

Elsewhere in *Table Talk*, Luther refers to the epistle to the Galatians as his "Katie von Bora."[33] While many wives might not find that the most romantic or flattering comparison, it is hard to imagine Luther paying anyone a higher compliment. Had he drawn a connection between Katie and the letter of James, one might have been given pause for thought.

On that matter, the evidence certainly suggests that Katie was able to give as good as she got from Wittenberg's most famous theological wit. Another table talk entry records the following exchange:

> [Luther declared,] "The time will come when a man will take more than one wife."
>
> The doctor's wife responded, "Let the devil believe that!"
>
> The doctor said, "The reason, Katy, is that a woman can bear a child only once a year while her husband can beget many."
>
> Katy responded, "Paul said that each man should have his own wife" [1 Cor. 7:2].
>
> To this the doctor replied, "Yes, 'his own wife' and not 'only one wife,' for the latter isn't what Paul wrote.

---

[31] *LW*, 49:399.
[32] *LW*, 54:7–8.
[33] *LW*, 54:20–21.

The doctor spoke thus in jest for a long time, and finally the his wife said, "Before I put up with this, I'd rather go back to the convent and leave you and all our children."[34]

Luther, like all bombastic, bull-headed, and brilliant individuals, must have been a difficult man to live with, but Katie seems to have been up to the task.[35] Certainly, the woman who always complained that Lucas Cranach the Elder's many paintings of her never managed to capture her true beauty was a woman of strong opinions and a force to be reckoned with.

Luther's home was always open to students and friends, and thus he and Katie came to be the archetypal pastor's family in Wittenberg. We should not underestimate the significance of this. In the Pastoral Epistles, the apostle Paul makes household management a key qualification for being an overseer in the church (1 Tim. 3:4–5; Titus 1:6). This does not make marriage compulsory for overseers, but it does point to the kind of leadership quality such a person is to demonstrate. Luther and Katie offered students for the ministry a beautiful and loving, if warts-and-all, picture of what a minister's household should look like.

Children

Luther loved children. Indeed, one might say that he himself retained a somewhat childlike quality, as demonstrated in his sense of humor. Certainly, he regarded being childlike as an extremely important characteristic in the Christian when it came to matters of faith. He spoke of the basic catechetical faith as something he never fully mastered, of being like a little child in terms of his need of instruction, and of learning with his own children when he prayed with them each day.[36] This was a point he made in the introduction to his Large Catechism: "I must still read and study the Catechism daily, yet I cannot master it as I wish, but must remain a child and pupil of the Catechism, and I do it gladly."[37]

This is of a piece with Luther's soteriology, which requires an attitude of trust and reverent humility before God—akin to that appropriate for a

---

[34] *LW*, 54:153.

[35] On another occasion, Luther was telling a group of friends of an encounter with the radical theologian Caspar Schwenckfeld and said that he was praying that Schwenckfeld would be struck dumb. Katie apparently had no hesitation in rebuking him for being too coarse. As with many ministers since, his wife was clearly an important moderating influence upon his language and attitude (*LW*, 54:470).

[36] "Though I am a great doctor, I haven't yet progressed beyond the instruction of children in the Ten Commandments, the Creed, and the Lord's Prayer. I still learn and pray these every day with my Hans and my little Lena." *LW*, 54:9.

[37] *BC*, 359.

child toward a parent—and also his theology refracted through the cross, which stands in opposition to worldly conceptions of power and knowledge. Theology masters the man; the man is never to master the theology. Luther even used the example of his own son Martin Jr. breastfeeding as a child as demonstrating the cheerful confidence that the Christian should have in the face of all that the world threatens against him.[38] Indeed, it appears that children as examples of simple, trusting faith fascinated him.[39]

When it came to the rearing of actual children, Luther had plenty of advice. Childbearing is a deeply honorable task and one to be understood within the context of a loving home. Indeed, Luther actually criticized the apostle Paul in 1 Timothy 2:14–15 for using the impersonal term "woman" rather than the familial "mother."[40] Children are part of families, and families are grounded in the love of man and wife. Thus, the context for child-rearing is one of familial love.[41] Indeed, when it came to discipline, even in the rather brutal times in which Luther lived, this was to be tempered by loving restraint: he thought that parents must not whip their children too severely, lest the children come to resent them. That may seem hard by our standards, but one can still appreciate the underlying sentiment.[42]

On the spiritual side, Luther appears to have had devotions every day with his children, focused, as we might expect, on the basic elements of catechetical Christianity: the Ten Commandments, the creed, and the Lord's Prayer. Again, typical of Luther, he saw this exercise not so much as a hierarchical one where he, the adult, taught the children, but as one where they all learned together, for he was in as much need of understanding what he prayed through with them as they themselves were.[43] Indeed, the spiritual education and health of the family was so important that, if the emperor himself were to try to inhibit or prevent it, the Christian would have an absolute duty to resist him—which, given Luther's respect for the office of magistrate, speaks eloquently of his passion in this matter.[44]

One aspect of family life in the sixteenth century that is less common today was infant mortality. Marriage, of course, is an interesting phenomenon: two people commit to live together till death parts them; yet few

---

[38] *LW*, 54:159.
[39] *LW*, 54:335, 428.
[40] *LW*, 54:223.
[41] *LW*, 54:432, 463.
[42] *LW*, 54:157.
[43] *LW*, 54:9.
[44] *LW*, 54:279.

have any understanding of the traumas of life they will be called upon to face together. Newlyweds rarely contemplate the darker side of life on their wedding day, and yet that darker side must sooner or later enter the stage.

Luther had a somewhat ambiguous attitude toward death. As a Christian, he was aware that death brings to a conclusion a life of suffering and setbacks. Thus, he opined at one point that he hoped his wife and children would not long outlive him because of the dark and dangerous times pressing in.[45] Yet death is brutally painful, particularly for those left behind, as he himself knew. Luther's marriage was indeed loving and joyful and filled with laughter; but it was also touched at points with terrible darkness and pain caused by the death of two of his children, Elizabeth and Magdalene.

Elizabeth died on August 3, 1528, less than a year after her birth. Luther alluded to the death in a table talk: "There is no sweeter union than that in a good marriage. Nor is there any death more bitter than that which separates a married couple. Only the death of children comes close to this; how much this hurts I have myself experienced."[46] Tragically, this was not to be the last time he suffered such bereavement. In 1542, he lost his beloved daughter Magdalene. A series of powerful table talks describe the impact upon him. When Katie, realizing the gravity of the child's illness, began to weep uncontrollably, Luther reminded her that children have simple faith, have little fear, and die as if going to sleep.[47] The *Table Talk* also records a conversation between Luther and the dying girl:

> When the illness of his daughter became graver he said, "I love her very much. But if it is thy will to take her, dear God, I shall be glad to know that she is with thee."
>
> Afterward he said to his daughter, who was lying in bed, "Dear Magdalene, my little daughter, you would be glad to stay here with me, your father. Are you also glad to go to your Father in heaven?"
>
> The sick girl replied, "Yes, dear Father, as God wills."
>
> The father said, "You dear little girl!" [Then he turned away from her and said,] "The spirit is willing, but the flesh is weak [Matt. 26:41]. I love her very much. If this flesh is so strong, what must the spirit be?" Among other things he then said, "In the last thousand years God has given to no bishop such great gifts as he has given to me (for one should boast of God's gifts). I'm angry with myself that I'm unable to rejoice from my

---

[45] *LW*, 54:319.
[46] *LW*, 54:33.
[47] *LW*, 54:428–29.

heart and be thankful to God, though I do at times sing a little song and thank God. Whether we live or die, we are the Lord's [Rom. 14:8]—in the genitive singular and not in the nominative plural."[48]

Here we see the existential agony of a father facing the death of a child. His theology tells him she is going to a better place, but his embodied creatureliness feels the pain of the unnatural intrusion of death as it takes his loved one from him. The pain was to continue, with the child dying in Luther's arms as he wept and prayed while Katie sat in the same room, apparently paralyzed with grief.[49] Then, the coffin was too small to contain her. Finally, at the funeral, the congregation sang Psalm 79:8, a reminder that even in the throes of mourning, Luther's understanding of God and salvation was a source of comfort to him.[50]

Concluding Reflections

One of the most attractive aspects of Luther's understanding of the Christian life is the manner in which it connects to the real world. For all of his focus on justification, on the need for the individual to be clothed by grace through faith with the righteousness of the Lord Jesus Christ, he also offers an account of human existence that does justice to the reality of life in this world. How to be a Christian in civic society—indeed, how to pursue a mundane, daily call in a manner that brings honor to God and makes the ordinariness of existence into something spiritual—that is a hardy perennial of Christian existence. As one is justified without reference to one's intrinsic righteousness, so one's earthly calling is made spiritual without reference to its intrinsic interest or specific value. This is powerful pastoral teaching. It turned the world upside down in the sixteenth century, and it has the power to revolutionize the way we think about the Christian life today.

For Luther, the Christian life was not simply the Christian life when one was in church or was evangelizing one's neighbors. It was the whole of life, sanctified by faith to God's glory and service. Nor was it thinking up arcane and clever Christian approaches to this or that artistic endeavor, as so often becomes the case in contemporary thinking about the Christian

---

[48] LW, 54:430–31.
[49] LW, 54:431–32.
[50] LW, 54:432–33.

view of the world. It was rather to be found in an attitude toward the world that was rooted in faith.

In addition, I would argue that Luther's view of the church and the world, like that of Augustine before him, is of increasing usefulness to the church in the West today. It is perhaps one hundred years since Christianity lost its grip on much of the civic sphere in Europe. The same phenomenon is, in many ways, now taking place in the United States. The elections of 2008 indicated just how tenuous the influence of conservative Christianity had become in the political realm. The powerbrokers of the Religious Right seem to have little power left to broker. The church is in cultural retreat before the tide of rising secularism or, if *secularism* is perhaps an inaccurate term, the rising tide of non-Christianity. Luther's modest vision of the church in relation to the political realm is surely the wave of the future. The church has at her disposal Word and sacrament; she should leave the sword, and the concomitant instruments and structures of power that go with it, to the God-ordained institution of the civil magistrate.

When we turn to the other great extra-ecclesiastical institution, the family, I would suggest that Martin and Katie offer a beautiful picture of a pastoral marriage and therefore of the kind of marriage to which all married Christian couples should aspire. It is surely significant that Paul makes good household management a prerequisite for holding office in the church. Further, in the analogy he draws between husbands and wives and Christ and the church, he points toward a pedagogical and paradigmatic significance of marriage that far transcends any other earthly institution. The married pastor has a huge burden laid upon him: in his family relationships, he is not only to show his flock that to which they should aspire in matters of domestic order; he is also to show them, in some dim, shadowy way, what it is for Christ to love the church.

Perhaps most touching of all is the way in which Luther's private grief was played out in the public sphere. For a man like him, there could be no truly private space. Everything he did had huge public significance. Imagine, for example, what the fate of the Reformation might have been if his first child had been stillborn? In that era such things had profound significance as signs of God's judgment. Thus, not only was the joy of Luther's wedding and even his wedding night a matter of public concern, but so too were the private traumas such as the deaths of his children. As we read the accounts of little Magdalene's final days, we see the breaking heart of a man who believed that she was departing for a better place but who also knew that death is an outrageous intrusion into this world and thus painful and devastating. Luther emerged from his family life as no less great a figure than his public ministry showed him to be, but as far more human. In this world, that is the kind of Christian pastor we should all long to be or to be pastored by.

Luther died in 1546 while away in Eisleben on pastoral business. Ironically, he passed away in the very town where he had been born. He died away from home and absent from the arms of his beloved wife. On a piece of paper he made a few final notes a day or so before his death. In them, he declared that no one could understand Vergil's agricultural, pastoral poems, the *Georgics* and the *Bucolics*, unless he had been a shepherd for four or five years; no one could understand Cicero unless he had been engaged in public life for twenty years; and no one could understand the Scriptures unless he had ruled the church for a hundred years. The text closed with the laconic statement, half in German, half in Latin: "We are beggars: this is true."[51] At the close of his own Christian life, as with Thomas Aquinas, it appears that the anticipation of eternity placed everything he had done and everything he knew into a modest and humbling light. Against the vast canvas of eternity, in the face of God, and in the context of God's gracious revelation of himself in Christ, Luther was but a small child, barely touching the surface of the ocean of God's mercy. Which is, one might say, exactly what he would have hoped to be.

We are all beggars. That is true.

---

[51] *LW*, 54:478.

LIFE AS TRAGEDY, LIFE AS COMEDY

We are beggars: this is true.

MARTIN LUTHER

Over twenty years ago, I was being interviewed for what would prove to be my first tenured appointment at a university. Halfway through the ordeal, one of the interviewers asked me, "If you were trapped on a desert island, who would you want with you—Luther or Calvin?" My response was reasonably nuanced for a reply to an unexpected question: "Well, I think Calvin would provide the best theological and exegetical discussion, but he always strikes me as somewhat sour and colorless. Luther, however, may not have been as careful a theologian, but he was so obviously human and so clearly loved life. Thus, I'd have to choose Luther." Later that day, I was offered the position of lecturer in medieval and Reformation theology.

Whether my answer to that particular question played a key role in the panel's decision, I know not. But that was the moment when I started on a career of teaching Luther's theology to generations of students on both sides of the Atlantic, and this story seems an appropriate segue into this conclusion. Writing this book has not quite been as traumatic as being marooned on a desert island with the man from Wittenberg, but there are similarities. As a Presbyterian, I do not have any friends who share quite my passion for Luther's theology; and I have realized as never before that his theological writings can be as infuriating as they are enlightening and entertaining.

Having spent my entire professional life reading and teaching Luther, I think it appropriate to close by reflecting on what I have learned in writing this particular book that has surprised or impressed me and has significance for the church today.

The first of these is Luther's great stress upon the priority and objectivity of God's revelation. When one reads Luther intensively, one is inevitably struck by his vision for the priority and awe-inspiring power of God as he acts in his Word. The Word is powerful, creative, destructive, and re-creative. The human response is as nothing before the Word's dramatic and powerful priority over all being. Whether the topic is God's spoken word the moment he suddenly brought the vast created cosmos into being from nothing, or the Word spoken from countless pulpits last Sunday, the objective power of God stands at the very heart of Luther's theology and indeed his view of reality. Only after one has grasped this does so much of his thought start to make any sense. This objectivity of God's action comes to its dramatic climax on the cross at Calvary. There, in the God who is clothed in human flesh and who dies cursed upon the tree, we see not only God's grace toward fallen humanity revealed in all its glory, but also every human thought and word about God brought into judgment and turned on its head. Power becomes weakness and weakness becomes power. The divine love, which we assume is responsive, is shown to be creative. Salvation is shown to be not an act of cooperation between God and the Christian but a sovereign act of God himself.

This objectivity of God undergirds those basic elements of the Christian life: the reading and preaching of the Bible and the reception of the sacraments. Indeed, Luther is careful to frame his understanding of the church and of church power strictly in light of the way God gives himself in, with, and under the forms of Word, water, bread, and wine. The church service is not a response of sinners to God's prior grace; it is itself an example of that grace in action. Church is a creature of God's grace; Christians are creatures of God's grace; and the life of the believer is marked out by the means of God's grace.

For the contemporary Christian, there is much to delight and encourage here. In an age marked by incredible confusion over the exact role of pastors, Luther provides clarity. If God comes first, if God decides how he gives himself to his people in grace, then pastors are to look to him as he shows himself in his revelation in order to know what their task is. And it is simply this: to let God be God, and therefore to proclaim in Word and sacrament that he has come in the person of the Lord Jesus Christ to deal graciously with those who will grasp him by faith. Therefore, the pastor need not fret overmuch about many things. The Word, after all, is not powerful because the preacher is godly; and while a certain clarity of speech is important, the real effect of the sermon derives not from the preacher's eloquence but from the God who really speaks the Word to the people. And when the preacher administers the Lord's Supper, he is not simply going through some empty ritual: he is giving the people Christ, God manifest in the flesh, and he should therefore be confident that the people will benefit through faith.

In an era when we are increasingly obsessed with technique and with the uniqueness of every individual person's problems and crises—with their own special *Anfechtungen*, we might say—Luther's God is disarmingly general. Human beings all face the same dilemma: they wish to stand before God in their own righteousness; and they all need the same solution— God manifest in the flesh, given to them in Word and sacrament, received by humble, contrite, dependent, *childlike* faith. Word and sacrament define the task of the pastoral office in simple, beautiful, and powerful terms.

If the pastoral office receives clear definition because of the objectivity of God, then so does the life of the Christian. Despondent? Flee to Christ. In despair? Flee to Christ. Struggling with sin? Flee to Christ. For Luther, the answer to life's *Anfechtungen* is not introspection but looking outward once again to the means of grace. Again, there is liberation for the Christian today. As alluded to above, we live in an age where everyone is taught to consider themselves unique. The downside of that is that every problem we face is thus unique and can be solved only by addressing matters of the person, individual circumstance, or biography. That is not the world according to Luther. Yes, the one who struggles with relationships may well be told by Luther, as by some Freudian psychologist, to look right back into childhood for the answer, but this would not be some attempt to unlock forgotten traumas; rather it would be to seek the significance of that moment of entry into the church: baptism, where Christ is first presented to the individual. And that will lead the individual to the promise attached to baptism, to Scripture, and to the regular reading and preaching of the Word in church.

Thus, as I reread Luther, I was struck both as pastor and as Christian believer by the immense confidence he had in the objective action of God in Christ and the objective reality this gives to both Word and sacrament. Yet Luther did not swallow up the whole of history in the cross of Christ. I was also impressed once again at the individual care this man had for the flock, whether in the touching and helpful treatise on prayer he wrote for Peter the Barber or in the misguided marital advice he offered to the troubled Landgrave of Hesse. The latter was a public relations disaster and fundamentally wrongheaded; but it is nonetheless testimony to a man who cared how people thought and acted in their individual concrete circumstances.

Even more, I was impressed at the way in which he outlined the existential struggles of life: joy, sorrow, illness, marriage, pain, and death. Luther saw God's hand in the particularities of life, and even as he understood them against the backdrop of the great objective actions of God, he gave them their due. Death was the gateway to resurrection, but he knew it was painful and heartbreaking. The funeral of his child was no place for one of those frightful "celebrations of life" that this present glittering, desperate age has developed as a means of lying about the one facet of human existence that remains stubbornly immune to our ambitions of control.

And this leads me to my last thoughts on Luther. One of the most striking things about the man is his sense of humor, and one cannot possibly write a book on his understanding of the Christian life without reference to this. In general terms, of course, Protestant theologians have not been renowned for their wit, and Protestant theology has not been distinguished by its laughter. Yet Luther laughed all the time, whether poking fun at himself, at Katie, at his colleagues, or indeed at his countless and ever-increasing number of enemies. Humor was a large part of what helped to make him so human and accessible. And in a world where everyone always seems to be "hurt" by something someone has said or offended by this or that, Luther's robust mockery of pretension and pomposity is a remarkable theological contribution in and of itself.

Humor, of course, has numerous functions. It is in part a survival mechanism. Mocking danger and laughing in the face of tragedy are proven ways of coping with hard and difficult situations. Undoubtedly, this played a significant role in Luther's own penchant for poking fun. Yet I think there is probably a theological reason for Luther's laughter too. Humor often plays on the absurd, and Luther knew that this fallen world was not as it was designed to be and was thus absurd and futile in a most significant and powerful way.

Thus, he knew that life is tragic. It is full of sound and fury. It is marked by pain and frustration. The strength of youth must eventually fade into the weakness of old age and finally end in the grave. We believe ourselves to be special, to be transcendent, to be unique and irreplaceable. And yet the one great lesson that everyone must ultimately learn in life is that they are none of these things, however much we want them to be true and however much we do things to trick ourselves into believing our own propaganda. We are fallen, finite, and mortal. We are not God. And because God is and has acted, because in incarnation, Word, and sacrament he has revealed and given himself and has thus pointed to the true meaning of life, our own pretensions to greatness are shown to be nothing but the perilous grandstanding of the absurdly pompous and the pompously absurd.

Indeed, in light of the fact that God is God and has revealed himself in the foolishness of the cross, the tendency of us all to be theologians of glory appears in all its risible futility. That we who cannot even escape our own mortality would assume that God is like us, that we are the measure of all things, including the terrifying and awesome hidden God who rides on the wings of the storm and calls all things into being by the mere Word of his power—that we poor, pathetic, sinful creatures would be so arrogant as to assume such a thing is surely the greatest and darkest joke of all. Luther knew that the tragedy and the comedy of fallen humanity is that we have such a laughable view of ourselves: one that would aspire to tell God who and what he must be. As humans are at once both righteous and sinful, so human existence is at once both heartbreaking and hilarious. Luther cites Psalm 2:4 on numerous occasions to make precisely this point: the tragedy of humanity is that God laughs at our ridiculous attempts at autonomy.

This is where I leave you with Luther. While the world, even the Christian world, remains populated by the self-important and the self-righteous, the figure of Luther, with his rumbustious theology and his cutting humor, will not cease to be relevant. Many of his writings have a refreshing and appropriately irreverent style to them, tearing down the pompous and the self-assured. They offer a breath of fresh air amid a forced and stale piety. And his emphasis on the objectivity of the action of God in Christ puts all things in perspective and exposes our lives outside of Christ for what they are, acts in a silly farce played out in the shadow of the beckoning grave.

Above all, Luther points us consistently toward God as he really is, the one who does not find but creates that which is lovely to him. The foolishness of God truly is greater than our highest wisdom.

AFTERWORD

Author Carl Trueman has done readers a favor by viewing Martin Luther through a particular prism, one whose perspective can help change lives. Had he simply written a biography, he could have performed a service to readers in general, people who seek to be informed about important topics. While researching he could have scaled the figurative Everest of the 120-plus volumes of Luther's writings and tried to condense his vision from there in the pages of this relatively short book. Additionally, he would have had to do justice to some of the literally thousands of writings about the man regularly measured to be among the five most significant figures in the millennium past. Readers might have thereupon been dazzled or benumbed by the amount of data served up by often profound and elegant biographers.

Trueman's acceptance of an assignment in this particular series meant that the authorial choices he made had to relate, as this book does, to Luther's ponderings on and expressions of the Christian life. It was to contribute to the living of lives among readers in our generation. Accepting that choice meant leaving out many tantalizing subjects, since Luther touched on so many dimensions, events, and themes of human existence. Let it also be said that the author's need to select also helped save him from having to deal with embarrassing or appalling Luther topics, for example, his late-in-life notorious anti-Semitism—on which, to be sure, Trueman does touch with some pain and much fairness.

Luther on the Christian life? More predictable and more easily handled themes could have been "Luther on Christian doctrine" or "Luther on Christian preaching," or . . . Think how much easier an author would have it if he dealt with a figure like John Wesley or Saint Francis or hundreds of others whose specialty is devotion to holiness, sanctification, or ethics, as

Luther's was not or has not often been perceived to be. Of course, Trueman could not have commented on the Bible, as he has done in discussing writings that make up much of Luther's works, without having dealt with the many incentives to, and models of, the Christian life.

What readers must by the end have found remarkable is the way Dr. Trueman has brought clarity and some sense of system to the often obscure, paradoxical, and anything-but-systematic writings of Luther on the Christian life. I would argue that Trueman has served well by keeping his feet on firm ground as he has stood on an approach to Christian life which he sometimes calls Presbyterian or Reformed or evangelical, often in differing combinations. He has never done that flat-footedly or heavy-footedly, but usually incidentally, since he was not writing a book of Presbyterian-Reformed-evangelical doctrine, which can easily be learned by consulting encyclopedias or works of polemics. His intent was not overtly to say, "Notice us! We're better than you are!" but always to sharpen his points and add color and clarity to his narrative through comparison.

What, we might ask, is the potential profit from his viewing Luther through non-Lutheran eyes? (Readers need little reminder that books on Luther through Lutheran eyes, for all their worth, can often miss much or distort some of what they display or argue!) The profit in this instance? Such an approach helps readers of various confessional, denominational, and personal stances to move from the known—their own understandings—to the relatively unknown "other." Elements of faith as they show up in the Christian life stand in sharper relief when the comparative approach illumines what was already known and probably taken for granted.

To take an example: when I deal with Muslim worshipers and theologians, as I have done in dialogue with Muslims or in an Islamic school, I later reflect with a greater awareness of the role of the doctrine of the Trinity, or witness to the incarnation when Muslim students show puzzlement about Christian Trinitarian and incarnational talk. Why are these two topics so important to us Christians, we are asked? What are the sources and consequences of our beliefs? In the case not of Christians relating to Muslims but of Christians-of-one-sort in relation to Christians-of-another-sort, as it shows up in ecumenical conversation or comparative courses on Christian ethics, the gulfs between commitments in various confessional camps may often look like mere nuances, subtleties, or subjects for Pecksniffian polemicists to distort. Yet in choices made about the life of Christians, these differences can be either alienating or positively informative. The book you have just read will contribute to your living of the Christian life. A reread-ing—which I picture will be an enjoyable exercise—will confirm this.

Martin Luther's pursuits thus jostle those who share them through the book's realistic readiness to deal with *Anfechtung*, a peculiar sort of doubting. After reading this, they may well be more ready to deal with their own doubts. Those who had been casual about drawing on Scripture to guide their daily lives cannot help but draw closer, thanks to this account of Luther's probes. Also, in the past century Roman Catholic devotion to scriptural studies is often acknowledged to have been enriched by Luther's drawing on the Bible for the deepening of the Christian life.

I live across the street from a strategic and compelling Presbyterian church and on occasion am able to attend worship there. As I listen to and share in the hymnody, prayer forms, ethical injunctions, and proc-lamations of the gospel, I join other non-Presbyterians in affirmation, celebration, and a feeling of being in company or at home. Yet there are not-infrequent moments when, for example, a preacher will explain some-thing to the diverse congregants on a particular day, while wrestling with a particular text, by making an explicit reference to the fact that something emphasized in the Presbyterian tradition can provide color and impetus for the living of the Christian life.

Such an approach magnificently stands out and is helpful in a world where Christians often have to settle for banal, wishy-washy expressions that do little to help inform the Christian life. For example, we who are not Mennonites can learn from their peace witness without becoming Menno-nites, or can draw closer to God through the liturgical and musical witness of Episcopalians without having to "jump ship" and sail on an Anglican vessel. As this book which you readers have just finished makes clear, the pursuit of the Christian life is not a matter of picking and choosing, or gazing through a kaleidoscope with jittery images, but is a serious busi-ness of seeking perspective and focus. Readers of many sorts will be more equipped than before to share that pursuit, and will want to join me in expressing gratitude to author Carl Trueman.

Martin E. Marty
Emeritus Professor at the University of Chicago
author of *Martin Luther*

GENERAL INDEX

transforming culture, 183
transubstantiation, 148
treasury of merits, 37
Treatise on Good Works, 125–26
Treatise on the New Testament, That Is, the Holy Mass, 147
Trinity, 202
two kingdoms, 179

ubiquity, of Christ's flesh, 153n46
Unigenitus (papal bull), 37
union with Christ, 73, 74, 145, 153n47
University of Erfurt, 32, 33
University of Wittenberg, 33

variata of Augsburg Confession, 145n21
venial sins, 58n2
Vermeer, Jan, 183
via moderna, 35, 59, 60, 62, 70
violence, 49
Visitation Articles, 165–66, 169
voluntarism, 62
Vulgate, 34

Wartburg, 46
weakness, strength in, 27, 64, 72, 76–77, 115, 196
Wesley, John, 132
Western culture, as self-absorbed and overindulged, 173
Whether Soldiers, Too, Can Be Saved, 182
will, impotent for salvation, 60–61
William of Occam, 13, 35

wisdom, 64–65
  in foolishness, 72, 115, 200
Wittenberg, 33–34, 40–41, 46–47, 49, 151–52
Word and sacrament
  corporate context of, 79
  define ministry, 197
  tools of the minister, 179
Word of God, 69
  in Christian life, 117, 118
  determines reality, 84, 85–86
  Devil seeks to distort, 127
  as external, 90–91, 119–21, 132–33
  in humble form, 113, 122
  never fails, 107
  power of, 81, 85, 89–90, 94–95, 96, 97
  public reading and hearing of, 113
  theology of, 79–97
words, nature and function of, 83–86
works righteousness, 33, 170–71
worldview, 183–84
worship
  as activity of God, 102
  aesthetics of, 101–4
  as catechetical exercise, 103–4
  drama in the routines of, 114
wrath of God, 170, 173–74

Zurich, 49–50
Zwickau Prophets, 47, 94
Zwilling, Konrad, 46–47, 94, 106, 151
Zwingli, Huldrych, 22, 24, 25, 29, 47, 49–51, 137–38, 144, 147, 150, 161
Zwinglians, on Lord's Supper, 152

SCRIPTURE INDEX

WISDOM FROM THE PAST FOR LIFE IN THE PRESENT

Other volumes in the Theologians on the Christian Life series

AUGUSTINE

BAVINCK

BONHOEFFER

CALVIN

EDWARDS

LUTHER

NEWTON

OWEN

PACKER

SCHAEFFER

WARFIELD

WESLEY

Visit crossway.org/TOCL for more information.